Rolf-Dieter Müller is Professor of Military History at Humboldt University, Berlin; Scientific Director of the German Armed Forces Military History Research Institute in Potsdam; and Co-ordinator of the 'The German Reich and the Second World War' project. He is the author of numerous publications on World War II.

THE UNKNOWN EASTERN FRONT

THE WEHRMACHT AND HITLER'S FOREIGN SOLDIERS

ROLF-DIETER MÜLLER

Translated by David Burnett

I.B. TAURIS

LONDON · NEW YORK

Reprinted in 2013 and first published in 2012 by I.B.Tauris & Co Ltd
6 Salem Road, London W2 4BU
175 Fifth Avenue, New York NY 10010
www.ibtauris.com

Distributed in the United States and Canada Exclusively by Palgrave Macmillan
175 Fifth Avenue, New York NY 10010

ISBN: 978 1 78076 072 8

A full CIP record for this book is available from the British Library
A full CIP record is available from the Library of Congress

Library of Congress Catalog Card Number: available

Printed and bound by CPI Group (UK) Ltd, Croydon, CR0 4YY

*The translation of this work was funded by Geisteswissenschaften International –
Translation Funding for Humanities and Social Sciences from Germany, a joint initiative
of the Fritz Thyssen Foundation, the German Federal Foreign Office, the collecting society
VG WORT and the Börsenverein des Deutschen Buchhandels (German Publishers &
Booksellers Association).*

Contents

PART III:
THE EASTERN EUROPEAN NATIONS
IN THE STRUGGLE AGAINST STALINISM

List of Illustrations

Despite diligent efforts, copyright holders could not be found in every instance.
If you own the copyright to photos used here, please contact the publisher.

List of Maps

The maps were drawn by Christopher Volle using material at the Military History Research Institute (MGFA) in Potsdam.

Abbreviations

ADAP	Akten zur deutschen auswärtigen Politik [Documents on German Foreign Policy]
ARMIR	Armata Italiana in Russia [Italian Army in Russia]
BA-MA	Bundesarchiv-Militärarchiv [Federal Military Archives, Freiburg]
CP(B)	Communist Party (Bolsheviki)
CSIR	Corpo di Spedizione Italiano in Russia [Italian Expeditionary Corps in Russia]
DEV	División Española de Voluntarios [Spanish Volunteer Division]
DNSAP	Danmarks Nationalsocialistiske Arbejderparti [National Socialist Workers' Party of Denmark]
LAF	Lietuvių aktyvistų frontas [Lithuanian Activist Front]
LVF	Légion des Volontaires Français contre le Bolchevisme [Legion of French Volunteers against Bolshevism]
MG	machine gun
NKVD	Narodny kommissariat vnutrennych del (People's Commissariat for Internal Affairs, USSR)
NOC	Nederlandse Oostcampagnie [Dutch East Company]
NSB	Nationaal-Socialistische Beweging [National Socialist Movement in the Netherlands]
NSDAP	Nationalsozialistische Deutsche Arbeiterpartei [National Socialist German Workers' Party (Nazi Party)]
OKH	Oberkommando des Heeres [Army High Command]
OKW	Oberkommando der Wehrmacht [Wehrmacht High Command]
OUN-B	Orhanizatsiya Ukrayins'kykh Natsionalistiv [Organization of Ukrainian Nationalists] ('Bandera faction')

OUN-M	Orhanizatsiya Ukrayins'kykh Natsionalistiv [Organization of Ukrainian Nationalists] ('Melnik faction')
ROA	Russkaya Osvoboditel'naya Armiya [Russian Liberation Army]
RONA	Russkaya Osvoboditel'naya Narodnaya Armiya [Russian National Liberation Army]
SA	Sturmabteilung (stormtroopers or 'brownshirts')
SS	Schutzstaffel (elite party troops)
USSR	Union of Soviet Socialist Republics
UPA	Ukrayns'ka Povstans'ka Armiya [Ukrainian Insurgent Army]
USA	United States of America
VNV	Vlaamsch Nationaal Verbond [Flemish National Union]

Preface

The opening of Russian archives in the early 1990s stirred the hopes of many historians, military historians included. Admittedly, there were no sensational discoveries. For Western historians at least, the key revelations merely confirmed what most knew already. That Stalin had claimed all of East-Central Europe for himself in a secret protocol with Hitler in 1939–40, and that in early 1940, near Katyn, he had ordered the murder of Polish officers taken as prisoners of war could now be read by former Soviet citizens in the files of their highest-ranking leaders. Meanwhile, the most important secret files from the Soviet era in Moscow are long since under wraps again or hard to access. A real surprise, on the other hand – insightful for historians of Germany as well – is the development of a new national historiography in the Baltic states, Poland and Ukraine. The new approach in these countries has cast a completely different light on life under German occupation during World War II and under the pressures of two successive waves of Stalinization (1939–40 and 1944–5). These nations' fight for independence did not come to a standstill during this period, but was carried on in a fatal alliance with Hitler's Germany, even after German defeat.

For Stalin, these were criminal activities by treasonous Soviet citizens. The term 'collaboration' had already acquired a negative connotation among the anti-Hitler coalition during World War II. The image of homegrown fascists, mercenaries and traitors has continued to hold in Western scholarship and was thoroughly cultivated for half a century by Soviet historical propaganda. The new national historiography of the last 20 years in East-Central Europe, however, has drawn a more nuanced picture, obliging us to say goodbye to a number of longstanding clichés. Only recently did intense riots break out in Estonia when a Soviet victory monument was relocated. For the majority of Estonians, the Red Army was an occupying force rather than a 'liberator', whereas the country's Russian minority still clings to the myth of the 'Great Patriotic War'. In commenting on the controversy, Russian President Vladimir Putin said he would not stand for any attempt to rewrite the history of World War II.

And yet it seems inevitable the dam will break. Thus, for example, in 2007 a Museum of Soviet Occupation was set up in Kiev – the second of its kind after Riga – and the 100th birthday of the former commander-in-chief of the anti-Soviet Ukrainian Insurgent Army (UPA) in World War II, Roman Shukhevych, was honoured with an exhibition. In many cities, commemorative ceremonies led to counter-demonstrations and a strong police presence. French President Charles de Gaulle is routinely cited as chief witness to the power of these Ukrainian nationalists and sometime Wehrmacht collaborators, having supposedly uttered (before taking office) that never would a German soldier have set foot on French soil had France had an army as committed as the UPA.[1]

Discussions like these should be reason enough to recapitulate these changing perspectives and ask ourselves if we have not been harbouring a much too biased view of the German-Soviet war. What part did local helpers play in Hitler's 'Crusade against Bolshevism', and what factors led them to do so?

Many historical accounts of the war in the East, the bloodiest struggle in world history, overlook the role of local helpers and thereby unwittingly play up to Stalinist propaganda. They also underestimate the importance of German-allied armies fighting on the Eastern Front, thus supporting Hitler's claims that his allies had ultimately failed him miserably and left him in the lurch, that they were military failures and a burden to the German Eastern divisions. In Hungary and Romania, these 'forgotten sons' were not rediscovered until after the fall of Communism in 1989. Up until then, the history of Hitler's allied armies on the Eastern Front had been taboo. In Fascist Italy, another ally, there does exist a vast postwar veteran literature, but even today the history of the Italian Army in Russia is hampered by biased accounts dealing primarily with the Resistenza and tending to view Italian soldiers as victims.

Hitler's opinion of a third group – foreign volunteers from Western and Northern Europe – was not as harsh, but this tiny group of individuals came from nations and states that Hitler likewise despised for the most part. The 'Germanic' volunteers may have been highly regarded by the SS but were ultimately just more 'cannon fodder' for the Eastern Front, and were viewed in their homelands as traitors and fascists. Not until the spring of 2007 did the Norwegian government commission an extensive research project to investigate the fate of its erstwhile combatants on the Eastern Front.

All three groups have generally been dealt with separately in specialized literature, balanced scholarly approaches being the exception rather than the rule. Many publications in Germany as well as in the Western homelands of these foreign volunteers – lately even in Russia – tend to glorify these helpers, some even adopting Nazi slogans. The theme of volunteers for the 'Crusade against Bolshevism' is standard fare among German and European right-wing radicals, a Fascist International still very much active.

This overview is the first attempt to describe and acknowledge the overall phenomenon of foreigners on the side of the Wehrmacht fighting against the Red Army. The differences between individual countries and groups lend themselves to a systematic approach, allowing readers to search for specific information without losing the overall context or a comparative perspective. Eye-witness reports and excerpts from important documents illustrate and deepen a previously neglected chapter in the history of World War II.

Introduction

Operation Barbarossa and Its Consequences

It was the most startling coup in world history.[1] News of the Molotov-Ribbentrop Pact fell like a bombshell. Had not the 'Brown' dictator, whose aggressive foreign policy put Europe on the verge of a second major war in a generation, always claimed that his Third Reich was necessary to save Europe from Bolshevism? And had not the 'Red' dictator portrayed himself since 1935 as a bulwark against fascism and its spread across the Continent? British and French military officers had engaged in protracted negotiations in the summer of 1939 over an alliance with Moscow to prevent the advance of the Nazis. Yet Stalin proved to be a wily tactician. His Red Army was not fully operational after the purges, the Soviet dictator having had almost his entire higher officer corps murdered to consolidate his absolute power. Hitler, by contrast, had to contend with an experienced and self-confident General Staff, and was surprised to find that his generals were less than enthusiastic about a large-scale war at that point in time. Some of them, in secret, even entertained thoughts of a *coup d'état*.

Stalin used the opportunity of discussing a new trade agreement to signal his interest in reaching a political accord with Hitler. Berlin saw the chance to break the Western Powers' policy of containment and was prepared to pay any price to do so. So both dictators discovered a long-standing German-Russian tradition: the obliteration of Polish freedom. Their mutual eagerness to annex the country through a fourth partition and wipe it off the map for good made Poland's worst nightmare reality. For Stalin it meant restoring the old borders of the Russian Empire, including Finland, the Baltic states and territories in eastern Romania. Hitler pursued his own strategic aims:

the expansion of his eastern perimeter so that after dealing with the Western Powers he could crush his rival in the East. Added to this was the exploitation of Poland's resources. Cheap labour, raw materials and grain were to relieve an economy overheated by rearmament and help overcome the wearying British blockade.

Hitler had just celebrated his 50th birthday. He now pushed his generals into action, wanting to see the birth of the 'Greater Germanic Reich of the German Nation' and world supremacy of the 'Germanic master race' in his lifetime. The sober-minded Soviet leader, on the other hand, was in no hurry with his World Revolution. Hitler was the first to invade Poland, accepting the Western Powers' declaration of war. Stalin chose to bide his time until it was clear that the French would stay put behind their Maginot Line. Then he set his own troops in motion, breaking the Polish army's back. The Western Powers grudgingly listened to the propaganda version of an alleged act of liberation and accepted the USSR's mock-neutrality. Open conflict with the two dictators would have meant the end of free Europe.

In Soviet-occupied Poland, Stalin's secret police and political functionaries waged a brutal class war. The acts of terror and murder they committed in the ensuing two years were harder on the population than the merciless and ever more intense race war unleashed by the Nazis in their own zone of occupation.[2] Stalin endeavoured to please Hitler and consolidate their secret alliance. He handed over German communists and Polish Jews to the Gestapo, while his Comintern set to work denouncing France and Great Britain as warmongers. He sacrificed dwindling Soviet stockpiles to make sure Hitler's tanks had fuel, and appeased German workers by putting bread on the table. Stalin financed Hitler's war and hoped to receive state-of-the-art weapons technology in exchange.

The division of the world seemed imminent, albeit not the way Hitler imagined. Though he wanted to teach the British a lesson, they were still entitled as a 'master race' to maintain their supremacy overseas. Hitler's India was Russia. This old idea re-emerged in the summer of 1940, once Germany had overthrown France and chased the British army across the Channel. That Stalin now demanded his share of the spoils and, given the unexpected lightning victories of the Germans, had an eye to his own territorial gains only strengthened Hitler's resolve to make a strategic about-face and look eastward. His generals had since become used to the idea. Though they had recently been hesitant and sceptical, the Führer's brilliant victory had fired their imaginations. Newly appointed field marshals swore allegiance to the 'Greatest Field Marshal of All Times' (*Grösster Feldherr aller Zeiten*, shortened in common parlance to the mocking acronym *Gröfaz*).

Any misgivings were disregarded in devising secret plans (Aufbau Ost) to attack his loyal ally, the Soviet Union. The 'giant on feet of clay', they believed, could be crushed in one fell swoop, thus paving the way once and for all for a 'New Order' in Europe and the world. Great Britain, the only country still putting up a fight, despite German bombs and threats of invasion, would be forced into submission, and the Americans, they assumed, would keep quiet in their isolation.

Preoccupied with his own plans for his western territories, Stalin let himself be hoodwinked. He took warnings about his allies in Berlin to be a feint of British imperialists, who happened to be taking a beating from Hitler. He pressed for a new set of agreements and was not immodest. He did not accept Hitler's dubious offer of South Asia. Negotiations dragged on, but Stalin trusted in the judiciousness of Hitler, who in his programmatic work *Mein Kampf* had acknowledged the foolishness of a two-front war. Economic aid from the Soviets to Germany was intended to keep Hitler's lust for power focused on the British. As long as the Wehrmacht was undefeated, the Red Army did not have a chance anyway, despite its considerable efforts to gird itself for war. Even when invading tiny Finland, Soviet soldiers had nearly made fools of themselves. Why should Stalin pull the chestnuts out of the fire for capitalist great powers?

The Soviet General Staff became increasingly nervous when in the spring of 1941 the Wehrmacht began its clandestine military build-up in the East. From a military perspective, a preventive strike against the German forces amassing in the East would perhaps have staved off the looming threat. But an overconfident Stalin opted against this. Instead, he offered words of encouragement to military academy graduates, telling them at their farewell banquet that they should not always admire and overrate the Wehrmacht, that his officers should return to their troops with assurance. Insufficient training and equipment – undoubtedly a major handicap – played no role in his decision-making.

Warnings from his General Staff mounted in March 1941. Communist master spy Richard Sorge, a German press correspondent in Tokyo, even knew the exact date of the offensive: 22 June. Yet Stalin was notoriously sceptical. He had no interest in becoming involved in the German-British conflict. Time, so he thought, was on his side. An offensive against the powerful

Wehrmacht would have been suicide and utterly foolish, because Hitler could have easily posed as defender of the West, possibly even reaching some kind of compromise with Great Britain after all. Indeed, what was Stalin to think of the mysterious flight of Rudolf Hess, who landed by parachute in Scotland on 10 May? We now know it was an intrigue of the British secret service, having convinced the already somewhat incoherent 'Deputy Führer' that there were circles in Britain willing to reach a peace agreement. Three weeks earlier, the British had inspired a *coup d'état* in Belgrade to deter German military efforts in the Balkans and make Hitler think that Stalin was behind it.

The confusion was settled during the night of 22 June 1941, when Hitler's Eastern Army, the greatest concentration of military strength in German history, attacked unsuspecting Soviet border troops. Stalin had courted Hitler's favour up to the very last minute. When hostilities began, he fled to his dacha, fearing arrest. But the Politburo begged its Comrade Chairman to take the country's defence into his own hands.

Though intensively prepared as a blitzkrieg, Operation Barbarossa remained a gamble. Wehrmacht leaders, however, were ready to go for broke. They had even made logistic preparations to shift their attention to Great Britain once the Eastern campaign was over. And yet the German Eastern Army was poorly equipped and full of gaps. Its numbers were not significantly larger than those of the troops who had taken France a year earlier. Apart from a few dozen elite divisions, the majority of soldiers headed east in the manner of Napoleon's Grande Armée – on foot or by horse and cart. Indeed, the Corsican had actually been faster than General Guderian's tank convoys, which only in December reached the outskirts of Moscow.

Napoleon's army had more foreigners than Frenchmen serving in it, and they were neither despised nor discriminated against. Hitler, on the other hand, overestimating his own capabilities, thought he could largely do without foreign help and the mobilization of his allies. Inducing Japan to open a second front in the Far East against Stalin would have seemed an obvious strategy, but Hitler chose not to. In the European theatre of war, he thought, only the Finns and Romanians at best could be counted on to provide him with flank protection in a planned blitzkrieg of approximately two months. He did not think them capable of more, and was not prepared, for political reasons, to arm his allies any better than they already were. Hitler was unrelenting on this point. He did not want to have to share the spoils, and in his future 'Eastern territory' (*Ostraum*) no one would bear arms but the Germans, lording it over their Slavic vassals. For this reason it did not even cross his mind in the summer of 1941 to arm Russians or other Eastern European peoples and win them as brothers-in-arms against the Red Army.

It was in this vein that Hitler declared the following in an internal meeting on 31 July 1941: 'No one but a German shall ever be allowed to bear arms! This is of utmost importance; even if it may seem easier at first to mobilize the military support of some foreign subject peoples, it is wrong! Because one day it will backfire, absolutely and inevitably. Only the German may bear arms, not the Slav, not the Czech, not the Cossack nor the Ukrainian!'[3] And yet the Führer had to make compromises and concessions from day one, at first for diplomatic-propagandistic and military-tactical reasons (the use of local recruits for defence commandos and as auxiliary police), but more and more due to increasing attrition on the Eastern Front and the unfavourable course of the war. Still, Hitler and his ideological stubbornness remained the biggest hindrance to enlisting the support of foreign volunteers for the Eastern Front despite the varied efforts of the more pragmatic-minded Wehrmacht, the Eastern Ministry (Ostministerium) and ultimately even the self-proclaimed guardians of Nazi racial ideology, the SS, who eventually abandoned their ideological scruples for the sake of recruiting 'cannon fodder'. Hitler's insistence on 'Germanic origins' as a condition for bearing arms was never taken so seriously, at least in the case of his closest allies, the Hungarians, Romanians and Italians.

Despite being outnumbered, Hitler's more experienced troops routed the Red Army in the first four weeks of the campaign. The newly developed blitzkrieg strategy seemed to be working. Stukas bombed key enemy positions, and hordes of tanks broke through the front and encircled enemy formations in daring operations. The Wehrmacht soon marched more than 3 million prisoners of war through the streets, and Stalin had lost practically his entire peacetime army of 5 million men. The Germans had planned to be in Moscow by August. Preparations were under way for a victory parade on Red Square, and Himmler's police had endless arrest lists at their disposal.

Hitler had ordered radical warfare as early as March 1941. Communists and political functionaries were to be shot summarily. Conflicts between the Wehrmacht and the SS – the kind that had arisen during the Polish campaign – were to be avoided from the outset. Whereas army leaders strove for a division of labour so as to concentrate on the 'war of arms' (*Waffenkrieg*), it was clear already in drafting occupation policy that the Wehrmacht would be deeply entangled in a racially and ideologically motivated war of conquest and extermination. Troops were expected to 'live off the land' in order to free up reinforcements. The death by starvation of 'umpteen millions'[4] was calculated into the equation quite matter-of-factly. Big cities such as Leningrad and Moscow were not to be occupied but destroyed and flooded, considered as they were to be breeding grounds of Bolshevism, inhabited by 'useless eaters'. Army command gave criminal orders to murder Soviet commissars. And German soldiers complicit in attacks on the civilian populace were no longer invariably tried by court martial.

Many administrative agencies, economic enterprises and university institutes were soon involved in the euphoria of planning and 'reorganization' (*Neuordnung*). Himmler, convinced that the East would belong to the SS, reworked his notorious 'General Plan for the East' for the settlement and Germanization of Eastern Europe. Hitler entrusted him with broadly defined 'special tasks'. Specially formed 'task forces', the so-called *Einsatzkommandos*, were not only responsible for murdering political foes, but, with the help of police and the Waffen SS, were to implement the 'Final Solution to the Jewish Question'. The genocide of Jews was only one task of the units engaged in 'worldview war' (*Weltanschauungskrieg*). The ethnic cleansing or 'land consolidation' (*Flurbereinigung*) of the East also included gypsies, the mentally ill and other 'life unworthy of life', along with the enforcement of a race hierarchy in the East. Millions of Germanic *Wehrbauer*, a free and militarized peasantry, were to form the 'master class' – a prospect officially held out to combatants even at this point in time. There was no lack of applicants, from enlisted men to higher nobility. Determining the hierarchy of Slavic 'auxiliary peoples' (*Hilfsvölker*) – potential work slaves for several generations – was a source of friction in many German administrative offices.

In April 1941, Hitler appointed Alfred Rosenberg, the Party's insipid ideologue, to the position of 'Reich minister for the occupied eastern territories'. His notions of giving preferential treatment to the Baltic peoples and the Ukrainians quickly collided with the actions of Reich commissioners appointed by Hitler to administer the territories. The latter were duty-bound to carry out Göring's goals of exploitation with the greatest brutality. Thus the sympathy Germans had initially enjoyed among parts of the local population was soon lost in the ensuing chaos of occupation policy. Particularly in former Soviet zones of occupation, many people had welcomed the invading Germans as 'liberators' in the hope of regaining their national autonomy.

But the pressures of economic exploitation and, later, the hunt for forced labourers to serve in the Reich drove many of them underground and into the ranks of the partisans.

Stalin's proclamation of the 'Great Patriotic War' on 14 July 1941 initially met with little response in the western USSR. Only NKVD agents and scattered Red Army soldiers organized isolated acts of sabotage in the German hinterland. Unlike in 1812, Russian peasants showed little inclination to fight a foreign occupier this time. Indeed, after the bitter experiences of Stalinism, many of them were prepared to make arrangements with the Germans, especially considering that the German army they had encountered in World War I was anything but a horde of barbarians. Hitler's order to shoot anyone 'who so much as looks suspicious'[5] resulted in a brutalization of the German 'pacification policy' (*Befriedungspolitik*), which nonetheless failed to fully contain a growing partisan movement. For Stalin, the partisans were particularly important for keeping the population in his German-occupied hinterland under pressure. Partisans killed more Soviet citizens than German soldiers did.

Instead of letting his army fall back into the depths of Russia as in the Napoleonic invasion of 1812, the 'Generalissimo', as Stalin now called himself, ordered fanatical resistance. Generals who allegedly failed in their duties were shot, as were retreating units. Time and again he managed to close up gaps in the front and hold the advancing Germans in check. Stalin, whose survival seemed unlikely to Washington and London, had meanwhile secured some powerful allies. US President Roosevelt, who still had to win the support of his reluctant countrymen for an anti-Hitler coalition, now promised huge amounts of aid. Churchill, too, did everything to get his detested adversary back on his feet. Stalin succeeded – contrary to German expectations – in evacuating a large part of his industry and mobilizing the formidable resources of his country. Behind the smoke screen of a fragile Western Front, he was even preparing strategic reserves for a counter-offensive. He drew these reserves from the Far East, since Japan – encouraged by Hitler – was preparing to attack the United States. Moscow and Tokyo had signed a mutually beneficial neutrality pact in April of 1941.

Two months after the invasion of the Soviet Union began, a feverish nervousness prevailed in the German Supreme Command. The breakthrough to Moscow had still not been achieved, and Hitler was pushing to finally shift the focus of operations to the Ukrainian 'breadbasket' and towards the oil wells of the Caucasus. In his new, mosquito-infested Führer Headquarters near the East Prussian town of Rastenburg, he paused to write a memorandum, his second since coming to power. He justified his decision to focus for the time being on vital strategic centres in the South, despite the opposition of army commanders. It is clear in retrospect that this doomed his military campaign to failure.

His soldiers marched their feet off in the hope of a swift victory. Guderian's tanks, with their ailing engines, changed course and headed for Kiev, engaging in the biggest battle of encirclement in military history. More than 600,000 Red Army soldiers were captured. The catastrophe, however, gave Stalin time to organize his defence of the capital. He placed his poorly armed workers' battalions at the forefront to give the impression that the Red Army was already down to its last reserves. Meanwhile, his strategic Siberian divisions were on their way. Sorge, the spy, had reported that Japan would uphold its pledge of neutrality.

The worst drama played out in the North. Hitler's troops prepared for the siege of Leningrad, determined to starve out and destroy the 'birthplace' of Soviet Communism and its millions of inhabitants. His Finnish allies, though, only marched to the old river border, the Svir, leaving the Red Army wide access to Leningrad via Lake Ladoga. But Stalin harboured age-old Muscovite suspicions towards the originally quite cosmopolitan city, the former St Petersburg, and for the most part left its starving inhabitants to their own devices. At the end of the war, the leaders of its successful defence were sentenced to death on spurious charges. The Generalissimo, it was clear, would suffer no other heroes beside him.

Stalin's ruthlessly organized defence campaign against the Wehrmacht in 1941 probably saved the Soviet Union from its downfall. Hitler resumed his Moscow offensive, his wearied troops breaking through Soviet lines once again. For a few days in October, Stalin considered fleeing from the Kremlin. But without sufficient reinforcements and equipment the German advance lost speed. Then, with the start of the rainy season in autumn, the *rasputitsa*, or Russian quagmire, effectively hindered any forward movement – a defensive advantage for Stalin. With the onset of frost, Hitler ordered one last-ditch effort to storm the enemy capital and bring the war in the East to a tentative conclusion. Victory, prematurely declared, was long in coming.

Events followed in rapid succession in early December 1941. Hitler's emaciated front units had to halt their offensive because of the snowdrifts. One day later they were hit by a massive counter-offensive. Stalin was unltimately saved by the Japanese attack on Pearl Harbour, which drew the United States into the war. Hitler, for his part, was seized by a dark presentiment of his inevitable downfall. Plans to annihilate the Jews were ripening, being laid out in detail soon afterwards at the notorious Wannsee Conference. The two dictators duelled it out in a fierce winter battle outside Moscow, a test of strength for Hitler this time. He relieved two dozen generals of their posts to overcome a confidence crisis. (Stalin, in a comparable situation, probably would have had them shot.) With fanatic orders to halt and the quick mobilization of reserves, Hitler managed to gradually stabilize a collapsing front and strengthen the self-assurance of his exhausted troops.

Stalin had been too bold in plotting his counter-offensive and was already making plans for the borders of postwar Europe. The Red Army wore itself out in weeks of heavy winter fighting, its head-on attacks producing nothing in the way of strategic advance. For the first time in the war, Hitler mobilized all his forces. Up until this point he had made sure that 'peacelike' conditions prevailed in Germany so as not to endanger morale on the home front. Now his indifference to the future of his people became apparent. Hitler was fighting to extend his own life and to fulfil his political and ideological ambitions – at any cost.

To show his resolve to his helpless generals, Hitler appointed himself supreme commander of the army and took over the planning and execution of the Eastern war. There would be no capitulation or compromise, as the secret opposition hoped for at home. Fritz Todt, chief engineer of the Reich and Reich minister for armaments and munitions, had lost his faith in the *Endsieg*, or 'final victory', and urged a political solution. He perished in a mysterious plane crash following an important meeting at the 'Wolf's Lair' Führer Headquarters. Three months earlier, Ernst Udet, the famed World War I fighter pilot responsible for air armament, had lost his life as well, a suicide likewise passed off by Nazi propaganda as a plane crash.

On 8 February 1942, Hitler appointed his senior architect and confidant Albert Speer as the new minister of armaments. Working closely with German industry, Speer was able to streamline armaments production without the interference of the military. His progress reports invariably assured the Führer of glowing military prospects ahead. Thus, Hitler, his confidence growing, focused on a renewed offensive in the East. His *Weltblitzkrieg* had undoubtedly failed, but there was still time to prepare his 'Fortress Europe' for defensive action before the Americans intervened.

Hitler knew he was dependent on oil. Aborting his offensive in the south towards the Caucasus and resuming the fight for Moscow at the insistence of his General Staff in September 1941 had presumably been a strategic blunder – one he was not eager to repeat. Hitler pulled together all his available forces in the spring of 1942 to go on the offensive in the Ukraine. He could not do much more, but it was enough to break through the front once again at isolated strategic points. Yet the Red Army – unlike in the previous year – would not be encircled so easily this time. The Germans were looking to the oil fields of the Caucasus – a marching distance of more than 1,000 kilometres from north to south.

The arduous advance to the south opened up a correspondingly wide flank to the east which Hitler safeguarded using his Romanian, Hungarian and Italian allies – a risk he had to take if he wanted to focus on his thrust into the Caucasus. He trusted that Stalin would stand his ground, defending his vital oil wells with all his might. Yet the Russian leader once again proved his farsightedness, skilfully luring his opponent into a trap. Just as Hitler's troops were about to begin their assault on the Caucasus, Stalin built up his position on the Volga. The armaments centre threatened Hitler's flank, but could be held at bay or destroyed with little effort. To the dismay of his generals, however, Hitler ordered his offensive to be split, steering his 6th Army towards Stalingrad.

Though German mountain infantry managed to conquer Mount Elbrus, the highest point in the Caucasus, and enfeebled German forces reached the first oil wells near Maykop, enemy fire and total destruction of the oil rigs prevented German petroleum experts from extracting more than a few tons of the precious resource. And it was still another 700 kilometres to the main wells of Baku. Thus, thirsty German tanks had to continue being supplied through camel caravans. In the steppe landscape of the Don as well, German tanks ran out of fuel, giving Stalingrad's defenders time to entrench themselves in the rubble. Hitler's Stukas had created an ideal fortress, effectively digging a grave for Paulus's 6th Army. The Germans managed to take 90 per cent of the city in gruelling house-to-house fighting – the so-called 'rat war' (*Rattenkrieg*) – and were utterly exhausted by the time Stalin launched his counter-offensive. His tank armies crushed Germany's helpless allied units at the flanks and encircled the 6th Army with its 250,000 men outside Stalingrad. Only several thousand of these men would ultimately escape with their lives. There was no talk in Hitler's Führer Headquarters of the hundreds of thousands of foreign casualties on the German side – the Romanians, Italians, Hungarians, Slovaks and countless Russian 'willing helpers' (*Hilfswillige*) – but at best snide and reproachful remarks about the supposed failure of Hitler's allies.

The ruin of the 6th Army was a bad omen for the Reich. Hitler had sacrificed his own soldiers to spoil his rival's triumph. He was furious when he heard that Paulus, freshly promoted to field marshal, had left his bunker and surrendered, instead of shooting himself. That would never happen to him. There are many indications that Hitler had long since abandoned the idea of 'final victory' and used the next two years to merely stage his own downfall. He was rightly convinced that he alone could bring his faithless cohorts, especially his generals, under control so as to draw out an obviously senseless war. While others, even high-ranking Nazi officials whom he blindly trusted, were increasingly racked with doubt and secretly sought a way out, Hitler succeeded in holding together his system of rule until the bitter end, dragging out its inevitable collapse by mobilizing ever more forces and radicalizing his strategy of war. Having sacrificed other peoples, he now offered up his own – millions of soldiers and civilians who, like a living wall, served to prolong his own miserable life by a matter of weeks or days.

Hitler was ever more unyielding after Stalingrad, fighting a simple holding action and consenting to evasive manoeuvres in the face of wave-like attacks by the advancing Red Army only after wrangling with his generals, and then for the most part too late. Field Marshal Erich von Manstein proved the most successful strategist in the East in 1943–4; some even hoped Hitler would give him supreme command over the Eastern Front. Yet the dictator held on to the reins. He interfered in daily briefings and always insisted on having his say, even down to the transfer of individual companies. He lacked any understanding of the generals' preferred strategy of a mobile defence against a vastly superior foe, though it was this very strategy that had enabled the Germans to inflict spectacular retaliatory blows on the Soviet army. Hitler saw to it that a bloody war of attrition took place in the East, with the Red Army paying dearly with hecatombs of casualties as Stalin ruthlessly pushed his armies forward in a westward surge. Despite its superiority in numbers, the Red Army took a multiple of losses compared to German casualties.

But the Wehrmacht, too, having had to shift its focus in the autumn of 1943 to defend against a possible invasion from the west, was gradually drained of its fighting strength by an unremitting series of heavy battles and withdrawals. Compared to 22 June 1941, it had since become a mere shadow of itself, propped up by the deployment of more than a million foreign soldiers and volunteers and by a brutal scorched-earth policy. To delay the Red Army's advance and compensate for its own losses, the abandonment of terrain in the East was coupled with ruthless plundering, the thorough destruction of infrastructure, and the deportation of millions of people westwards as forced labourers for the construction of defence fortifications or in the Reich's military economy. The treks included hundreds of thousands of Soviet citizens – Russian Germans, Caucasians, Ukrainians and other nationalities – all fleeing from Stalinism. Countless other political or racial 'undesirables', prisoners of war, partisans and concentration camp slaves were murdered by the SS and police at the last minute.

The drama in the East progressed to its bloody finale. The Eastern Front had all but collapsed following the spectacular breakdown of Army Group Centre in July 1944, and by autumn of that year the Red Army had practically reached the point from which the Wehrmacht had launched its Operation Barbarossa three years earlier, confident of victory. The Germans had taken about five months to cover a stretch from Brest-Litovsk to the outskirts of Moscow. The Red Army, by contrast, needed more than three years for its counter-offensive, despite its constant superiority in manpower and supplies, even as it moved further from its industrial base, and despite its having the most powerful allies on earth. This might explain why the military competence of the Wehrmacht, though serving a criminal regime, still managed to command the respect of its foes right up to the end of the war, even after suffering catastrophic defeats. But this admiration came also as a result of the deployment of over 2 million foreign soldiers on the German side, a fact that Hitler denied to the very end and that is also generally overlooked by historians. The Führer, to whom many had sworn their allegiance, thanked them with contempt. In his New Year's announcement of 1 January 1945, he publicly declared himself the 'victim of betrayal by our allies', who had supposedly forced him to withdraw from entire fronts. Behind closed doors he later called his allies weaklings, whom he had made the mistake of treating as 'equals'. The 'Romance peoples' had failed him the worst: France was a 'down-at-the-heels courtesan', and Italy had always been in his way.[6] Except for the desolate group of foreign SS volunteers still defending the Führer Bunker in the centre of Berlin during the final hours of the war, his former allies and their recruits had fought in the East for their own national interests, he fumed, abandoning the struggle at an opportune moment or switching sides altogether.

Part I

THE ALLIES

Introduction

The still young great power in the middle of the Continent had no wealth of experience in organizing and steering a wartime system of allies. The mastery of an Otto von Bismarck was not shared by his successor in ruling over the Reich. During World War I it became apparent how difficult it was to co-ordinate the interests of allies. This was true not only in strategic and political terms, because of the frequent need to hold one's own ambitions in check and enter into compromises; the inclusion of allied armies with varied skills and equipment in joint military operations was an impediment to conducting warfare as well. Austria-Hungary, in particular, complained about the supposed arrogance of German officers who felt their general staff were superior. Snobbery and nationalism were rampant on both sides.

The Prussia admirer Adolf Hitler was an heir to this impatience towards and even inability to accept his weaker and less efficient allies, as well as a tendency to fault his allies for his own problems and failures. The Führer showed a deep-seated aversion, both internally and in dealing with foreign powers and leaders, to sitting down at the conference table, or even larger gatherings, and discussing current problems and strategies. When high-level discussions or negotiations could not be avoided, he preferred a direct personal dialogue, or monologue as it were, where his skills at commanding those around him could be brought to bear. His allies were mostly monarchies, so that those he dealt with were the representatives of an 'old order' and an often older generation of elites. The Finn Mannerheim, for example, had been a Tsarist cavalry general, whereas the Hungarian Horthy had been an admiral in the Austro-Hungarian Navy during World War I. The former lance-corporal was surely troubled by such encounters.

Unlike the German Empire at the start of World War I, Hitler's state of foreign affairs in 1939–40 was much more favourable. He was able to reactivate traditional contacts and old military alliances, as in the case of Hungary. To counteract the loss of Turkey, a huge strategic disadvantage, he was able to win the support of erstwhile enemies such as Romania and Italy and, above all, Japan which – so Hitler hoped – would keep the United States preoccupied in the Far East. A new ally was Finland, allowing him to considerably expand the front for his secret plan to attack his strongest ally, the USSR. Intent on using a blitzkrieg strategy to win the war in the East, he was not particularly interested at first in the difficult task of integrating allied armies into the campaign. His strongest and oldest military allies, Japan and Italy, with whom he had signed an Anti-Comintern Pact in 1936/7 and a Tripartite Pact in 1940, he planned on leaving out entirely, encouraging them instead to engage in diversionary attacks in the Mediterranean and the Pacific. These were decisions that proved fatal to the Eastern campaign and which Hitler was unable to correct after the failure of his blitzkrieg. Instead he took to reviling his allies in a wholesale manner, finding in them the cause of his own failures, despite their having served him loyally on the Eastern Front, where far too much was demanded of them anyway.

Anti-Bolshevism as the ideological linchpin of his system of allies proved to be weak and fragile, especially considering that Hitler himself was not exclusively guided by this principle, treating his allies arbitrarily, sometimes ruthlessly, as well as playing favourites.

1

Finland

This land in the far north with only 3.7 million inhabitants (little more than Berlin) was a strategically vital partner of the Third Reich if only for its long border with the Soviet Union. In principle, Hitler could have decided to ignore the Scandinavian flank of his Operation Barbarossa altogether, as the expansion of the German Front from the Memel to Murmansk brought no real advantages for conducting a blitzkrieg. And even if Finland had been neutral, Stalin could not have freed up his units on the Northern Front (three armies) fast enough or even completely. In other words, a German-Finnish operation in this area to tie up Soviet forces was strategically meaningless. From a German perspective, only the capture of Leningrad or Murmansk would have made it worthwhile. As it later turned out, the Germans wanted to take the former but found themselves unable to do so, whereas the Finns were supposed to take the latter but did not want to.

This – as popular opinion would have it – 'natural' alliance reveals a number of additional peculiarities upon closer examination. There was never a formal wartime alliance between Finland and the German Reich. Helsinki, by its own account, was waging its own war – a 'continuation' or parallel war – against the Soviet Union. It was the only state in the 'Hitler Coalition' to assume a section of the long front between the North Cape and the Black Sea under its own command, a 600-kilometre stretch in Karelia. Of Germany's allies, only the Finnish Army was fully utilized in the war against the Red Army. Finally, Finland was the only fully functioning democratic system in the German sphere of influence and did not undergo a fascist transformation. With the exception of the region of Petsamo, rich in nickel-ore, an important resource in the war effort, the country was of scant economic importance to Germany and essentially became a deficit region during the war. In terms of ideology, too, the Finnish Republic shared little with Nazi Germany. According to the Nazi's obscure racial theories, the Finns were actually quite problematic.

And yet Finland was Hitler's most valued partner during World War II. He rated the Finns' military prowess higher than that of all his other allies, despite the fact that their battlefield performance was, from the German standpoint, the worst on the whole Eastern Front. The Finns advanced barely more than 250 kilometres in Karelia before becoming bogged down for three years in swamp and tundra. It was not just the difficult terrain with its thousands of lakes and a brief summer that made the going tough but also the excessive demands Hitler placed on them strategically and militarily.

None of this, however, even to the present day, has detracted from the image of an apparently heroic ideal. Along with North Africa, the Finnish theatre of war was the only one in which a 'normal war' was waged during World War II, and not a Nazi war of plunder and extermination. The myth of an unusual brotherhood-in-arms between Germans and Finns, which was only marred by Helsinki's about-face in the autumn of 1944, had emerged already during World War I. As early as 1915, the creation of a Finnish Legion had begun near Hamburg with the purpose of weakening the Tsarist Empire and fanning the flames of revolution in Finland.[1] The Finnish Jäger Battalion fought on the Eastern Front near Riga in 1916–17. When the homeland declared independence on 6 December 1917, the soldiers swore an oath to the 'White' government in Helsinki. Landing on 25 February 1918, they were greeted by the Finnish commander-in-chief, General Carl Gustaf Freiherr von Mannerheim, and formed the backbone of the new Finnish Army, which would hold its own against the 'Reds' in the civil war. Until well into the 1950s, the Finnish military elite was moulded by former members of the Jäger Battalion. In short, the myth of Finnish independence goes back to this age-old brotherhood-in-arms.

In the period between the wars, the country played its part in the circle of Scandinavian democracies. Only in the autumn of 1939 was Finland suddenly and acutely threatened by its Soviet neighbour to the East. In late June, German Chief-of-Staff Franz Halder had paid the Finnish Army a visit. He was impressed by the anti-Russian mood and their willingness to make common cause with the Germans. The visit of General Walter Kirke, commander of the British Territorial Army, just prior to this did little to change this.[2] The Finns felt secure in their defence efforts against the Red Army, though according to the assessment of a German military attaché their artillery was primarily captured Russian equipment from World War I and the development of their own armaments industry had not yet progressed sufficiently. Arms supplies from the Germans, especially modern aeroplanes and tanks, so greatly sought-after in Finland, had not yet been effected due to the Germans' high asking prices.

The fact that Paris and London showed interest in a military pact with Moscow to curb German expansion made the Finns somewhat cautious towards the Western Powers. What they did not know in Helsinki was that only weeks later Hitler would be willing – in a secret protocol to his pact with Stalin – to cede not only the Baltic states to the Soviet 'sphere of influence' but Finland as well.

Hitler cold-shouldered the Finns when the Soviet dictator was prepared to collect his spoils and, on 30 November 1939, ordered an invasion of his little northern neighbour with 30 divisions and 750,000 troops. Even fellow fascist Mussolini was willing to lend his support to the courageous little army in its fight against Bolshevism. But Hitler would not budge. It was up to the Western democracies to help out the Finns. Indeed, it almost came to a direct military confrontation with the USSR. But Helsinki, after surprising initial victories against a clumsy Red Army which suffered heavy losses, ultimately yielded to pressure from Moscow and surrendered on 13 March 1940. In a peace treaty the Finns never really accepted, they were forced to cede large parts of Karelia to the Soviet Union along with strategic bases in the Baltic Sea. With 132,000 dead and 330,000 wounded, the Red Army paid a high price for this victory. The 5,800 Soviet prisoners of war allowed to return to their homeland were led through Leningrad to cheering crowds before being secretly executed. 'Father' Stalin granted no pardon to 'losers'.

When the Wehrmacht began its own offensive in Scandinavia, occupying Denmark and Norway four weeks later, the Finnish multiparty government under Prime Minister Risto Ryti banked on a rapid dissolution of the German-Soviet alliance. The German victory against France seemed proof that a revision of Finland's eastern border could only be hoped for in co-operation with the Reich. Hitler, on the other hand, would only gradually drop his 'cool and distanced, essentially anti-Finnish policy'.[3] It was his decision to attack the Soviet Union in the coming spring that induced him to resume supplying German arms to the Finns in August of 1940. His only concern for the time being was to bolster Finland against the possibility of another push by Stalin. Germany's interests were mainly to protect the strategically vital nickel mines in northern Finnish Petsamo, which Helsinki cleverly brought into play. About 2,000 German soldiers were permitted to be stationed in the country to protect a supply route to northern Norway passing through Finnish territory.

On his visit to Berlin in November 1940, Soviet Foreign Minister Molotov insisted that Finland 'once and for all [be considered] an inalienable part of the Soviet sphere of influence' – which basically boiled down to the right to annex the country Baltic style.[4] Hitler left his demand for a German withdrawal unanswered. And yet they acted in unison to foil plans for a proposed Swedish-Finnish defence pact. German sovereignty in the Baltic Sea region forced the Swedes into compliance, and the Finns even more so given the pressure they faced from the East.

German generals were extremely sympathetic towards Finnish soldiers. Thus, from the very beginning their operational plans included the participation of the Finns. The German Army of Norway was preparing Operation Reindeer, its attack on Murmansk, with the potential support of Finland. The formation and supplying of even just a few German divisions at the North Cape required transport through Swedish territory, however.

Baron Carl Gustav Emil von Mannerheim, commander-in-chief of Finnish armed forces, 1939–44.

By late 1940, reconnaissance activities had intensified on both sides, as well as talks on a military level. Revising his previous plans, Hitler now gave priority to capturing Leningrad over Moscow so that Finnish territory gained in importance. A second focal point of attack in central Finland was envisaged as part of a pincer operation to cut off the Murman Railway, which connected Murmansk with Leningrad and was built during World War II by German prisoners of war. Moreover, Hitler had already made plans for the Finnish Army – without consulting Helsinki beforehand – to engage in operations on both sides of Lake Ladoga, tying up Soviet forces there to the greatest possible extent, in conjunction with German Army Group North, and facilitating the attack on Leningrad. A visit by the Finnish chief-of-staff, Lieutenant-General Erik Heinrichs, to Berlin in late January 1941 was used to reach non-binding agreements as avowed precautionary measures against the USSR. Hitler was already convinced of this 'solid brotherhood-in-arms'.[5]

It was impossible, however, for more German forces to be deployed in this theatre of war, because a British naval thrust towards Lofoten in early March of 1941 made Hitler more concerned about defending Norway. What is more, German-Finnish forces were split up from the start. At his notorious 'Führer conference' of 30 March 1941, where he disclosed his ideological conception of war, Hitler was extremely sceptical in assessing his potential allies. He praised the Finns, though, for their valiance, even though he considered their army rather weak in terms of leadership and equipment. This weakness notwithstanding, he was still willing to give overall command of the operations to their supreme commander, Field Marshal Mannerheim. As Mannerheim later declined for political reasons, a unified command structure never materialized.

The deployment of German troops could no longer be disguised by April–May 1941. Concrete plans had already been made at the lower levels and reconnaissance activities had been carried out as well. And yet the political situation was still unresolved. Here too, Hitler sought to avoid concrete contractual negotiations, keen as he was to retain sole command over the Eastern campaign. Official military talks did not begin until 25 May 1941. There was talk of a 'Crusade against Bolshevism', but no binding agreements as of yet. Only two weeks before the German attack were there any negotiations in Helsinki about more detailed agreements. The Finnish government deemed Hitler's intention 'an historical sign of a great era'. The time was now ripe to take up arms against Finland's arch enemy.[6]

Granted, for reasons of domestic politics and constitutional law Helsinki refused to wage war against the USSR without provocation. There were also fears that the Germans might intervene in the country's internal affairs. Finnish volunteers had been running recruitment ads for the Waffen SS for some time,[7] and Hitler, 'with all due precaution', was secretly preparing the 'annexation of Finland as a federal state'.[8] The Nordost Battalion was set up in Vienna on 15 June 1941. A total of 373 men, among them active soldiers of the Finnish Army, were assigned to the Wiking Division. They were part of the Russian campaign from the very first day of fighting. The volunteer battalion was comprised of 834 Finns and received its own flag in October. After completing its training, it was attached to the SS Regiment Nordland. The battalion included army chaplains as well – quite unusual for the SS.

The volunteer battalion was utilized in December 1941 in the fight against partisans and for defending positions along the Mius River in southwest Russia. The Finns fought in the Caucasus in the summer of 1942, survived the retreat and were transferred to Bavaria in May 1943 to recuperate. From there they were sent back to Finland where the battalion was disbanded and the volunteers rejoined the Finnish Army.

One week before the war began, the III Finnish Corps were made subordinate to the German Army of Norway under Colonel-General Nikolaus von Falkenhorst. Field Marshal Mannerheim assumed independent supreme command over 16 divisions with around 200,000 men in the south of the country as well as over the German units reinforcing the attack on the Soviet base of Hanko. The Finnish Air Force with its 307 front aeroplanes was also under Mannerheim. The German Liaison Staff North, led by Infantry General Waldemar Erfurth, was to co-ordinate.[9]

Thus, on 22 June 1941 German armed forces set out from Finnish soil against the Red Army while the government in Helsinki declared its neutrality. It was only the repeated Soviet attacks on Finnish cities and military facilities that finally prompted them on 25 June to declare a defensive war. The Finns did not at all identify with Hitler's racially motivated war of extermination against the USSR, as much as they adopted its anti-Communist propaganda. Indeed, Jewish officers and soldiers served in the Finnish Army until the end of the war.

Brothers-in-arms! Follow me one last time, now as Karelia rises up and
the dawn of a new day for Finland approaches![10] (From Mannerheim's
order of the day to his soldiers on 28 June 1941)

From a Finnish perspective, it was a completely normal power-political
process to seize the opportunity and, in a 'Continuation War', pick up where
the Winter War of 1939–40 had left off, reconquering the territories Stalin had
stolen from them. While it is true that initial military successes gave rise to
territorial expectations bordering on the notion of a Greater Finland, these
never became a binding political programme shared by all political parties in
Finland, and were soon put aside, as concerns about being drawn too deeply
into a struggle between great powers sharpened the Finnish government's
realism. In this they could count on the sympathy of their Swedish neighbours,
who were determined, despite voices to the contrary in their German-friendly
officer corps, to hold on to their neutrality at all costs. The Swedes, however,
bowing to considerable German pressure, did permit occasional German
military transports across their territory.

At the war's beginning, the most important strategic task in the far north
was assumed by the German Mountain Corps Norway under Mountain Troop
General Eduard Dietl. Two reinforced mountain divisions and subordinate
Finnish border troops were supposed to take Murmansk. But Operation
Platinum Fox became the first real failure of the Russian campaign. The
heavily fortified Rybachy Peninsula could not be captured, so that as early
as July 1941 a permanent defensive position had to be set up in this area.
German attacks on deeply echeloned Soviet defence lines along the Litsa River
incurred heavy losses in the middle of the month and likewise failed to achieve
their objective. Though Hitler authorized reinforcements, the 6th Mountain
Division stationed in Greece did not arrive in northern Norway until October,
at which point resuming the offensive was out of the question on account of
severe weather. Mountain Corps Norway ultimately suffered the highest losses
on the entire Eastern Front in 1941.

The German XXXVI Army Corps offensive in the Salla region, advancing
towards the Murman Railway, also encountered bitter resistance. The 169th
Infantry Division and the SS Nord Division became stuck outside Salla. Only
with the help of the Finnish 6th Division – part of the XXXVI Corps – could
Soviet fortifications be broken. The general lack of reserves and supplies meant
that the utterly exhausted units at the Verman Line had to go on the defensive

just 30 kilometres before the Murman Railway. The Finnish III Army Corps joining them from the south was hardly more successful, split up as it was in central Finland. In hard-to-access areas with thick, primeval forest-like vegetation, Soviet defenders could rely on reinforcements via the Murman Railway, whereas the Finns led by the Army of Norway were given no such back-up despite heavy enemy counter-attacks. The German liaison command found it much too difficult to ask Mannerheim for help. Hence, supplying a good 200,000 troops was dependent on a difficult transport situation, requiring the consent of Sweden and with no winterproof supply lines in Lapland.

The ebb of the Finnish attack in this sector is probably also related to the efforts of the United States to negotiate a separate peace between Helsinki and Moscow. The USA threatened severe consequences should the Finns interrupt arms supplies to the Soviet Union via the Murman Railway.[11] The Luftwaffe alone could not effectively block the railway. Their feeble units were split up along the various sectors of a long front and also had to provide support for the naval war at Kirkenes. The Finnish Air Force with its 'cosmopolitan' fleet (mostly American, British, French and Italian makes) was focused on securing the successful advance of the Finnish Army in Karelia.[12] Its fighter planes even gained air supremacy against an opponent that vastly outnumbered them but was focused on the Germans and on defending Murmansk.

The Finnish Army's independent operation aimed, in concert with Berlin, at an attack on both sides of Lake Ladoga. It began on 10 July 1941 and advanced with surprising speed against the main forces of the Soviet northern front. Contrary to Halder's expectations, Mannerheim shifted the focus of his attack to the Karelian Isthmus towards Viipuri (Vyborg). The city was captured on 30 August, and soon the old border was reached. In the Army High Command (OKH) more importance had been attached to the attacking wing east of Lake Ladoga so as to threaten Soviet troops to the rear of Leningrad and relieve the advance of Army Group North.

The attack on the left wing could not begin until mid-August, once the Finns had regrouped and the German 163rd Infantry Division was added. Here, too, Soviet troops were pushed back across the old border all the way to Lake Syam, but German units suffered heavy losses, not having been equipped for forest fighting. Thus, the division went back into reserve. Unlike at the Romanian front sector in the south, in Karelia the Wehrmacht did not have sufficient forces to accelerate the offensive itself. Mannerheim did not seem inclined to press forward deep into Russian territory beyond the old border. Direct pressure on Leningard was therefore modest, whereas an envelopment from the east across the Svir was totally uninteresting from a Finnish perspective and impossible on their own. Hitler's requests to this effect were rejected by Helsinki out of hand. Berlin was now paying the price for avoiding binding agreements before the start of Operation Barbarossa.[13]

The Finns were, however, willing to continue their advance into East Karelia in early September 1941 to gain a better strategic position, having failed, after all, to protect the old border in 1940. Advancing towards Lake Onega and the Svir, they improved their defensive positions and were able to disrupt a siding of the Murman Railway. With the capture of Petrozavodsk and the occupation of the western shore of Lake Onega on 1 October 1941, the Finnish offensive scored another great victory. Defensive positions were set up along the Svir at the start of winter.

Hitler again urged Mannerheim in September to at least let the German 163rd Infantry Division make an attack across the Svir towards the mouth of the Volkhov, where it could join up with the German 18th Army and enable the total encirclement of Leningrad. His announced intention to level the city once it was captured and give the area north of the Neva to Finland found little sympathy in Helsinki, however.[14] Rather, Mannerheim responded by reorganizing and reducing the size of the Finnish Army from 500,000 to 150,000 troops by the spring of 1942. It would be up to the Germans to take Leningrad; they could talk about future operations of the Finnish Army later. The signing of the Anti-Comintern Pact by Finnish Foreign Minister Rolf Witting on 25 November 1941 and the subsequent British declaration of war did nothing to alter this stance.

Finland achieved the territorial aims of its Continuation War by occupying the naval base at Hanko on 3 December 1941, made possible thanks to the withdrawal of the beleaguered Soviet garrison, whereas the German Eastern Army became visibly more exhausted with the loss of Tikhvin on 8 December 1941. Helsinki was therefore uneasy about the German declaration of war on the United States, and endeavoured not to jeopardize its own contacts with Washington.

This is the reason why Mannerheim, during a visit by Keitel in February 1942, refused to offer any support whatsoever in attacking the Murman Railway, which was being used for American aid shipments to Stalin. He insisted on a clear division of responsibilities and the dissolution of German-Finnish command posts. The Finnish Army reorganized itself into three fronts: at the Karelian Isthmus under Lieutenant-General Harald Öhquist, the Svir-Onega Front under Lieutenant-General Karl L. Oesch and the Maaselkä Front under Lieutenant-General Taavetti Laatikainen.

Even with Mannerheim's unambiguous policy of demarcation, Hitler continued to pay him respect. Thus, Hitler used the occasion of the general's 75th birthday – on 4 June 1942 – to make his only visit abroad, extending his personal congratulations to the newly appointed 'Marshal of Finland'. In Berlin the plan was now to move Manstein's 11th Army north after conquering Sevastopol and, with its help, to force the capture of Leningrad (Operation Northern Light). Then they could establish a liaison with the Finns in Karelia and on the Svir. But Manstein's forces were tied up and exhausted by Soviet counter-attacks on the Volkhov. The Finnish Front remained stable.

Snow positions on the Kollaa Front, winter 1941–2.

The country had long been suffering the consequences of mobilization and war. German foodstuffs were indispensable, whereas only a very limited supply of war material, fuel and raw materials was provided by Berlin. The German war economy, on the other hand, profited immensely from the strategically valuable nickel supplies from Petsamo and Germany's IG Farben concern had long since been expanding its influence. The pressure of German economic hegemony was a heavy burden for Finland – unlike Sweden, which was able to distance itself increasingly from the Third Reich. Finland's plans to exit the

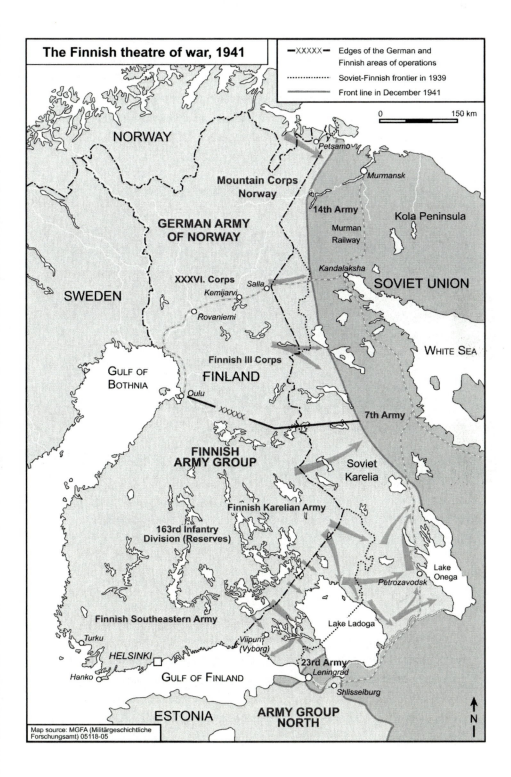

The Finnish theatre of war, 1941

Legend:
- —×××××— Edges of the German and Finnish areas of operations
- Soviet-Finnish frontier in 1939
- Front line in December 1941

0   150 km

NORWAY

Petsamo

Mountain Corps Norway

Murmansk

GERMAN ARMY OF NORWAY

14th Army

Kola Peninsula

Murman Railway

SWEDEN

XXXVI. Corps

Kemijärvi

Salla

Kandalaksha

SOVIET UNION

Rovaniemi

WHITE SEA

Finnish III Corps

FINLAND

GULF OF BOTHNIA

Oulu

×××××

7th Army

FINNISH ARMY GROUP

Soviet Karelia

163rd Infantry Division (Reserves)

Finnish Karelian Army

Lake Onega

Petrozavodsk

Finnish Southeastern Army

Lake Ladoga

Turku

HELSINKI

Viipuri (Vyborg)

Hanko

GULF OF FINLAND

23rd Army

Leningrad

Shlisselburg

ESTONIA

ARMY GROUP NORTH

N

Map source: MGFA (Militärgeschichtliche Forschungsamt) 05118-05 war were in jeopardy. Though the government was reshuffled in February 1943, the Social Democrats were still represented. During his visit to Berlin, the new foreign minister, Henrik Ramsay, refused to agree to consulting the government of the Reich first before signing any separate peace treaty with the USSR. Among the more spectacular political signals in the summer of 1943 were the disbanding of the Finnish volunteer battalion in the Waffen SS and Finland's criticism of the deportation of Danish Jews.

Finnish Waffen SS volunteers: f. l. t. r. SS Obersturmbannführer Hans Collani, SS Gruppenführer and Lieutenant-General of the Waffen SS Felix Steiner, and General Malmberg, Commander of the Finnish Defence Corps, June 1943.

The Finnish Front was almost quiet throughout the whole of 1943. But there was a good chance that a Soviet counter-offensive would threaten the country's very existence. Politically they relied on the support of the Allies against further Soviet moves, yet they wanted to be strong enough to hold their own militarily as well. Mannerheim therefore pushed to strengthen and modernize the army, particularly their artillery. To bolster its positions in the especially precarious Karelian area he therefore ordered the construction of several lines of defence at the end of 1943: a forward position on the Karelian Isthmus at the border of 1939, the VT position (Vaamelsuu–Taipall) 20 kilometres behind it, and finally the VKT position (Viipuri–Kuparsaari–Taipall), likewise on former Finnish territory; that is, before the Soviet incursion of 1940. At a distance of 150 kilometres behind the front on the Svir and Lake Onega, they constructed the so-called 'U line' along the border of 1940.

News from Washington gave the Finnish government little cause for hope. Though the Americans sympathized with the Finns, they were not prepared to jeopardize their much more important relations with Stalin. Unconditional surrender and an at least partial occupation of its territory seemed the inevitable outcome for Finland.[15] At the Teheran Conference of 1943, the Soviets signalled their willingness to respect Finnish independence so long as the Finns were willing to recognize the borders of 1940 and pay reparations; Finland, of course, would have no choice but to break off relations with Germany, expel the Wehrmacht from the country and demobilize its army. Yet Helsinki refused to negotiate on the basis of the Moscow Peace of 1940.

By early 1944, there were clear indications that a Soviet offensive was in the making. The Wehrmacht was forced to withdraw from Leningrad. A war of nerves had begun which would prompt the Finnish government to change sides. But the Finns still had an intact army of about 350,000 men on enemy territory, whereas the German 20th Mountain Army with its circa 200,000 soldiers, though defending Petsamo, at the same time posed a threat to Finland. There was nothing the Germans could do politically to put their brothers-in-arms under pressure. Thus, in the spring of 1944, they resorted to curbing the supply of grain and cutting off arms exports to Finland. Helsinki merely reacted by reining in its rebellious press.

The Wehrmacht had to be prepared for Finland's about-face. Logistical reasons alone made it impossible for the Lapland Army to intervene in the south of the country. More than a withdrawal securing northern Norway and the nickel mines in northern Finland seemed unrealistic. Finland's situation changed dramatically on 9 June 1944, three days after the Allied invasion of Normandy began. The Red Army surprisingly launched a major offensive on the Karelian Isthmus, with fewer forces than in 1939–40 but still vastly superior to the Finns in terms of numbers and supplies. A rapid breakthrough led to the capture of Viipuri on 20 June 1944. Mannerheim was left no choice but to ask the Germans to assemble six to eight divisions and provide more weapons. Hitler's foreign minister, Joachim von Ribbentrop, made a visit to Helsinki and demanded that Finland first renounce the possibility of a separate peace. One day later, Moscow called on the Finnish government to request a declaration of peace. Only then would they receive a Finnish delegation.

The Finnish government faced a tough decision. On 26 June 1944, President Risto Ryti signed the Ribbentrop letter. This secured them considerable German military aid and reinforcements, particularly anti-tank defences, giving Finland the possibility of stabilizing its front and strengthening home defence, psychologically as well. It also laid the foundation for Mannerheim – who succeeded Ryti as president – to pull his country out of war under more favourable conditions.

Despite considerable territorial gains, the Red Army had not succeeded in breaking down the Finnish Army. On the contrary, the militarily outmatched Finns managed at Tali-Ihantala to lure Soviet troops into a trap through a feigned withdrawal, destroying them in a battle of encirclement. It was Finland's greatest military achievement in World War II, indeed the greatest battle ever fought in Scandinavia. Five Finnish divisions took up arms against twelve Soviet ones, inflicting losses of 20,000 men and 600 tanks. Two squadrons of German Stukas and fighter bombers played an important role here.

After reaching the front line of 1940, Stalin withdrew his larger units to reinforce the attack on Germany. Berlin was completely at a loss. Keitel presented Mannerheim with the Oak Leaves to his Knight's Cross, but Mannerheim did not feel bound to Ryti's letter. The Finns had obviously fooled the Germans. However one viewed it in legal terms, the country was given a significant breather.

In a letter to Hitler of 2 September 1944, Mannerheim announced for his part that their paths would 'most likely diverge quite soon', as Finland could not allow the war to continue.[16] Three days later, the guns went silent on the Finnish-Soviet Front. An armistice was signed in Moscow on 19 September after hard negotiations. Berlin was in a stupor, above all from the loss of political prestige. Yet it was not unthinkable that parts of the Finnish Army would rally behind the German cause, and there was even talk of a Finnish volunteer corps as part of the Waffen SS. An urgent task was vacating German headquarters in southern Finland, which could be accomplished across the sea. The 20th Mountain Army was concerned about making a peaceful retreat. This was especially true of the two mountain corps units in central Finland, whereas the northern corps could remain in their positions before Mumansk.

The armistice commission forced the Finns to actively expel the Wehrmacht, which, following a few initial mock battles ('autumn manoeuvres'), led to the first real clashes at the end of September. At the same time, a Soviet offensive on the Murmansk Front resulted in the surprisingly rapid collapse of German positions there. The Mountain Army, threatened by a potential British landing to their rear, preferred to exit Finland in a 1,000-kilometre disengagement plan, withdrawing to the Narvik region. The scorched-earth policy they used in doing so would encumber German-Finnish relations for years to come.

Around 84,000 Finns were killed in World War II. The Treaty of Paris (1947) imposed the loss of 12 per cent of Finland's territory and payment of US$300 million in reparations. More than 400,000 refugees from Karelia had to be taken in as well – over 12 per cent of the total population, a figure proportionately comparable to the number of German war refugees. But the country was not in ruins, and its army was still fit for action. Finland was Hitler's only European ally to avoid being occupied and which managed to preserve its political culture.

2

Hungary

The Kingdom of Hungary was the oldest ally of the German Reich. Hungarian troops fought against Russia in the Austro-Hungarian Army, on the side of the Central Powers, until 1918. The collapse of the Austrian dual monarchy left behind a barely cohesive Hungarian state which, after the Treaty of Trianon, belonged to the losers of World War I. More than 70 per cent of its national territory was amputated and more than 3.5 million ethnic Hungarians suddenly found themselves under the sovereignty of newly formed neighbouring states. The country was left with only 8.6 million citizens. Viewed in this light, Hungary was the biggest loser of World War I. Reclaiming the borders of 'Greater Hungary' became the doctrine of its new army, the Royal Hungarian Honvéd. Formed in 1919, the army initially comprised 4,000 officers who, under the leadership of Miklós von Horthy, the last commander-in-chief of the Austro-Hungarian Navy, overthrew the communist revolution of Belá Kun. Thus anti-Communism became the second doctrine of a state which clung to the fiction of a monarchy and was ruled by its 'Vice-Regent' Horthy.

The victorious powers had imposed severe military restrictions on Hungary, similar to those of the Weimar Republic. In the 1920s, Budapest became the hotbed of a 'right-wing international' which followed the example first of Fascist Italy, then of National Socialist Germany. Though hindered by reparation payments and economic depression, Hungarian army leaders sought opportunities for systematic rearmament as of the early 1930s. Mussolini's Italy was willing to help, and later Hitler's Germany. In early 1939, the feverish build-up of Hungary's armed forces began; they were already 120,000 strong. Shortly before, Czechoslovakia had been pressured by the Axis Powers to return southern Slovakia to Hungary, and in March 1939 –

following the occupation of Prague by the Wehrmacht – Carpathian Ruthenia, too, became Hungarian territory once again.

Horthy, surrounded at first by the states of the French-backed Little Entente, pursued his policy of revisionism cautiously. In September 1939, more than 150,000 Polish refugees were permitted to cross the new Hungarian-Polish border, among them tens of thousands of soldiers who, via Budapest, made their way to France, where they established a Polish army-in-exile. Berlin, in the autumn of 1939, was more interested in 'peace' in the Balkans. But already in early 1940 there were plans for a possible German invasion of Romania, in which Hungary, naturally, would be indispensable as a deployment zone.[16] Budapest picked up on its changing strategic role. The German-friendly chief-of-staff, Colonel-General Henrik Werth, mobilized his country for an attack on its hated neighbour. At the very last minute, on 30 August 1940, Hitler decided to divide Transylvania between Hungary and Romania with the Second Vienna Award. But the Hungarians were still not satisfied by this compromise, and throughout the war there would be frequent gun battles along the new Hungarian-Romanian border.

This giant step towards restoring Greater Hungary was impressive, however, to military leaders, who trusted that, in future, the Germans would give them preferential treatment over Romania. But their urgent interest in modernizing the Hungarian Army was met with reserve in Berlin. Hungary was still considered 'unreliable' and received aeroplanes, tanks and guns from Germany's giant arsenal of captured weapons no different from those given to Romania; care was taken to give neither side a notable advantage over the other so as to avoid a potential invasion in either direction. To be sure, Hungary's industry was able to produce its own armaments under German licence and could even think about raising its own tank divisions. But this was not enough, by 1941, to wage any kind of serious war for an extended period of time.

Hungarian Prime Minister Count Pál Teleki was therefore extremely apprehensive. When events in the Balkans came to a head in the spring of 1941, he informed London and Washington that he hoped to keep his country out of war:

The Hungarian government's main task in this European war is to preserve Hungary's military, material and national strength until the end of the war. We must keep ourselves out of the conflict at all costs. The outcome of the war is doubtful. What is most important for Hungary, in any case, is to stand unscathed in the concluding period of the European war. It can easily happen, particularly in the case of Germany's total defeat, that in all of Europe at the end of the war conditions become chaotic, which would pose the greatest threat to those states that are unprotected, that have sacrificed their material means and their army before the conclusion of the European war. ... The country, our youth, our army must be risked solely for ourselves and for no one else. (From a letter of Count Pál Teleki from 3 March 1941)[17]

Army leaders assessed the situation more optimistically and could not elude the pressure emanating from Romanian Prime Minister Ion Antonescu's attempts to curry favour with Hitler. If Hungary wanted to protect its territories from Romanian revisionism, it could not fall behind in the arms race. Thus, it immediately showed its willingness to take part in the German invasion of Yugoslavia. Hungary committed itself with an entire army and was able to reconquer Bácska, the Mur region and the Baranya triangle with a total of 1 million inhabitants. Resistance among the local population was met with brute force, to which Serbs, Jews and even ethnic Germans fell victim. Driven to despair by these political developments, Prime Minister Teleki shot himself on 3 April 1941 just before the invasion began. Three days later, Great Britain broke off relations with Budapest. The British waited with their declaration of war until the end of the year, when Stalin pressed them to put an end to the double-track policy of Germany's allies.

Army reforms in Hungary were making progress by the spring of 1941. The number of troops was increased, but a tight economic situation did not allow their equipment to be upgraded to any significant degree. The Honvéd now had three high commands at its disposal and the command of the I Mobile Corps with a potential war strength of 600,000. The continuous build-up of reserves, on the other hand, was lagging behind, as was the procurement of modern aeroplanes, anti-aircraft guns, tanks and anti-tank guns. The army tried to hide these deficiencies through the intense indoctrination of troops. Army propaganda touted its own soldiers as the best in the world. Revisionism and anti-Communism were guiding principles, particularly in the officer corps.

Although Berlin recognized the importance of Hungary as an indispensable transit zone in planning Operation Barbarossa, Hitler, in December 1940, was still opposed to its direct involvement. Budapest would be informed at the last minute to avoid a potential disclosure to the British. The OKH lobbied in vain for a Hungarian thrust across the Carpathians. Horthy was long unsure of Germany's intentions, but assumed that defensive measures along the border to the USSR would be of use to Berlin. One week before the start of the Russian campaign, Colonel-General Werth was pressing Germany for a formal offer to take part in the war against the Soviet Union. The new prime minister, László von Bárdossy, however, was anxious that his country might divide its forces in the face of hostile neighbours (Romania and Slovakia).

The bluffing on both sides verged on the ridiculous. While the Hungarians waited for the Germans to ask them for help with the hope of negotiating services in return later on, Berlin remained tentative to the very last minute. Chief-of-Staff Halder explained this stance as follows: 'One doesn't make demands, because these require payment, but one would be grateful for any support, especially mobile troops. German train transports may under no circumstances be disrupted'.[18] When the Wehrmacht began its attack on the USSR on 22 June 1941, the Hungarian-Carpathian border was thus omitted for the time being. The border was secured by a mere four brigades, up against a vastly superior 12th Soviet Army. The latter, with its armoured units, formed part of the point of main effort in the Lemberg (Lviv) area. From the perspective of the OKH, Hungary's initial non-involvement was quite welcome, because its own attack against the bulge in the front line at Lemberg was to target the flanks. But frontal pressure by the Hungarians in the near future could perhaps prevent an evasive manoeuvre by the Soviet grouping.

In the political arena, Hungary's reserve was attracting attention. Mussolini was astonished, what with 'all of Europe in combat fever'.[19] To this day it is still a mystery whose aeroplanes bombarded the northern Hungarian city of Kassa (Košice). Moscow denied its involvement immediately, and would indeed have had little interest in such a provocation. The Hungarian government, in any case, had found its *casus belli*. The Royal Hungarian Honvéd received the order to undertake 'appropriate retaliatory measures'. Following Hungarian air strikes on the Soviet hinterland, two border brigades and the Mobile Army Corps with around 45,000 soldiers began their advance. In the first two weeks they encountered little resistance. Border troops stayed behind as an occupying force.

The Mobile Army Corps under Major-General Béla von Miklós, the most modern major formation in the Hungarian armed forces with around 25,000 men, was incorporated in the 17th German Army. The nine tank companies comprising 160 light tanks of the 'Toldi' and 'Ansaldo L 5' varieties were unsuitable for major combat tasks. But as long as the corps were merely supporting the German advance as a second echelon, their poor equipment was enough, even to secure the Uman pocket where severely exhausted Soviet units had hardly any armoured forces left. Hungarian troops were euphoric, advancing along the Bug through Pervomaisk and towards the Black Sea. The defeated enemy in its indefensible position was long since beating a retreat behind the river. By mid-August, the Hungarians had reached the sea near Nikolayev.

The morning found us in heavy combat with a fiercely resisting opponent firmly entrenched along a high railway embankment. Four times we attacked, four times we got clobbered. Our commander swore in every key. Our company commanders were desperate. Urgently requested artillery support was always coming but never did. A Hungarian Hussar regiment came instead. We smiled. What did the Magyars want here? What a shame to lose such nice, elegant horses! Then suddenly we turned to stone. These fellows had obviously gone mad! Squadron after squadron moved forward, approaching us. A loud command. Like lightning the lean, suntanned riders were in their saddles, a tall colonel with a shiny gold collar actually drew his sabre. Four, five armoured scout cars barked along the flank, and already the entire regiment was roaring across the wide earth, flashing sabres gleaming in the afternoon sun. This must be how Seydlitz charged! Throwing all caution to the wind, we leapt from our holes.

It was all like a magnificent close-up for a cavalry film. The first, oddly thin rounds cracked from the embankment. … And then we watched, amazed and laughing, as the same Soviet regiment which had resisted our company's attacks so furiously and fiercely jumped to their feet and rushed backwards like mad, driven away by the howling Hungarians whose shining sabres had a rich and abundant harvest. The sight of their glaring sabres was simply too much for the nerves of these Russian muzhiks. (German eye-witness report of an attack by Hungarian cavalry in southern Ukraine)[20]

Whereas the older officers might have been reminded of their service in the Ukraine 23 years before, their commander-in-chief was more sober in his estimation. A quick German victory receded into the dim distance while the Romanians entrenched themselves with the mass of their army in the southern Ukraine. Berlin had always endeavoured to keep the two mutually hostile allies as far apart from each other as possible. Horthy now insisted on the rapid withdrawal of his elite corps. Chief-of-Staff Werth, on the other hand, wanted to send more troops to the Eastern Front and was prompted by the Vice-Regent to resign as a consequence. His successor, Colonel-General Ferenc Szombathelyi, was pessimistic about Hitler's prospects in the East and made the case for Hungary to keep its armed forces in the homeland.

But the German dictator demanded the Hungarians' continued commitment. Their Mobile Corps joined those of the Italians to support the thrust across the Dnieper near Dniepropetrovsk, and marched with the 17th German Army in October 1941 all the way to the Donets near Izyum. Then, by stages, it was allowed to retire from the front and return to the homeland. The loss of nearly 10 per cent of its personnel was less acute than the loss of almost all of its armoured cars and vehicles, worn-out as they were by the long march. Apart from four infantry brigades that were quite welcome as an occupying army in Galicia – that is to say, in Hungary's backyard, on former territory of the Austro-Hungarian Empire – the Hungarian contribution to Hitler's war in the East seemed for all intents and purposes to be over.

The setback before Moscow in December 1941 changed the situation dramatically. Hitler needed the Hungarians to prepare another summer offensive. There was no balking now. In late January 1942, Keitel began negotiating the modalities in Budapest. Szombathelyi could not dismiss the comment about Romania's huge commitment. Instead of the 32 divisions requested he ultimately offered 17, 10 of them front-line units which would march into battle as the 2nd Hungarian Army under the leadership of Colonel-General Gusztáv Jány. Keitel's promise to supply them with German equipment was less than credible, but Budapest liked to believe that it had bought its way out of any further commitments.

The Hungarian contingent was undoubtedly the core of the country's military strength. The 2nd Army was made up of 200,000 troops with nine weak infantry divisions and a tank division equipped for the most part with outdated German models (38 t and P III). An air-force brigade with 90 aircraft increased its reach. Seven occupying divisions – the Germans, by comparison, had a total of 12 security divisions at their disposal in 1941 for the entire occupied territory – took charge of large areas in northern Ukraine, thereby freeing up German security units. With regard to local populations, the Hungarians acted just like the Wehrmacht. On the homefront they increased anti-Semitic measures under pressure from the Germans. This did not stop Hungarian recruits of the Jewish faith, however, from being assigned to fatigue duty in labour-service companies, on the Eastern Front and elsewhere, where they counted among the regular units of the Royal Hungarian Honvéd.

Hungarian infantrymen occupy a
village in the Ukraine.

The 2nd Hungarian Army arrived in the zone of Germany's Army Group South by the end of July. Here, along with the Italians and Romanians, they were supposed to secure the flank on the Don, a defensive task that was about the limit of what Hitler expected from them. The Hungarians, moreover, were to secure the northern section near Voronezh, which they had helped capture in mid-July 1942. The chief of the Operations Department of the 2nd Hungarian Army, Colonel Gyula Kovács, was sceptical of the operation. 'Neither the army marching into battle nor – I presume – our motherland itself can see any point, any meaningfulness in this war and our participation in it. … You can't fight a war if you're not convinced of its meaningfulness.'[21]

With the German armies marching off to the South, the Hungarians were largely left to their own devices in a section 200 kilometres wide. The river was not a sure defence, the Soviets having held a number of bridgeheads on the western bank. Hungarian attacks suffered high casualties and were halted in September. They now went on the defensive.

While the battle for Stalingrad was raging and the Soviet counter-offensive in November of 1942 succeeded in encircling the 6th Army, a tense calm reigned on the Hungarian Front in the north. The Hungarian infantry divisions positioned there were each supposed to occupy an expanse of nearly 20 kilometres, twice as much as normal. Heavy weapons had to be deployed at the main line of resistance. Individual German divisions stationed as reserves behind the Hungarian lines were withdrawn in December and January in order to close the enormous gap in the southern front. Honvéd soldiers received rations from German depots that were lacking in fat and flavour compared to those they were used to. Their commander-in-chief, however, had other things on his mind.

Relations with the German liaison staff under Major-General Hermann von Witzleben were extremely tense. With the withdrawal of the last German divisions from the main line of resistance, Jány declared that his entire army had apparently been betrayed beyond redemption and that he was considering marching his troops back home. Promises of heavy anti-tank weapons were enough to detain him for the time being. Behind the scenes, the Germans made no secret of their opinion that the Hungarians were unreliable and not particularly fit for combat. The Army Group, at any rate, provided a general command with a tank corps as a reserve. But most of these fighting vehicles had to be given up when the Hungarians surrendered their tank division – which later turned out to be a disastrous decision, the 2nd Hungarian Army losing its single most powerful unit.

In early January 1943, as the 6th Army was on its last legs in the Stalingrad pocket, the Hungarians observed the Soviets preparing for an attack at the Uryv bridgehead. The offensive at the Voronezh Front began on 12 January and extended along the frozen Don across the entire breadth of the Hungarian sector. Within three days, large parts of the 2nd Hungarian Army were on the retreat. The neighbouring Italian section began to falter at exactly the same time. Hitler forbade any sort of fallback and was evidently prepared to sacrifice his allies in a hopeless situation so as to gain time for reorganizing his line of defence. The remains of the 1st Hungarian Tank

Division secured the disorderly retreat of two army corps near Alexeyevka, among them the Jewish labour-service companies, some of whom had armed themselves to make their way back home. Landing in the hands of Wehrmacht soldiers or Ukrainian militias, the latter were unprotected by the law and could be robbed or killed indiscriminately. The chief-of-staff of the 2nd Army, Gyula Kovács, who had meanwhile been promoted to Major-General, described the desperate situation as such: 'In the Oskol Valley, 17,000 men have gathered who are still in possession of rifles. I cannot speak of battalions, because these are no longer existent. There is only a giant dung heap to speak of. ... What I've seen here has been the biggest disappointment in my life.'[22] Commander-in-Chief Gusztáv Jány was beside himself, and accused his troops of being cowardly and dishonourable in an order of the day (which he later revoked after returning home): 'Our front sector was taken over by German troops worthy of the greatest admiration. We don't deserve it, and should not expect it until we become a fully operational unit once again.'[23] Hitler rewarded this attitude by bestowing a Knight's Cross on Jány.

The III Corps deployed on the left flank was hit even harder. Whereas the rest of the other two army corps had already been removed from the front line, the northern grouping and the 2nd German Army remained in their positions for the time being, securing the bulwark of Voronezh. Hunger and cold undermined combat morale, as did constant friction with the Germans. The order to retreat from the Don was not issued until 26 January 1943. The decimated Hungarians were expected to bring up the rear to cover the retreating Germans. Major-General Count Marcell Stomm disbanded his army corps on the spot, advising his soldiers to act 'as the situation requires'. With the exception of some smaller groups that were able to fight their way through, his unit went under and Stomm himself was taken prisoner. All in all the 2nd Hungarian Army lost more than 100,000 men and all of its heavy equipment in the winter battles of early 1943.

With their suspicious co-allies the Romanians having suffered similar losses, the security situation of Hungary had at least not worsened in this respect. From the viewpoint of Hungarian leaders, it was now more crucial than ever to find a way out of the war in co-operation with the Western Allies and without provoking the Germans. But that was like trying to square the circle, for every reinforcement of home defence could be requisitioned by Berlin to shore up a wavering Eastern Front. It was therefore rather

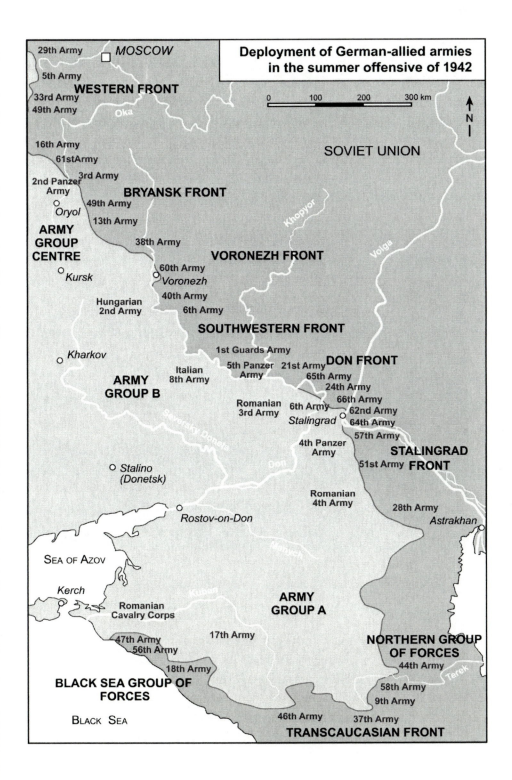

Deployment of German-allied armies in the summer offensive of 1942

29th Army
MOSCOW
5th Army
WESTERN FRONT
33rd Army
49th Army

0   100   200   300 km

N

SOVIET UNION

16th Army
61stArmy
3rd Army
2nd Panzer
Army
Oryol
BRYANSK FRONT
49th Army
13th Army
ARMY
GROUP
CENTRE
38th Army
Kursk
VORONEZH FRONT
60th Army
Voronezh
40th Army
Hungarian
2nd Army
6th Army
SOUTHWESTERN FRONT
Kharkov
1st Guards Army
Italian
8th Army
5th Panzer
Army
21st Army
DON FRONT
ARMY
GROUP B
65th Army
24th Army
Romanian
3rd Army
6th Army
66th Army
62nd Army
Stalingrad
64th Army
57th Army
Stalino
(Donetsk)
4th Panzer
Army
STALINGRAD
FRONT
51st Army
Rostov-on-Don
Romanian
4th Army
28th Army
Astrakhan
SEA OF AZOV
Kerch
Romanian
Cavalry Corps
ARMY
GROUP A
NORTHERN GROUP
OF FORCES
47th Army
56th Army
17th Army
44th Army
18th Army
BLACK SEA GROUP OF
FORCES
58th Army
9th Army
BLACK SEA
46th Army
37th Army
TRANSCAUCASIAN FRONT

Oka
Khopyor
Volga
Seversky Donets
Don
Manych
Kuban
Terek

expedient that Hitler had lost all confidence in the Hungarians militarily after their disaster on the Don. Only the Hungarian occupying army in western Ukraine remained, though a growing Soviet partisan army made this chore a tough one indeed. And while leaders in Budapest were increasingly concerned about withdrawing troops back close to their own border, the Germans viewed their allied Hungarian occupying divisions as front reserves, deployable, if necessary, in the struggle against Red Army units which had broken through. Thus, a tough political struggle ensued, demanding a good many compromises from Hungarian leaders.

The Hungarian Honvéd's retreat
from the Don on 20 January 1943.

Contact with the Western Powers was consolidated. In a secret agreement of 9 September 1943, Hungary promised to reduce its military commitment to Nazi Germany. Military engagements against the Allies were to be avoided whenever possible. Allied prisoners of war who had fled to Hungary would not be handed over to Germany. The government would aid the departure of Polish military internees and thereby contribute to the formation of an army-in-exile. On the other hand, Berlin put Hungary under increased pressure to export more to Germany, and this on a credit basis. The suggestion to do so by expropriating Hungarian Jews was roundly rejected by the government of Kállay, even while discrimination against this economically powerful minority was accelerated.[24]

Hitler complained about Hungary's lack of commitment in the war against Bolshevism and Jewry during Horthy's visit in Klessheim on 16 April 1943. The Vice-Regent affirmed his absolute loyalty but said 'he couldn't just kill the Jews'.[25] He had expected more German support, at least in rebuilding the Hungarian Army. But Berlin retained its signature reserve. Eight divisions with increased firepower would be activated by October 1944. This time frame most likely took into account expectations of an Allied advance. Though lacking still in equipment, the Honvéd increased the number of its troops significantly, enough at least for national defence. By the end of 1943, eight reserve divisions, two tank divisions, one cavalry division and eight specialized brigades were at its disposal as well. The arms industry in Hungary, a country not yet affected by the air war, was far from meeting demand. Sixty per cent of its capacities were working for the Germans, who ordered increasing supplies of armaments, especially aeroplanes.

Mobilization plans had to be drastically cut back as a result in the spring of 1944. Only one quarter of those eligible for military service could be drafted, but even these 500,000 soldiers did not have sufficient arms. Heavy equipment was technically outdated. Turán 40 and Turán 41 tanks with their 40 and 75 mm cannons did not stand a chance against the Soviet T-34s. An additional problem with regard to combat morale was the high proportion of recruits of Romanian, Slovakian, Ukrainian and Serbian nationality. These soldiers were primarily used in units behind the lines, which hardly improved the Germans' opinion of their ally.

The Hungarian western and eastern occupying groups with their nine divisions to a large degree bore the brunt of the war in the East in 1943–4. Around 90,000 troops were expected to secure large areas behind the lines for the German Army Groups Centre and South. Hungarians thus comprised about 30 per cent of overall occupying forces. Group East was to control the eastern part of the Pripyet swamp between Kiev and Priluki, while Group West was to monitor the rail lines between Brest-Litovsk and Gomel.

There in the Bryansk Forest the partisan war was particularly fierce. Residual parts of the Soviet Army, provided with continuous air cover, developed a combat technique for which the lightly armed and poorly trained Hungarians were no match. Permanently overburdened, the latter reacted by creating 'dead zones', with harsh reprisals against the civilian population. In terms of brutality, the Hungarians were surpassed only by the SS.[26] Insufficient discipline encouraged arbitrary shootings and attacks, or so the Wehrmacht units which had been allocated Hungarian subunits complained. Such behaviour was not of an ideological mould. Sixty per cent of the soldiers were recruits of non-Hungarian nationality, commanded by overtaxed reserve officers. They felt like mere 'guests' in the German theatre of war, and saw no reason not to be ruthless to the Russian-Ukrainian population.

As of 1943, Hungarian occupying troops were increasingly passive. They failed miserably against Soviet troops when the latter managed to penetrate the front. The Hungarians in Group West, in former eastern Polish territories, respected their traditional friendship with Poland. They also made local truces with the anti-Communist Ukrainian partisan army, the UPA. But the Hungarian occupying troops were still a kind of security for the Germans.

By the spring of 1944, the front was approaching northeastern Hungary. A critical situation and mistrust of his allies forced Hitler to act. Plans devised long before to occupy the strategically and economically important country were taken out of reserve.[27] These took for granted a considerable willingness of the population and army to collaborate. Any resistance was to be met with brute force, but they expected a largely 'co-operative' occupation. The desperate situation of Horthy-loyal officers was expressed in a radio message by Lieutenant-General Bakay, commanding general of the III Corps: 'The Russian before us, the German behind us, the Englishman above us, give me orders.'[28]

On 18 March 1944, Horthy was pressured by Hitler in Klessheim. He ultimately had no other option than to accept the occupation of his country by eight German divisions and to dissolve the government of Kállay, so loathsome to Berlin. The Germans did not disarm the Honvéd, but they did institute a dramatic change of policy towards Hungarian Jews. Adolf Eichmann's special unit moved in and, with the support of a right-wing opposition jockeying for power, organized the deportation of 437,000 individuals to Auschwitz. It was not only the Germans who profited from the confiscation of their estates but also countless Hungarian citizens who helped themselves to Jewish property, rendering the alliance with the Reich more 'productive'.[29] To be sure, an increasing number of Jewish men were conscripted into labour service in the Hungarian Army, momentarily avoiding their extermination.

Hungarian military leaders accepted this change of policy with an 'almost Oriental fatalism' – or such was the impression of the German General Staff.[30] The Germans massively intervened in army organization. Higher staffs were eliminated and new reserve divisions formed. Special emphasis was placed on the recruitment of Hungarian Germans. About 120,000 were mobilized by the Waffen SS, most of them forced recruits. Himmler assembled no less than five divisions this way, as well as reserves for his police regiments, where the less able-bodied recruits ended up.

Of immediate military importance was the use of the newly activated 1st Hungarian Army in April 1944 to defend the Carpathian foothills. Around 150,000 troops under Colonel-General Géza Lakatos fought in the units of the German Army Group Northern Ukraine led by Field Marshal Walter Model. With a steady stream of reinforcements from Hungary, the army, on 22 July 1944, encountered a Soviet offensive on a 150-kilometre front which within two days forced the Hungarians to retreat to their position in the Carpathians. The 1st Hungarian Army lost about 30,000 men in the process – dead, wounded and missing in action. But the marshalling of two German divisions enabled them to hold their deeply echeloned defence lines against multiple Soviet attempts to break through, especially at the all-important Dukla Pass. The difficult terrain alone was enough to keep the Red Army from exerting its superiority in tanks and artillery on this secondary front.

With Romania's change of front on 23 August 1944, Hungary had to use its 2nd Army to defend Transylvania in the southern Carpathians. It was able to mobilize about 190,000 soldiers. One way of obtaining the necessary manpower was by shortening a front of the 1st Army. Occupying troops, as well, were now given permission to return home from Poland.

Hungary was suddenly an important theatre of war. Its oil fields, the only ones Hitler now had, were imperilled. Hence several major offensives were begun here from September 1944 to March 1945. Hitler deployed a large part of his mobile reserves (15 tank divisions, 4 armoured infantry divisions, 4 cavalry divisions, 6 infantry divisions) to try and regain the initiative. The largest massing of German tank units on the Eastern Front required the support of infantry forces, most of whom were Hungarians.

Friction with the OKH was not uncommon, as the Germans preferred to send higher staff, and not troops, to lead the Honvéd units themselves. The

Hungarians were in fact quite daring in their offensive near Kolozsvár (Cluj) against their 'arch-enemy' the Romanians, who were preparing, with Soviet backing, the 'liberation' of northern Transylvania. With the deployment of Soviet armoured forces, however, the General Staff in Budapest thought it advisable after only two weeks to go on the defensive again. The Red Army tried to break through via Nagyvárad (Oradea) and Debrecen in order to advance on the Hungarian capital. One of the hardest-fought tank battles of World War II took place there in early October 1944.[31] German-Hungarian forces with 11 divisions crushed the spearhead of an opponent three times stronger, inflicting heavy casualties. Thus, the attempt of the 2nd Ukrainian Front to encircle the 8th German Army along with the 1st and 2nd Hungarian Armies had backfired. The bulk of these armies was able to make an orderly retreat to the Budapest area.

Horthy, thoroughly despising the Soviets, had actually wanted to avoid negotiations with them at all costs. But the Western Allies rejected a separate armistice. Following the lead of Finland, the Vice-Regent was seeking a way to get out of the war by mid-September 1944. He even sent a delegation to Moscow and in a letter to Stalin pleaded for the lenient treatment of his country. On 11 October, he declared his willingness to accept the Soviet demand for an immediate declaration of war on Germany. The Germans were well informed, though, and organized a putsch in Budapest. Under the leadership of Otto Skorzeny, separate commandos arrested important Horthy-loyal officers and kidnapped Horthy's son. A brief exchange of gunfire with household troops ensued, and then the castle was taken. On 16 October, Horthy signed his abdication.

The radical 'Arrow Cross Party' now took the reins in Hungary, mobilizing the entire country and intensifying anti-Jewish measures. They promised the Germans four additional divisions while even their regular troops were disbanding. They therefore disbanded their divisional headquarters and formed mixed German-Hungarian regimental groups. Hungarian artillery remained operational. In early 1945, the ration strength of Hungarian forces in the field was 280,000, along with 500,000 rearward troops. Hungarian commanders had the frequent impression that the Germans had no scruples letting untrained or exhausted Hungarian units be 'led to the slaughter'.

While the country was sinking in the maelstrom of war, Berlin at least wanted to secure some troop reserves. The rear installations and training regiments of the Honvéd with their circa 200,000 men were distributed

Morale-boosting propaganda for the ethnic German minority in northern Transylvania, August 1944.

Arrow Cross leader Szálasi after seizing power in Budapest with German assistance in October 1944.

throughout Germany and Denmark. About 16,000 youths were used in German anti-aircraft units. Individual Hungarian battalions fought in 'fortresses' on the Eastern Front such as Breslau (Wrocław), Kolberg (Kołobrzeg) and Posen (Poznań), and ultimately in Berlin as well. At the end of the war, a good 110,000 Hungarian soldiers were still deployed, mainly in Army Group South.

The attack on Budapest was of great strategic importance to Stalin. The attempt at a rapid capture in early November 1944 failed, and the Germans used the opportunity to reinforce their lines of defence with the help of Jewish forced labourers. Attacks along the 2nd Ukrainian Front gained ground very slowly against outnumbered German-Hungarian defenders. Several German counter-offensives jeopardized Soviet victory. The Hungarians did not expect to defend their capital city for long, but Hitler ordered the 'fortress' to be held at all costs, without regard for civilian casualties. Thus, the battle for Budapest turned into a 'Stalingrad on the Danube'. By the end of the year about 100,000 soldiers had been surrounded, half of them Germans, half Hungarians. They managed to hold the city for 52 days against superior Soviet forces.

The worse a hopeless military situation became, the more frequent were the German reports about the supposedly low morale of the Hungarians and their high rates of desertion. That the Germans themselves contributed to this by virtually disabling Hungarian officers and treating them condescendingly, giving them no real reason to urge their troops on, was left unmentioned. The SS units recruited from Hungarian-Germans did not give a much better impression. Machine-gun positions were set up behind the 8th SS Police Regiment, for example, to keep the soldiers from deserting. Hungarian Arrow Cross fascists, on the other hand, found the SS to be a valuable support in their mass murder of the remaining Budapest Jews. The battles outside the city, with their ultimately failed relief offensives, were conducted almost exclusively by German units. On 11 February 1945, the attempted escape of the last defenders ended in a catastrophe. Honvéd and Arrow Cross troops were supposed to follow in the second group. Instead they were shot to pieces by murderous Soviet defensive fire. Thousands died on the march to prisoner-of-war camps.

With the failure of the last German offensive on Lake Balaton in mid-March 1945, the Red Army continued its campaign to occupy the country. Its vastly superior forces crushed the Hungarian defensive front in the Vértes

Mountains and pursued the 6th German Panzer Army westward. The German-Hungarian bridgehead near Esztergom, held by the 3rd Hungarian Army, was evacuated just in time. The defence of German-Hungarian positions north of the Danube near Komárom likewise collapsed on 25 March. The complete dissolution of Hungarian units was looming on the horizon. The chief-of-staff of the Szent László Division defected to the Soviet side and encouraged his soldiers to do the same.

Hungarian troops were subsequently disarmed in the operational area of the 6th German Army. They had to hand over their vehicles and make their way on foot to specified quarters. Many Hungarian refugees, including ministers and generals, were ruthlessly robbed. Protests by the Honvéd Ministry went unheard. In the chaotic last days of the war, German and Hungarian commanders alike were mainly concerned with avoiding Soviet captivity.

The country paid a high price for its alliance with the Third Reich. In terms of its national borders of 1941, it suffered an estimated 360,000 deaths, more than a third of these (120,000 to 155,000) on the Eastern Front and at least 55,000 in captivity. The remaining 155,000 soldiers cannot be accounted for. The last prisoner of war, András Thoma, returned home in 2001. In addition, 590,000 civilians perished in the war, 490,000 of these persecuted and murdered as Jews. About 20,000 died in allied bombings, another 30,000 during fighting in the last months of the war. Around 290,000 civilians were deported to the Soviet Union.

Hungary spent four decades in the Soviet sphere of influence. Its national uprising of 1956 was bloodily suppressed. In the Paris Peace Treaties of 1947, the country was trimmed back to its territorial status of 1920. Moreover, it was forced to pay US$300 million in reparations. An open debate about guilt and responsibility never took place under the communist regime.

3

Romania

Romania, a Hohenzollern monarchy, could well have chosen to join the German-Austrian coalition at the start of World War I. But the British landing at the Dardanelles, which opened the perspective of a new front, made Bucharest the object of Allied wooing too. Berlin had no real political and economic perspectives to offer, given the overlapping interests of its other allies. Under pressure from the Austro-Hungarian monarchy to the south and west and Germany's ally Bulgaria to the south, the little kingdom could scarcely maintain its neutrality. The German Supreme Command, wanting to secure its strategically important ties to Turkey, decided to act in the summer of 1916. Romanian troops were taken by surprise in their defensive positions in the Carpathians. Many young German officers, among them Erwin Rommel, learned how to fight a blitzkrieg there. The Romanian Army retreated behind the Dniester and joined forces with the Tsarist Army. Romania suffered from a harsh German occupation policy and was ruthlessly plundered.

The Romanians knew how to profit from the collapse of the Russian Empire in 1917–18, having troops stationed in Bessarabia, a region predominantly settled by Germans and Romanians and which Russia had snatched from the Ottoman Empire a century before. Berlin supported this annexation. In the turmoil of the Russian Civil War, the river Dniester on the border was salvation for defeated anti-Bolshevist groups. Romania was magnanimous in granting asylum to former White Guardsmen and the country suddenly enjoyed the most fortunate moment in its history. It could pride itself on having belonged to the victorious powers of World War I, which paid off in the form of enormous territorial expansion – to the detriment of its neighbours. The country's national territory increased threefold, primarily through the annexation of German and Hungarian-populated Transylvania and the former Russian province of Bessarabia, and the number of inhabitants grew to almost 20 million (1938). Bucharest became the bulwark of the so-called Little Entente, the Central European zone of influence France used to secure its hegemony on the Continent.

Romania pursued a moderate policy towards its minorities. Ethnic Germans, who had lived in the region for nearly 800 years, viewed themselves as a bridge to the German Reich, the latter soon becoming the principal market for Romanian exports once again. Predominantly agrarian, the Balkan great power with its strategically important oil fields was enticing for a German policy of revision that, as of 1933, pushed for a massive expansion of economic relations with Bucharest under the banner of 'defence economics' and 'autarky'.[1] Berlin offered the Romanians extremely advantageous conditions, too, but the country's political orientation towards France could not be so easily swayed. Its vibrant cultural life in the 1930s turned Bucharest into a 'Little Paris'. Romania's Royal Army was also greatly influenced by its French ally and felt strong enough to keep in check with the Hungarians, who demanded the return of Transylvania.

While Hitler was busy breaking up Czechoslovakia with the consent of the Western Powers, Romania's authoritarian regime under King Carol II hoped to maintain its neutrality with the help, especially, of British guarantees. Co-operation with Stalin was out of the question for ideological reasons, as was dependence on Germany for fear of total domination. The country's ethnic Germans had already been systematically infiltrated by the Nazis and were interested in maintaining their identity against growing Romanian nationalism.

The subjugation and division of Poland by Hitler and Stalin in September 1939 put Romania in an increasingly precarious position. The country offered asylum to the remnants of the Polish Army, its former ally, enabling their passage to France. No one in Bucharest knew about the secret protocols signed by German Foreign Minister Joachim von Ribbentrop in Moscow. Immediately following the military defeat of France in June of 1940, the Soviets issued an unexpected ultimatum. Stalin demanded the return of the former Russian territories of Bessarabia and northern Bukovina. Mobilization of the Romanian Army was ultimately a helpless gesture. The German government 'recommended' they comply with Soviet demands, despite the fact that Berlin, in the Oil-for-Arms Pact of 27 May 1940, had just agreed to pay for Romanian oil supplies in 'hard currency'; that is to say, in weapons.

A serious political crisis erupted in Bucharest. The previously neutral country now found itself in complete political isolation. The king ordered the disputed area to be evacuated. His new government asked Germany to protect the new border and provide military training assistance – just in the nick of time, because Hungary and Bulgaria were now making claims as well. By mid-August 1940, open warfare was imminent. It was the intervention of Benito Mussolini that finally helped turn the tables. The Italian dictator had designs of his own in the Balkans, following in the footsteps of the old Roman Empire. Of course he also had tangible economic interests in mind, which were hard to assert, however, against his German ally and competitor.[2]

But it was Hitler who set up a German-Italian commission in Vienna to decide the fate of Romania. The Vienna Award of 30 August 1940 divided Transylvania between Hungary and Romania. Just a few days later, southern Dobruja was ceded to Bulgaria. Though not reverting to the borders of 1914, Greater Romania nonetheless lost half of its national territory in 1940 along with nearly 7 million citizens, 50 per cent of them ethnic Romanians. To this day, historians in Bucharest still talk about the cessions as stolen territory. At the time, indignation in the Romanian heartland was huge, exacerbated by the stream of refugees from these lost territories. The ethnic Germans from these areas were immediately resettled, or sent 'back home to the Reich' (*heim ins Reich*), in accordance with German-Soviet agreements.

The Romanian nationalist 'Iron Guard', a right-wing extremist movement, succeeded in whipping up popular resentment. Anti-Communism and anti-Semitism were among their ideological pillars, not unlike the National Socialists. Their radical nationalism, however, jeopardized the autonomy of the Romanian Germans, the bastion of a future 'Greater Germanic Reich of the German Nation' (*Grossgermanisches Reich deutscher Nation*) according to the Germanization plans of Berlin. To avoid a possible *coup d'état* by the fascist Iron Guard, the king appointed Colonel-General Ion Antonescu as head of a 'government on a military basis'. The constitution was suspended and the king stepped down in favour of his son Mihai. As erstwhile chief-of-staff and defence minister, Antonescu had been one of the monarchy's harshest critics and maintained murky relations with the Iron Guard. Appointed head of state, he held the reins of power tightly until 1944.

Antonescu played the German card unequivocally. Hungary, a power of equal rank, did not impress him, Antonescu having played a part in overthrowing the Hungarian Soviet Republic in 1919 and the temporary occupation of Budapest with Romanian troops. Indeed, he felt equal to the task of competing with the great powers in their bid for the Balkans. The general had apparently divined Hiter's next move and shifted his focus of national defence to the east. The Romanian request to send a military mission was fulfilled by the Germans in September 1940, so rapidly and massively, in fact, that Romania became the springboard for larger operations. More than 20,000 troops were certainly not just 'instruction units' for the Romanian Army, and powerful anti-aircraft units were more than protection for the strategically vital oil fields of Ploiești against potential British air attacks. In December 1940, a German tank division arrived as well.

A possible assault of German forces across the Romanian border towards Kiev was planned in the very first drafts of Operation Barbarossa. The Red Army's strongest forces, after all, were stationed in the Ukraine. The dirty work, in any case, was to be done by fast-moving German tank units. Hitler entrusted the Romanian Army with little more than security tasks. But Antonescu had his ambitions. He longed to be the Führer's ally and render 'services' that would enhance Romania's position in the Balkans. Thus, Bucharest joined the German Tripartite Pact and promised to arm itself for war by the spring of 1941. When street violence precipitated by the Iron Guard got out of control, Antonescu crushed it with brute force. The fascist Legionnaires and their leader Horia Sima, former deputy prime minister, were given asylum in Germany but no political support.

From a German perspective, maintaining the military efficiency of Romania was of prime importance. But a fascist seizure of power would have posed a potential threat to the status of the 800,000 ethnic Germans in the country. In this respect, Antonescu seemed the ideal ally. Some saw it differently – for example, Artur Phleps, who opted for the Reich in 1940, like many of his ethnic German compatriots. Indeed, the Waffen SS found welcome recruits among the Bessarabia Germans, who were sent 'back home to the Reich' – as agreed with Stalin – along with other Romanian citizens of German ancestry. Phleps was even an experienced career officer. Romania experienced shifting boundaries four times between 1918 and 1945, so that officers there had to change uniforms as many as three times. Phleps, too, had served in the Austro-Hungarian Army, then joined the Romanian Army in 1919. Disappointed by his career perspectives and indignant at the corruption he encountered, he retired from the army in 1940. In 1941, he decided to join the Waffen SS, where he made a new career for himself as a general and adopted the requisite ideology as well. It was apparently financial considerations and the professional appeal of a modern army, however, that induced him to take this step.

King Mihai (front) and General Ion Antonescu (right) following the abdication of Carol II.

By the time the Wehrmacht began using Romania as a hub for lightning campaigns against Yugoslavia and Greece in March–April 1941, the secret concentration of German troops for an offensive against the USSR was already underway. The Romanian Army comprised 29 divisions, almost exclusively infantry, and was lacking in motorized vehicles and heavy artillery. With the exception of three divisions retrained according to German principles of warfare, these troops were virtually World War I vintage in terms of their equipment. Antonescu had hoped to receive modern German arms, but German armaments production was not even able to meet the needs of the Wehrmacht. Captured weapons from the Western campaign and outdated models of various makes were all they could provide the Romanians with. This not only conflicted with the planned modernization of the army and its alignment to German standards, but actually weakened the fighting potential of the Romanians, putting them at a disadvantage logistically as well as in terms of munition supplies and spare parts. The air force with its 400 aircraft found itself in the same situation. Measured against the Hungarians, however – who were no better off with Hitler's support and, indeed, were the real reason for Romania's arms build-up – their equipment was sufficient. The Germans would have preferred it, of course, if Romanian military leaders had been content with a smaller, better-equipped army.

Officially Bucharest had not been cued in on Operation Barbarossa until just before the invasion began. German preparations for the planned spearhead from Romania towards Kiev had to be modified anyway, as the forces allocated for this manoeuvre were unexpectedly tied up in Yugoslavia and Greece. Hitler did not count on military support from the Romanians for the time being. His internal assessment of their capacities was in fact quite devastating. On 30 March 1941, he flatly stated to his generals: 'Cowardly, corrupt, rotten'. Romanian troops were fit for use only when protected by broad rivers. There was no relying on them.[3]

The 11th German Army ultimately assembled on Romanian soil was made up nonetheless – and this was unusual – of two-thirds infantry and cavalry divisions supplied by Antonescu. When the latter was officially informed by Hitler about German plans for attack, only days before it began, he spontaneously offered the whole of Romania's armed forces for deployment against the Red Army. His country would never forgive him, he felt, 'if he left the Romanian Army on alert while German troops in Romania marched against the Russians'.[4] On the very same battlefield where, 25 years before, Romanian soldiers had fought alongside the Russians against German invaders, a major formation was now hastily assembled out of the 3rd and 4th Romanian Armies and the 11th German Army, nominally under Antonescu's leadership.

Romania's interests were obvious: restoring Greater Romania along the eastern frontier as well as its hope – through unconditional support of the Wehrmacht – of impressing the Führer to such a degree that he might be willing to rethink the Vienna Award, especially if Romania's contribution to the war effort were bigger than Hungary's. Moreover, Bucharest had declared its willingness to more than double its fuel supplies to Germany in 1941 compared to the year before, giving the Wehrmacht the means to consider more expansive undertakings in the first place. Agricultural deliveries, on the other hand, were declining, even though the Germans were expecting miracles here. The Wehrmacht, which paid on credit, brought inflation to the country in 1940–1. The Romanian government had an understandable interest in not letting the country be destroyed if it entered the war, and demanded that Germany make good its growing debts by providing them with massive arms supplies, fast. Antonescu trusted in the Führer's good will – credit of trust which, it seemed, would only pay off in the case of a rapid German victory.

The Marshal ordered his German-Romanian troops to march on 22 June 1941, without a declaration of war against the USSR. In his appeal to the soldiers, he demanded the liberation of territories occupied by Bolshevism, swore upon honour, church and fatherland, and did not so much as mention that German aims went much further. The Romanians were not involved in the plan-making in Berlin anyway. But even if Romanian leaders – not unlike the Finnish government – were convinced they were fighting a war of their own, there was no thought of reining in troops once Bessarabia had been reconquered, because only by advancing eastward would Antonescu be able to render those 'services' which, to his mind, would secure Hitler's goodwill in creating a 'New European Order'.

With a national population of 13.5 million, Bucharest reckoned with a maximum of 2.2 million able-bodied men at the start of the campaign. The mobilization of all forces on 22 June 1941 yielded a total of 686,244 troops.[5] Of these roughly one half, or 325,685, saw action on the Eastern Front, namely, the 3rd and 4th Armies as well as the II Army Corps. The front troops comprised 151 infantry battalions, 53 cavalry troops, 4 tank battalions, 32 anti-tank companies, 19 anti-aircraft companies, 203 gun batteries, 61 light howitzer batteries as well as 27 batteries with heavy howitzers. Their equipment was mainly made up of antiquated firearms, artillery and vehicles. Under-equipped with light French battle tanks, the Romanian Army was never capable of conducting a German-style blitzkrieg. But Romanian troops were able to take on important tasks and relieve the Wehrmacht – light security tasks, for instance, or mopping-up of towns and villages following German tank attacks, as well as the pursuit of retreating enemy troops. The active units of the Romanian Air Force with their 209 aircraft were sufficient for this purpose. Of limited use were the 39 navy warships stationed in the Danube Delta and along the coast. The Romanians were no match, however, for the powerful Soviet Black Sea Fleet.

Weak Romanian troops faced Red Army forces of the Odessa Military District. Three mechanized and/or armoured army corps were stationed between the Dniester and Prut alone. This implied a potential clash between

Romanian cavalry and Soviet tank brigades in the battle for Bessarabia. As the main forces of the Red Army were expected in the Ukraine, Antonescu could consider himself lucky that his army group did not have to go on the offensive just yet. The Germans retained responsibility for operations anyway.

Thus, on the 600-kilometre Romanian Front, the war launched on 22 June 1941 began with merely a few local, isolated attacks with the aim of establishing bridgeheads on the other side of the Prut. Both sides bombed cities and garrisons in the hinterland of their opponent. The Soviet air fleet attacked Bucharest and nearby oil fields. Within a week, the Romanians had lost 1,000 men. In the provincial capital of Iaşi (Jassy), a pogrom broke out in which more than 12,000 Jews were murdered. Romanian anti-Semitism was directed mainly towards foreigners at first.[6] Later, hundreds of thousands of Romanian and Ukrainian Jews were deported to the newly conquered province of Transnistria. An estimated 300,000 Jews and 20,000 Roma were murdered in the Romanian Holocaust.

By 2 July 1941, the time had come – from a Romanian viewpoint – to commence the struggle for the territories 'stolen' by Stalin a year before. The better-equipped 3rd Army managed within a period of two weeks to occupy the hills of northern Bukovina against a delaying opponent, ultimately reaching the western bank of the Dniester. The 4th Army offensive against the Bessarabian capital of Kishinev (Chişinău) was successful thanks to German support. The Red Army left a trail of destruction in retreating from the city. The Romanian majority in the city welcomed the invading troops. Russians, Ukrainians and Jews who had come to the city in the course of Sovietization were deported to the other side of the Dniester by the new administration. In the course of 'clean-up' operations, the Germans saw to it that around 10,000 Jews were killed within a period of two weeks, the first great massacre on the Eastern Front.

On 22 July, German 11th Army headquarters gave Antonescu sole responsibility for capturing the crucial seaport of Odessa, despite cautious estimations of its ally's fighting potential. In the heart of the Ukraine, a battle of encirclement began once Army Group South, with its single assault group, had reached the Kiev area and headed south. Two weeks later, the fate of several Soviet armies near Uman was sealed. The 11th German Army, formed mainly from Romanian units, and the 3rd Romanian Army were badly needed to complete the encirclement. Thus, only the 4th Romanian Army remained for the fight against Soviet forces in southwest Ukraine.

The soldiers of Antonescu's army
were greeted with cheers by
Romanian compatriots in July 1941.

Antonescu's task would have been impossible had the three Soviet armies opposite him not hastened to retreat behind the Bug. The Romanian leader had much at stake, not only militarily. The occupation of southern Bessarabia – his actual war aim – was easy, being completed by the end of July. By capturing Odessa, however, the Romanians would be crossing the old Russian border, becoming a party to Hitler's far-reaching military objectives. The German dictator felt compelled to praise Antonescu for his military achievements to date and to thank him for his decision to 'choose to fight it out to the bitter end' on the side of Germany in the war against the USSR.[7] At the same time, he proposed that Romania take on the task of 'securing' the area southwest of the Bug – which ultimately boiled down to territorial spoils beyond the Romanian border. Finally, he bestowed the Knight's Cross of the Iron Cross on 'Führer' Antonescu, though puzzling over him in his inner circle: 'Racially certainly not Romanian, but Germanic, Antonescu is a born soldier. His misfortune to command over Romanians.'[8]

Indeed, the Romanian leader's euphoric military expansion did not obtain the unanimous approval of his populace. The leaders of the democratic opposition warned about crossing the Dniester. Not a single Romanian soldier should be sacrificed for foreign aims, they asserted. The Army should be reserved for achieving 'Greater Romania'.[9] Antonescu's position on the domestic front was by no means secure,[10] and conservative elite leaders had clearly picked up on signals suggesting the USA might enter the war. Antonescu could not overstretch his anti-Bolshevik philosophy as a rationale for his military ventures, even if he described his actions as an obligation to civilization. Completely mistaken about Hitler's racial-ideological objectives, he was worried that, freed from the yoke of Bolshevism, a 'Greater Slavic Empire' might emerge as a consequence of the war. The Romanian government was therefore relieved when the Germans incorporated occupied Galicia into the General Government, giving Romania an immediate border with the Greater German Reich. Hitler also made plain that he was not considering Ukrainian independence of the kind the Germans supported back in 1918.[11]

Overestimating his actual military capabilities, Antonescu soon offered to take not only Odessa but the sea fortress of Sevastopol and the Crimea as well with the aim of eliminating Soviet air-force bases there. His troops did in fact play a much greater role on the battlefields of the Ukraine than the tiny Hungarian contingent did. This might have lent him the audacity to declare candidly to German Ambassador Clodius in mid-August 1941 that he was determined 'to march against Hungary at the next available opportunity'.[12] For his chief interest was in undoing the cession of northern Transylvania to their hated neighbours, the Hungarians, and he trusted in the 'fairness of the Führer' after the end of the war in the East.

No sooner had the Romanian 4th Army encircled Odessa from the mainland than Hitler asked him to assemble troops for future operations east of the Dnieper. Antonescu was delighted at the opportunity to 'help save civilization, justice and the freedom of nations' with his own troops.[13] He offered 15 divisions, which first had to be replenished and newly equipped by the Germans, who had plenty of captured French arms with which to supply Antonescu.

The political slogans of the Romanian government seemed to allude quite consciously to the principles of the Atlantic Charter, proclaimed by US President Roosevelt and British Prime Minister Churchill on 12 August (and which included the self-determination of nations and their right to live in peace and happiness within secure borders). Bucharest, after all, had an interest in following the Finnish example, securing international recognition for the restoration of sovereignty in 'liberated' areas. US Secretary of State Cordell Hull received the Romanian Chargé d'Affaires Brutus Coste in Washington on 4 September 1941.[14] Coste explained that, from Romania's point of view, going to war against the USSR had merely served to win back the areas occupied by Stalin. The continuation of operations on foreign territory was necessary for strategic reasons and did not aim for annexation, but served to protect against the 'Red Peril'. Hull characterized the spread of Communism as a separate problem. His government, he said, viewed 'Hitlerism' as the current enemy. And his warning was unmistakable. If Romania – unlike Finland – carried the war beyond its own borders on the side of Hitler, it was opposing American interests.

Contrary to official declarations, the 4th Army – reinforced to 11 divisions with 160,000 men – was given the task of conquering a new province for the monarchy. The area between the Dniester and Bug was to be given the name 'Transnistria', with Odessa as its capital. About 34,000 Red Army soldiers, in well-consolidated positions and supported by the Black Sea Fleet, defended the seaport 'until the end', just as Stalin had ordered. Even four weeks of attacks by Romanian forces superior in number were completely unsuccessful, despite heavy casualties. The siege had to be interrupted at the end of September 1941 due to a change in army leadership. The Germans had meanwhile captured Kiev and fought the greatest battle of encirclement in history. The 3rd Romanian Army was already marching towards the Sea of Azov as part of Army Group South. Before the Germans could assemble two divisions of their own for the attack on Odessa, the Soviet garrison there withdrew on the quiet, across the water, during the night of 15 October 1941.

Romanian stormtroopers occupied the port around noon with no resistance. The 4th Army had lost nearly 100,000 men, including more than 20,000 dead, during the seven-week siege. This says less about the soldiers' bravery than about the lack of good leadership and training among troops made up predominantly of older, less enthusiastic reservists.[15] Odessa was a decisive battle in the Romanian war, for it ended the brief initial phase marked by an unwarranted feeling of superiority over the Red Army and occasioned military leaders to redouble their efforts to modernize the army.

A new administration was to turn the Ukrainian city of Odessa into a Romanian one. Co-operation with SS Einsatzkommandos went smoothly. When a division headquarters (that of General Ion Glogojeanu, commander of the 10th Romanian Infantry Division) was blown up by saboteurs on 22 October 1941 in Odessa – the same as had happened in Kiev four weeks earlier – a massacre of 25,000 Jews was organized in retaliation. Half of them were locked up in four giant warehouses. Three of the buildings were set on fire; those who tried to flee were mowed down by a hail of bullets. Women threw their children out of the windows in desperation. The fourth warehouse was torn to shreds by artillery fire. In the following days, an almost equal number of Jews were driven out of the city and shot to death on the edge of anti-tank ditches – all in all nearly 50,000 victims (at Babi Yar near Kiev, the single largest massacre, the German 'Sonderkommando 4 a' murdered 33,000 Jews in one go).

From a Romanian perspective, the campaign was over. The 4th Army went back home again to slowly fill up its ranks. The 3rd Army, having suffered not so negligible losses of 10,000 under the command of Army Group South, which made it the farthest on its eastward drive, was disbanded. The only troops to stay behind in occupied Soviet territory were four occupying divisions in Transnistria as well as a cavalry and a mountain corps belonging to the 11th German Army and deployed on the Crimea. The latter would later take part in besieging the fortress of Sevastopol.

Hitler, fearing his Eastern Front might fall apart in the face of a Soviet counter-offensive in December, could not blame this setback on his allies. Instead, he fired two dozen of his generals. The Führer's trust in Antonescu seemed justified. After legitimizing his regime through a plebiscite in November 1941, the Romanian Marshal followed Hitler into the war. On 7 December, Great Britain, pressured by the USSR, declared war against the Balkan state. And five days later, under German pressure, Antonescu declared war on the United States. War Minister and Chief of the Romanian General Staff in Bucharest Colonel-General Iosif Jacobici pointedly took his leave. The lesson learned at Odessa, where he last commanded the 4th Army, spared him the optimism of his Marshal. Antonescu described his own, self-willed interpretation of the war situation as such: 'I am an ally of the Reich against Russia. I am neutral between Great Britain and Germany. I support the Americans against the Japanese'.[16]

Having sufficiently mastered the crisis on the Eastern Front by the end of the year so he could now consider a new summer offensive, Hitler wrote a friendly letter trying to enlist the support of Romania. Without their support – alongside the help of Italian and Hungarian troops – not even the limited offensive planned in the zone of Army Group South was feasible. Antonescu alone was asked to marshal up 27 divisions as fast as possible – two-thirds of his army – for Operation Blue. German arms and equipment were promised, but what the Romanians needed the most was what it was hardest to provide them with, namely, modern battle tanks and heavy anti-tank guns. Supplies, in fact, would be even fewer than in the previous year. But Berlin was quite conscious of the persistent tensions between Romania and Hungary, and found it advisable not to overarm either one of its allies.

The Romanian General Staff found ways to safeguard its own interests despite German reservations. Whereas outwardly it seemed that Romania's border in Transylvania was wholly unprotected, because all war materials were being sent to the Eastern Front, in secret they were making sure that the troops marching east towards the Volga were thinning out and that the mass of their artillery stayed behind on the homefront. Officially this material was supposed to be used to prepare a second eastward thrust, but no such formation was ever sent marching.[17]

The Germans were well aware that the Romanians actually needed a more obliging partner in the economic sphere as well, so as 'not to [have] a lead weight but a valuable ally' at their side.[18] The Wehrmacht's unscrupulous bulk buying threatened to plunge Romania into ruin. And yet an increase in Romanian oil production was badly needed. Göring explained to Vice-Prime Minister Mihai Antonescu that 'after the blood of its soldiers, the most valuable contribution Romania can make to the common cause is therefore its petroleum'.[19]

But what was their 'common cause' once Romania had expanded its territory at the expense of the USSR? The Marshal was anticipating a 'day of reckoning with the Slavs'[20] and was prepared to march to the Caucasus or even the Urals. Antonescu was prudent enough to insist that the Hungarians, too, should make a more active contribution to the Eastern campaign, and the Führer agreed that neither Bulgaria nor Hungary would be allowed to take up arms against Romania once the war was over. The anti-Bolshevist war cry had long since faded. King Mihai viewed the deployment of his troops as a 'German affair', and was looking for an opportunity to relieve Antonescu of his duties and lead his country out of its alliance with Hitler.[21] Only when heavily pressured by the Marshal could the king be induced later on to reluctantly pay a visit to his soldiers on the Crimea, which the Germans, of course, did not fail to notice. There was growing doubt in Bucharest whether Hitler would really be willing to reward Romania's wartime commitment with the return of Transylvania. The SS had meanwhile begun to recruit volunteers among the ethnic German population, and other German organizations as well were employing an increasing number of Romanian citizens of German descent. From the government's point of view these men were deserters, and were threatened with being treated as such when on home leave or returning.[22]

Romanian infantry before Sevastopol, June 1942.

The renewed deployment of two Romanian field armies on the Eastern Front was dragging. Only when deployment was complete was Antonescu willing to assume supreme command himself again. But this would never come to pass. Reinforcements were sent first to the Crimea, where in June 1942 they participated in the conquest of Sevastopol. Six divisions were supporting the advance of Army Group A towards the northern Caucasus. These troops formed the core of the 3rd Romanian Army, which in August assumed the task of securing the coast along the Sea of Azov, in the Kuban region and on the Taman Peninsula. The advance guard of Panzer Group 1 in the middle of the army group penetrated to the edge of the High Caucasus near Nalchik, supported by the 2nd Romanian Mountain

Division. With that the Caucasus offensive was exhausted, though Hitler still envisioned the capture of oil fields as a turning point in the war. The OKH had wanted to avoid a greater Romanian commitment in the Caucasus, as incursions by allied troops against the local population had in some cases soured the mood there. The quartermaster general noted: 'expecting more of the worst: looting, rapes on a daily basis, especially on the part of the Romanians and despite strict countermeasures'.[23]

> We had some noisy neighbours: the Romanians. Their officers came to join us sometimes, wearing caps that looked like tarts. Nearly all of them spoke a sing-song and lisping French. Their soldiers produced an infernal din. There were more than 20,000 of them on our left wing. They constantly fired their guns. But we weren't even under attack! We scorned their incessant, careless fire. It merely provoked the Russians, bringing needless reaction. In a single night, the Romanians used up as many cartridges as all the rest of the sector did in two weeks. This was no longer war. It was disturbance of the peace! … Thousands of Romanian soldiers were subverted by communist propaganda. The Romanian soldiers had unquestionably performed many exploits since June 1941. They had liberated Bessarabia and conquered Odessa. They had fought gloriously in the Crimea and in the Donets. But they had a savage nature and massacred their prisoners, thus bringing about reprisals in which everyone suffered. (From the memoirs of Léon Degrelle) [24]

Instead of heading to Baku, a large part of the deployable units marched towards Stalingrad, in effect little more than flank protection on the Don and Volga. The Führer's need for prestige, however, had led him into a trap: the big city bearing the name of his rival. In mid-September 1942, the mass of the 3rd Romanian Army was transferred to the area north of Stalingrad where they were obliged to take on the most arduous section of the new front on the Don, across from a powerful Soviet bridgehead on the western bank. Colonel-General Petre Dumitrescu requested German tank and artillery support to eliminate the threat.

With an overextended front sector of 180 kilometres and insufficient supplies and equipment, considerable German pressure was required to persuade him to take over another sector from the Italians. He was given reassurances that the Red Army would not risk an offensive and some German units were even withdrawn. Receiving no clear instructions, Dumitrescu was exposed to small but continuous Soviet attacks which by 19 November had cost him 11,000 men. The Germans provided a hastily formed tank corps at the very last minute as a reserve detachment for the 3rd Army.

A front sector south of Stalingrad, extending over 250 kilometres in the Kalmykian Steppes, had been reserved for the advancing Romanian 4th Army. These circa 100,000 troops arrived just three weeks before the start of the Soviet counter-offensive. They trusted that in a crisis situation they would be given support from the German 4th Panzer Army, parts of which were tangled up in the fight for the city. At a visit to the Führer Headquarters in Vinnitsa on 22 September 1942, Deputy Prime Minister Mihai Antonescu asked not to have Romanian forces stuck between the Crimea, Caucasus, Volga and Don. 'It is unfair to expect the Romanian people to defend the most difficult sector of the Eastern Front; this task is too hard for our soldiers. I told the Führer that, in my opinion, the concentration of our units in one single area and their preparation for the coming winter would help protect us, otherwise we risk losing our army.'[25]

The deployment of Romanians on both sides of Stalingrad, the focus of attention, was a great relief to Moscow. That Hitler chose to use his weakest allied units to defend his threatened flanks was a boon to Stalin's planned counter-offensive. By encircling the German grouping at Stalingrad and destroying the Germans' allied troops, he would even gain political capital. Following a massive artillery strike, on 19 November 1942, he smashed the 3rd Romanian Army Front from his bridgeheads. The 5th Army Corps, surrounded at Raspopinskaya, tried to break out on its own. Only 3,500 men managed to reach the German lines. Antonescu abandoned his troops; it was the Germans, he said, who were giving orders. The Germans did pull out three divisions from the Stalingrad Front in order to support the Romanians and set up a new defensive line on the Chir. But the belated counter-attack of the XXXXVIII German Panzer Corps was ineffective in the face of Soviet tank masses, which the shocked remains of the 3rd Romanian Army tried to elude in a westward retreat. With no food or ammunition, they strayed through an icy winter landscape.

Their comrades from the 4th Army south of Stalingrad did not fare much better. They had been in action non-stop for almost a year, and less than half of them were fit for action. Winter equipment and supplies had not been delivered to the front on German-controlled railways. In the open steppe, the Soviet counter-offensive hit them even harder. In a matter of hours their units were wiped out, despite sometimes desperate resistance. Romanian cavalry did not stand a chance against modern T-34 battle tanks. In only four days they were enveloped near Kalach. Two Romanian divisions were caught in the Stalingrad pocket. Having lost their baggage trains and depots, all they had left to keep them from going hungry were around 5,000 horses. General Nicolae Tataranu, commander of the 20th Infantry Division, was awarded the Knight's Cross on 25 December, but considered Paulus's strategy of holding out wrong. On 18 January 1943, he was flown out of the pocket to give a report and refused to go back. Around 3,000 Romanian soldiers, among them two generals and several dozen officers, were ultimately taken prisoner. All in all the two Romanian armies lost upwards of 150,000 – dead, wounded and missing in action – in the battle for Stalingrad, in other words, the bulk of its expeditionary forces.

Antonescu and Hitler at Führer Headquarters in Vinnitsa on 26 September 1942.

Romanian troops on the march
towards Stalingrad, summer 1942.

Of the original 22 Romanian divisions only four were more or less still capable of deployment when it came to taking on a front sector as part of the new Army Group Don led by Manstein and supporting the relief attack on Stalingrad. Meanwhile, the Great General Staff in Bucharest had taken affairs into its own hands and given its own remaining troops strategic orders. German command posts accused their Romanian allies of failure. Romanian demands for sufficient supplies of anti-tank defences were met with mistrust; to the Germans these sounded like just more excuses, as Romanian soldiers already equipped with heavy anti-tank guns had in some cases simply left them behind when the Soviets attacked.[26]

In a letter to Manstein, Antonescu complained for his part that German officers had shot Romanian soldiers or disarmed them.[27] That his rival in domestic politics, Horia Sima, could escape from an internment camp in southern Germany was interpreted by the Marshal (correctly, it would seem) as an indirect threat by Hitler. It was after a personal conversation between the Romanian leader and Hitler, in which the latter, apart from making reproaches, promised additional arms supplies, that Goebbels put an end to public statements about the supposed failure of Germany's allies.

Despite the disaster of his two eastern armies, the remains of which (135,000 men) were brought back home, Antonescu appeared optimistic about the possibility of building up his military potential in Romania if the Germans would only deliver a larger supply of modern arms and vehicles. In a memorandum to Hitler, he openly declared that 'Romania's war against Bolshevism and Slavdom for the liberation of its own territories invaded and occupied illegitimately by the Soviets [was] a war of its own'. His country had its own responsibility towards history and should expect to receive some guarantees for its national security in return for participating in the war in the East.[28] His claims against Hungary were expressed again quite directly.

In pursuing events on the Eastern Front, an increasing war-weariness can be observed in parts of the Romanian Army as well as in the population. This war-weariness is due for one thing to heavy casualties, for another to the frequent and noticeable loss of confidence in the possibility of Russia ever being overpowered. The people have obviously not yet realized the true magnitude of the Bolshevist peril. The masses perceive the war as nothing but a nuisance on account of the numerous restrictions, rising prices, mobilization and bitter losses. They in no way appreciate the magnitude and significance of the war in the East. Thanks to an age-old 'hereditary enmity' nourished down to the present day by Romanian propaganda, Hungary is still viewed as the enemy. Even in the Romanian units fighting in the East, chauvinist elements in the officer corps have made out the Hungarians as the chief adversary, suggesting that the real purpose of the Romanian fight in the East is the eventual reintegration of their detached territory – as a thank-you, so to say, for Romanian assistance. (From a report of the German General in the High Command of the Romanian Army on 5 March 1943)[29]

The cabinet in Bucharest decided to rebuild the army, not for the benefit of the Wehrmacht but to defend Romanian interests. The aim was to have a strong army at the end of the war. Two lists were drawn up by the General Staff regarding Romanian equipment and war supplies. The one received by the Germans disguised the fact that a considerable amount of arms was stockpiled on Romanian territory. By autumn of 1943, 24 fully equipped divisions were ready for action in the homeland. And they did, in fact, succeed in delaying their deployment to the Eastern Front. These troops were a means of maintaining secret contacts with the Western Powers, with the ultimate aim of securing a separate peace. Bucharest hoped for an Anglo-American invasion in the Balkans and offered '45 carloads of gold, huge amounts of grain and 1 million armed soldiers'.[30] The British Prime Minister was quite interested in keeping Stalinism out of Southeastern Europe. But US policy favoured good relations with Stalin and an invasion of Western Europe.

Part of the Romanian Army remained on the Eastern Front. This was especially true of the air force, whose 1st Romanian Air Corps with circa 100 aeroplanes was flying continuous missions in the southern Ukraine in 1943–4. Almost half of the troops that ventured an advance in the Caucasus were Romanian units. They were lucky, following the Stalingrad disaster, to be able to make a timely retreat. Six divisions of cavalry and mountain troops ultimately entrenched themselves on the Taman Peninsula together with the other units of the 17th German Army. Several intense battles were fought to defend this Kuban bridgehead, Hitler being intent on keeping a springboard into the Caucasus. The war of position and retreat lasted

Romanian soldiers meet with Finnish volunteers on the Eastern Front.

until early October 1943, when Hitler finally agreed to withdraw. In the end, 177,355 German and 50,139 Romanian soldiers with some of their equipment were evacuated on 240 ships to the Crimea. The Wehrmacht suffered losses of approximately 47,000 dead, wounded and missing in action, the Romanians about 9,000.

In only three weeks' time, these troops were in trouble again on the Crimea. Soviet armies had reached the Isthmus of Perekop by land and cut off the peninsula. Five German and seven Romanian divisions fought a losing battle here in the winter of 1943–4. A Russian offensive broke through thin enemy lines on 7 April 1944 and crowded German-Romanian forces into the area around the old fortress of Sevastopol. This time they did not get off so lightly in an evacuation ordered much too late. Though two-thirds of the troops (a total of 137,000 men, 40,200 of them Romanians) were transported across the sea to Constanța, they had to leave all their equipment behind. Saving human lives was the priority for German-Romanian naval forces. Total losses on the Crimea totalled about 100,000 men, 25,800 of them Romanians.

Arrival in Constanţa after evacuation
from the Crimea.

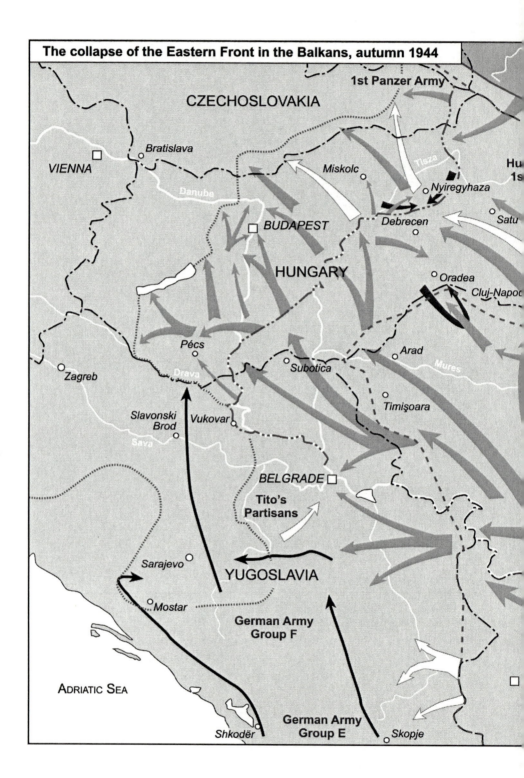

The collapse of the Eastern Front in the Balkans, autumn 1944

CZECHOSLOVAKIA

1st Panzer Army

Bratislava

VIENNA

Miskolc

Nyiregyhaza

Danube

BUDAPEST

Debrecen

Satu

HUNGARY

Hu
1s

Oradea

Cluj-Napoc

Pécs

Arad

Zagreb

Subotica

Mures

Timişoara

Slavonski
Brod

Vukovar

Sava

BELGRADE

Tito's
Partisans

Sarajevo

YUGOSLAVIA

Mostar

German Army
Group F

ADRIATIC SEA

German Army
Group E

Shkodër

Skopje

Tisza

Drava

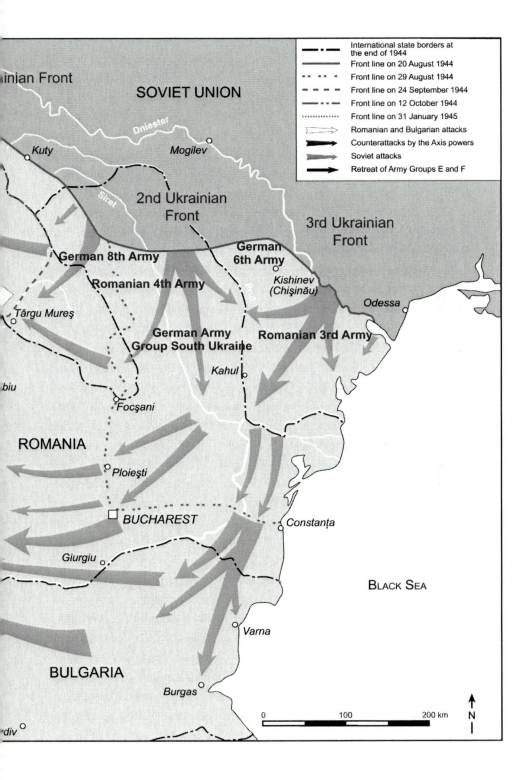

International state borders at the end of 1944
Front line on 20 August 1944
Front line on 29 August 1944
Front line on 24 September 1944
Front line on 12 October 1944
Front line on 31 January 1945
Romanian and Bulgarian attacks
Counterattacks by the Axis powers
Soviet attacks
Retreat of Army Groups E and F

...inian Front

SOVIET UNION

Dniester

Kuty

Mogilev

Siret

2nd Ukrainian Front

3rd Ukrainian Front

German 8th Army

German 6th Army

Romanian 4th Army

Kishinev (Chişinău)

Odessa

Târgu Mureş

German Army Group South Ukraine

Romanian 3rd Army

Kahul

...biu

Focşani

ROMANIA

Ploieşti

□ *BUCHAREST*

Constanţa

Giurgiu

BLACK SEA

Varna

BULGARIA

Burgas

...div

0   100   200 km

N

The rapid advance of Soviet armed forces in the southern Ukraine pushed the 6th German Army back to the Dniester. But the Romanians did not mourn the loss of Transnistria for long. It was more imperative to hold their old eastern border until the British and Americans attacked in the Balkans once they had advanced through Italy. These were desperate hopes, dashed at the latest with the start of the Soviet summer offensive on 22 June 1944. Already a year before, the Americans had called in massive air attacks against the Romanian oil industry, showing their resolve not to spare the country at all. It was the longest bombing raid flown during the war, 178 bombers being launched from far-away North Africa. They encountered well-prepared air defences, particularly the considerable anti-aircraft units near Ploieşti, and with 67 aircraft downed, it was the greatest loss of planes, percentage-wise, suffered by the Allies during the entire war. On 24 April 1944, 290 US bombers repeated their attacks from Italy, not stopping short of Bucharest this time.

The Germans made some efforts to strengthen the defences of its ally, but had the impression that Romania itself was 'not deploying all its resources in the joint war effort'.[31] Endeavouring to discourage Bucharest from approaching the Western Powers and hoping to keep Antonescu in the war, Berlin decided to offer some special economic concessions. Coal supplies were increased, gold from the Reichsbank deposited in Switzerland was offered to them, along with promises of extensive war materials. While German deliveries increased, Romanian ones began to dwindle. The Romanians knew how to politically appease a failing hegemonic power without losing sight of their own interests. They even cut their military spending by 60 per cent for 1944. Unlike other Hitler allies, they managed not to sell out and ruin their country before switching sides. In 1944, the Germans had to supply three to four times the amount of goods to Romania in exchange for one ton of oil compared to at the start of the war.[32]

Nevertheless, even Bucharest saw the need to order general mobilization and deploy its two remaining field armies to protect the eastern border. These were subordinate to the German Army Group South Ukraine under Colonel-General Hans Friessner, each of them being attached to one German army (the 6th and 8th). At first glance, it was quite an impressive army, with 900,000 men in 27 divisions. The 2nd and 3rd Ukrainian Front opposite them was clearly superior in terms of heavy artillery, but improvements had been made on the Romanian side – the re-equipping of two cavalry and tank divisions, for example. And yet Friessner was still concerned. Hitler had ordered the withdrawal of eleven entire divisions and nearly all mobile reserves from Army Group South Ukraine because of the collapse in the centre of the Eastern Front in July 1944.

The conspicuous replacement of officers in Romanian staff and command functions made him suspicious as well. It had the look of a conspiracy, but the German embassy in Bucharest seemed confident that the situation was totally under control. Antonescu paid Hitler a visit at his 'Wolf's Lair' in East Prussia on 5 August 1944, two weeks after Stauffenberg's aborted assassination attempt. Both sides feigned mutual agreement. Hitler could not promise the requested reinforcements for the Romanian Front. The Marshal avoided any commitment to a potential fight 'to the end' and maintained that his army and people were firmly behind him.[33]

When the major Soviet offensive began on 20 August 1944, its thrust was against the two Romanian armies, just as it had been two years before on the Don and Volga. The reconstituted German 6th Army was now outflanked on the Dniester and encircled. Hitler again forbade an attempted break-out – a new Stalingrad which even fewer soldiers would survive than in 1943. Antonescu had paid a brief visit to Friessner's headquarters and was visibly shaken.[34] Romanian troops were ordered by their royalist officers to keep out of the fighting as far as possible. King Mihai decided to take immediate action. His negotiators, with allied assistance, had already come to terms in Cairo on a possible armistice with the Soviets.

On 23 August, he summoned Antonescu and had him arrested, immediately handing him over to representatives of the hitherto prohibited Communist Party. The German units by this point in time were already at a desperate pass. Around 20 divisions were encircled and lost with no prospect of setting up a new line of defence in Romania. The multitude of German headquarters in the country could apparently no longer be evacuated either. The Great General Staff in Bucharest ordered its troops to cease fighting on the side of the Wehrmacht and begin operations with the armies of the 'United Nations'. This wording was obviously an attempt to assuage fears about the Red Army and not give up hope that the Western Powers would feel responsible for Romania's subsequent fate. With the reorganization of Romanian armed forces, an offensive was to begin against German-Hungarian forces with the aim of winning back northern Transylvania, thereby achieving the key national interest which had led the Romanian Army to fight on the side of the Wehrmacht in the first place back in 1941. On 25 August 1944, the government declared war against the Third Reich.

The change of front did not happen without bloodshed. Hitler was neither willing to freely withdraw his troops nor to give up his economic basis in Romania so easily. Friessner's attempt to suppress the putsch in Bucharest failed miserably. Not a single Romanian general was willing to break with the king. The bombing of the capital by the Luftwaffe only increased local resistance. The powerful anti-aircraft defences near Ploieşti were not mobile, and the advance of weak German units collapsed as Romanian troops, equipped in part with modern German 'Tiger' tanks, quickly gained the upper hand. Within a matter of days, 5,000 Germans had been killed and 56,455 taken prisoner, including 14 generals.[35]

A Romanian general making contact with the Red Army, c. late August 1944.

The Romanians were soon disillusioned. Their attempt to withdraw the 3rd and 4th Army to the Danube Delta and thus elude being disarmed by the Red Army came to grief. The Russians took more than 150,000 Romanian soldiers prisoner and shipped them off to the USSR as forced labourers. The navy was confiscated and all war material treated as booty. Officers and bourgeois elements were the victims of political purges. Some officers preferred to commit suicide, among them the ethnic German General Hugo Schwab. Looting and rape were the order of the day. The surrender of German prisoners of war was barely averted. The government under Colonel-General Constantin Sanatescu asked the Western Powers in vain to occupy the country with airborne troops. Instead, on 31 August 1944, a Romanian volunteer division made up of former prisoners of war marched into Bucharest with Soviet troops. The royal government had to send an armistice delegation to Moscow. On 12 September 1944, with no prior negotiation, the Soviets signed a prepared agreement on behalf of the Western Powers as well. Romania agreed to pay reparations of US$300 million, to recognize the border of 22 June 1941, and to provide at least 12 divisions in the fight against Germany.

In the ensuing months, between 17 and 28 Romanian divisions would be fighting in two field armies within Soviet Front groups. In this way the Romanians were given the chance to loosen the bonds of the Allied Control Commission and Romania was no longer treated like a zone of occupation. In terms of the number of personnel, it was the fourth most powerful army in the anti-Hitler coalition behind the USSR, the United States and Great Britain. Yet it ultimately played the same subordinate role as it did before in relation to the Wehrmacht. The Romanian economy had to supply Soviet troops with larger amounts of foodstuffs and war material than their own soldiers were receiving. Romanian soldiers fought with élan, particularly when faced with Hungarian troops, finally in the battle for Budapest. Their losses were high, comparable to what they had suffered before on the Eastern Front. In the end they fought near Vienna and Prague. According to official numbers, between 22 June 1941 and 23 August 1944 the Romanian Army on the Eastern Front lost a total of 71,585 dead, 243,622 wounded and 309,533 missing in action. On the Western Front it officially lost 21,035 dead, 90,344 wounded and 58,443 missing in action.[36]

While Romanian soldiers were being celebrated as victors, having 'liberated' northern Transylvania, the Communists were busy organizing a political struggle against the bourgeois government in Bucharest. Churchill had agreed to let Stalin have '90 per cent' influence in Romania. This was not without consequences. Within three years the country was transformed into a 'people's democracy'. Marshal Ion Antonescu, former Deputy Prime Minister Mihai Antonescu and other representatives of the old regime were shot on 1 June 1946 in the wake of a show trial.

The peace treaty of 10 February 1947 handled the armed forces like those of a defeated nation, cutting them back to seven divisions with a total of 138,000 men. Though 40 years of communist dictatorship did provide some measure of latitude in terms of foreign policy, and under Ceauşescu Romania developed into the most headstrong member of the Warsaw Pact, the revolt in 1989 to overcome this dictatorship was the bloodiest in the Eastern bloc.

Bulgaria

Romania's neighbour Bulgaria could have been a desirable partner of the Wehrmacht on the Eastern Front. The Balkan country, after all, had proved a loyal ally of the Reich in World War I and was ruled by a Hohenzollern dynasty. Bulgaria, under Tsar Boris III, officially joined the Tripartite Pact on 1 March 1941. It became a German deployment zone for the invasion of Yugoslavia and Greece, and though not involved in the military campaign, shared in the division of territorial spoils. As Greater Bulgaria, the country expanded its territory by 50 per cent, surely reason enough to be open-minded towards Hitler's Eastern campaign. The Führer, for his part, was hardly interested in the impoverished country, which in exchange for German weapons primarily supplied tobacco and pigs. A deciding factor in Bulgaria's neutrality was an assessment by the government in Sofia that historical ties to Russia, which Bulgaria thanked for its independence from the Turks in the nineteenth century, would preclude the possibility of a war against the USSR due to popular sentiment. Anti-Bolshevism could do nothing to shake this pro-Russian orientation.

Though Bulgaria did provide convoy escorts in the Black Sea against Russian submarines in Bulgarian waters and took advantage of pilot training, it nonetheless remained neutral *vis-à-vis* the Soviet Union. On the other hand, Sofia did not hesitate to join the Axis Powers' declaration of war against Great Britain and the United States on 13 December 1941, which led to fighting in the Aegean and air strikes against Bulgaria. US bombers, having conducted air-raids on the Romanian oil industry in 1943–4, were attacked over Bulgarian territory on their return flight by Bulgarian fighter pilots trained in Germany. Allied attempts to bomb Bulgaria out of the war caused 300,000 inhabitants of the capital Sofia to abandon the city in January of 1944, marking the beginning of political decline. The about-face in autumn of 1944 culminated in the communist putsch of 9 September. More than 20,000 representatives of the old order were murdered, and Bulgaria had to take part in the campaign against Hungary and Germany on the side of the Red Army. About 30,000 Bulgarian soldiers were killed. Its cultural and religious ties to Russia, preserved even in the face of Hitler, did not protect the country from brutal Stalinization.

4

Italy

Like Romania, Italy, too, had disappointed German policy-makers in World War I by defecting to the enemy. The battles on the Alpine Front, however, were not the cause of hatred or embitterment among the Germans (with the Austrians it was a different story). The Italians were not considered good for much, militarily speaking. Military planners in Berlin were less impressed by their behaving like a victorious power and insisting on the annexation of South Tyrol than they were by the growing Italian-French conflict in the Mediterranean. While German right-wing parties were mourning the loss of South Tyrol, Hitler, in his book *Mein Kampf*, was developing the concept of a strategic partnership with Germany's former wartime enemy. In a future war with France and Britain, Italy was to keep the Mediterranean at bay. In exchange he was willing to grant his ideal partner not only South Tyrol but also a new Imperial Rome.

The rise of Mussolini and his Fascist Party had raised Hitler's hopes for a change of course for the traditionally Anglophile country. The 'Duce' had long been a role model for him and a personal inspiration until his own seizure of power. Indeed, the ideological proximity between German National Socialism and Italian Fascism was plain to see, coinciding above all in their vehement anti-Bolshevism and their imperial designs, which did not shy away from the use of military force in altering the distribution of power in Europe. Whereas Italy sought its future in the Mediterranean, Hitler's Third Reich was intent on conquering its own 'Lebensraum' to the East.

And yet their common cause was burdened, as Italy, concerned about its newly acquired South Tyrol, defined itself as the protector of a neutral Austria, whereas Austrian National Socialists were already attempting a putsch in Vienna as early as 1934. The confrontation was soon resolved when one year later Mussolini conquered Abyssinia, setting the League of Nations in Geneva against him. Germany refused to be cowed by the threat of sanctions and quickly assembled a foreign alliance against the Western Powers, nominally as a Berlin-Rome 'Axis' against Bolshevism, and expanded in November 1936 to include Japan in an Anti-Comintern Pact. In the Spanish Civil War, the German Condor Legion fought alongside an Italian expeditionary corps against Republican forces.

Although Mussolini was celebrated in Berlin during his spectacular visit in 1937, and Hitler, too, was acclaimed in Italy on his return visit in 1938, conflicts of interest would continually erupt between the Axis partners. While Hitler was gearing up for war during the Sudeten crisis, the Duce made a name for himself as a negotiator at the Munich Conference. When Hitler occupied the remainder of Czechoslovakia – the so-called Rest-Tschechei – in March 1939, Mussolini followed suit with the surprise occupation of Albania on 7 April. German-Italian military talks ensued, culminating in the Pact of Friendship and Alliance (the so-called 'Pact of Steel') on 22 May 1939. Hitler led Mussolini to think that a period of peace lay ahead, one which Italy, weakened by its foreign wars and with a mere 44 million inhabitants, badly needed. But he was counting on Italy's support as an automatic ally in the event of war and considered their alliance a binding contract.

Thus, when Hitler, following the surprising conclusion of his pact with Stalin and his subsequent invasion of Poland, also took up arms against the British and the French, he assumed he had Mussolini on his side. But the Duce sent him a list of unfulfillable material and arms requests as the condition for his entry into the war. Thus, to Hitler's annoyance, Italy kept to the sidelines at first. The Duce endeavoured to underline his independence and was not afraid of torpedoing German-Soviet friendship at every opportunity.[1] His motivations here were not primarily ideological, but were based on a well-founded suspicion that Hitler and Stalin might have agreed on a division of interests in the Balkans as well. Rome saw its own interests jeopardized and offered massive support to Finland's defensive war against the USSR in the winter of 1939–40. Hitler had a difficult time explaining to an outraged Mussolini that he had by no means abandoned his anti-Soviet programme, but merely needed some backing in the East to wage his war with France and Britain.

Hitler had to accept the fact that Italy would only enter the war after further German successes on the battlefield. The time had come by April–

May 1940, with the enemy nearly defeated in Germany's Western campaign. The Italian Army, upon closer inspection, was hardly prepared for a modern war. About 1.6 million soldiers were mobilized, with equipment worse than in World War I. Army and air force were being re-equipped. The 67 divisions were insufficiently motorized, lacking in tanks, modern anti-aircraft and anti-tank guns, as well as in supplies. They were deployed in scattered locations from the Red Sea to the Balkans, inadequately supported by a nonetheless quite powerful navy. Upon entering the war in June 1940, Italy had 1,796 operational military aircraft and three tank divisions which were not up to Mussolini's expectations in terms of power and efficiency.

On 10 June 1940, Rome declared war on the British and the French. Just days before the armistice in France, Italian units on the Alpine Front were not faring so well any more. And yet Mussolini insisted on being France's rightful heir in the Mediterranean. Italy's ambitions hindered Hitler in his attempt to put up a strong front in the South against Great Britain by reaching a settlement with the Vichy regime in unoccupied France as well as with Franco's Spain. He needed this support if he wanted to conduct his next campaign against the Soviet Union. Of course, there was no strategic planning with Rome. Italy was now fighting its own parallel war against Britain and found itself in an increasingly precarious situation. Already in the autumn of 1940, it had lost its colonial territories in East Africa, and in Libya, too, the Italians soon found themselves on the defensive. In October, Mussolini even attacked Greece, without consulting Berlin beforehand. When his army nearly failed, Hitler had no choice but to bail out his most important European ally with the help of the Wehrmacht.

German leaders thus had good reason not to include Italy in their initial planning of Operation Barbarossa. It was in Germany's interest that Mussolini should keep his limited forces active in the Mediterranean, thereby indirectly supporting the German war in the East. But by May of 1941 at the latest, Rome was well aware of Berlin's next steps. The two dictators met at the Brenner Pass on 2 June 1941 where Mussolini was officially informed about Germany's intentions. The Duce pressed Hitler hard to finally solve the 'Russian question', but was unable to accept the fact that Germany was determined to conduct its campaign without the aid of the Italians.[2] Hitler was satisfied with the participation of the Balkan states, without taking into account that the Italians also had political and economic interests in

Southeastern Europe and would not sit back and watch the Germans gain supremacy there.

Mussolini had decided as early as 30 May 1941 to join the eastern campaign right from the outset. Though nominally about the 'struggle against Communism', in reality it was a matter of proving Italy's claims as a great power. Thus, three motorized divisions with the best possible equipment were to be assembled – a considerable challenge given the army's overall weakness. The Comando Supremo decided to deploy its Corpo d'Armata Autotrasportabile under General Francesco Zingales, made up of a partly armoured mobile division and two motorized infantry divisions.

From a German perspective this was not a noteworthy increase in offensive power, which is precisely what Army Group South was lacking in. And yet there was a certain merit in putting the Italian corps between the Romanians and the Hungarians, as a kind of partition and bridge between these two rival allies. The Italians, unlike the Romanians, were not assigned any independent operations, however, given their minimal fighting power. They were definitely to be kept away from the Crimea, because this is where Hitler planned to settle the South Tyroleans.[3] Mussolini, for his part, ardently hoped that the campaign would last long enough for his troops to prove their mettle – and for Hitler to bleed sufficiently in his struggle with the USSR so as not to feel entitled to map out the post-war order on his own.[4]

The Duce had varied motives for an enterprise that was quite controversial among Italian leaders. Added to ideological and power-political aspects were the material spoils – coal, iron, petroleum and grain – they could hope to find in southern Russia and which the Italian war economy sorely needed. The Italians produced a mere 10 per cent of the steel volume that Germany had, meaning they lacked the material basis to reinforce the ambitious and scattered operations of the Italian Army.

Their greatest weakness was in terms of personnel, however. Its education and training system did not produce enough specialists to meet the military's needs. Many soldiers could barely read or write, the inordinately small number of NCOs was not sufficient to offset serious training deficiencies, and officers were often hypersensitive and driven by a need for recognition which tainted relations with their own men as well as with their German allies.[5]

General Giovanni Messe, who replaced an ailing Francesco Zingales, led the Corpo di Spedizione Italiano in Russia (CSIR) in the full awareness of deploying an elite unit of the Italian army despite its many failings. This expeditionary force was, to his mind, 'wonderful. Enormously rich in motor vehicles and the finest weaponry which never fail to astonish the locals as well as the troops of our allies'.[6] Was this self-deceit or propaganda? The 9th Pasubio Infantry Division and the 52nd Torino Infantry Division were – compared to the Wehrmacht – weak units with their approximately 10,000 men, but were supposedly easy to transfer with the use of motor vehicles, and each had a motorized artillery regiment as well as a motorized baggage train. In reality there were too few motor vehicles to transfer both divisions at once, so the infantry either had to march on foot or ride on unprotected trucks when going into battle.

The 3rd Principe Amedeo Duca d'Aosta Mobile Division was the only one with armoured components, consisting of 60 tanks of the L 3–33 variety which, a mere three tons and armed with machine guns, were hopelessly outmatched by the enemy's battle tanks. The Savoia Cavalleria Milano Regiment attached to the division as well as the motorized 3rd Bersaglieri Regiment, on the other hand, lent the formation considerable fighting power, which to a certain extent also applied to the division's cavalry. Rome had equipped the CSIR with unusually strong corps troops, providing support for independent combat missions with sapper, anti-aircraft and anti-tank units. The volunteer militia, as well, took up the anti-Bolshevist slogan with three battalions of the motorized 63rd Tagliamento Legion. A total of 62,000 men with 220 artillery guns, 92 anti-tank guns and 5,500 motor vehicles were deployed, supported by 83 aeroplanes.[7]

All in all, the CSIR was certainly in a position to relieve German offensive units, at least in the second echelon. Four weeks after the beginning of the Russian campaign, the first Italian units arrived, initially in Hungary, where they were greeted with sympathy by the local population. The units had to cross the Carpathians on their own, where they would then hook up with the 11th German Army, forming a reserve for the time being. Though not yet fully assembled, the CSIR was prepared to send its Pasubio Division to cut off Soviet troops retreating from the Bug.

With these successful first engagements, the Germans were willing to give their allies more responsibility. The expeditionary corps was made subordinate to Panzer Group 1 and, covering the left flank with its Pasubio Division, freed up German divisions for the spearhead. With some effort they managed to bring the mass of the CSIR all the way to the Dnieper, where in late September 1941 they were even able to encircle some sizeable Red Army units near Petrikovka. The Italians took more than 10,000 prisoners of war. Following this impressive victory, the corps once again took on the task of securing the left flank of Panzer Group 1 when the latter advanced towards Rostov and the Donets Basin in early October.

Italian troops advancing in the Ukraine, 1941.

In addition to increasingly stiff Soviet resistance, weather-related supply disruptions weakened their further advance. Heavy rainfall caused the convoys to become stuck, and no relief was possible by rail due to the destruction of the Dnieper bridge. Logistical problems became a disaster for the Italians, which their feeling of being deceived and disadvantaged by the Germans did little to ameliorate. Despite Italian objections, the German High Command held firmly to its operational objectives. Together with the XXXXIX German Mountain Corps, the CSIR captured the industrial centre of Stalino on 20 October, whereas Pasubio units took the iron and steel works of Gorlovka in the Donets province on 2 November 1941. With the onset of winter, they set about stabilizing their own front sector and preparing defensive positions. In the last week of December, the severely weakened 3rd Mobile Division was hit by a fierce Soviet counter-offensive. Though faltering under this pressure and the extreme winter weather, the Italians received support from the 1st Panzer Army just in time.

Mussolini examines the situation
in late August 1941 in the area of
Army Group Centre.

The 'Christmas Battle' was hailed as a victory given the fact that the enemy was driven back. Of course it also became clear that Italian troops left to their own devices were vulnerable. Léon Degrelle, the leader of the Walloon legion deployed in the neighbouring sector, found these 'fellow soldiers' quite loathsome. 'One saw them everywhere, from the Dnieper to the Donets, small, swarthy, funny-looking in their two-pointed forage caps, or looking like birds of paradise under their bersagliere helmets from which projected, amidst the gusts of the steppe, a stately crop of rooster and pheasant feathers!' He also noted that 'they detested the Germans [who] couldn't abide the Italians' light fingers or their ardent amours in the ruined isbas. Neither could they tolerate the Italians' whimsical demeanour and quaint Latin carefreeness, so full of irreverence, indolence, persiflage and natural grace, so different from Prussian stiffness'.[8]

One night, in the southern part of the sector, strong detachments of Cossacks glided on their high-strung horses across the deep snow. At dawn, they were easily able to encircle three villages occupied by the Italians, but unprotected by the guards, who were busy sleeping or making love. They were taken completely by surprise. The Soviets particularly detested the Italians. They hated them even more than they did the Germans, and on the Eastern Front they always treated them with an extraordinary cruelty. In the twinkling of an eye they seized the three villages. No one had the time to react. The Italians were then dragged to the coal pits, where they were completely stripped of their clothes. Then the torture began. The Cossacks brought large buckets of icy water. Roaring with laughter, they emptied them on the bodies of their victims in cold which hovered 30 to 35 degrees below zero centigrade. The poor wretches in the three villages all died, frozen alive. No one escaped, not even the doctors. Not even the chaplain, who, stripped like a Roman marble, also suffered the torture of water and ice. Two days later, the three villages were recaptured. Naked bodies lay everywhere in the snow, twisted, contorted, as if they had died in a fire. From that time on, the Italian troops of the Donets were reinforced by German armour. (From the memoirs of Léon Degrelle regarding his encounters with the Italians)[9]

The CSIR survived the hard winter of 1941–2 remarkably well, most likely thanks to their experiences in the campaign against Greece the previous winter. In larger battles in the Izium area to the north, the Italians, at the behest of the Germans, repeatedly provided individual combat groups, who stood the test in both defensive and offensive functions.

The success of the small Italian expeditionary corps was not least of all thanks to the unflagging commitment of its commander General Messe. Born in 1883, the career soldier had worked his way up from NCO in the Royal Army to become a major and variously decorated shock-troop commander in World War I, thereafter gaining political influence as an aide-de-camp to the king and an admirer of Mussolini. His role as commander in Russia, where his charisma never failed to motivate his soldiers and increased the efficiency of the Italian Army, was to earn him the rank of Marshal of Italy. His ambivalent attitude towards his German ally notwithstanding, he was deeply convinced of his mission against the USSR, though the highest of values in his estimation would always be national prestige and the 'honour of one's own arms'.[10]

Messe had the full support of the Duce, who had promised him three additional divisions before the evacuation of the CSIR. Mussolini would not let up, offering Hitler a second and even a third army corps for the Eastern Front. But the German dictator showed no interest until the turning point before Moscow. He seemed to sense that Mussolini was counting on his own forces being involved in a possible thrust across the Caucasus in 1942, in which British positions in the Middle East were to be attacked in a pincer movement starting from Italian Libya and the Caucasus. From a military perspective, the offer to send the Alpini seemed to make sense, being as they were the last available elite unit of the Italian Army and given the fact that Rome was unable to provide additional tank divisions for the Russian steppe. The Foreign Ministry in Rome was already devising plans to take part in the economic exploitation of the Ukraine and Caucasian oil fields – demands that were less than welcome in Berlin.

By December 1941, Hitler no longer closed his eyes to the necessity of bulking up Italian troops on the Eastern Front. Italians, too, along with Hungarians and Romanians, would now be deployed in army strength in the planned summer offensive of 1942.[11] But it soon turned out that Rome did not have enough modern equipment and vehicles at its disposal to upgrade two additional army corps to the level even of the CSIR. Italian generals became increasingly irritated at having to weaken their positions in North Africa, the Mediterranean and the Balkans in favour of the Eastern Front. Having declared war on the United States, they considered it more important to hold the ground they had gained already and to distance themselves from their German ally if necessary.

Since Berlin refused to arm the Italians, presumably due to problems equipping its own armies, Mussolini had no choice but to outfit his additional divisions with supplies of his own. Thus, the Armata Italiana in Russia (ARMIR) was activated in the spring of 1942 with two corps in northern Italy: the II Army Corps with its Cosseria, Ravenna and Sforzesca divisions, and the Alpini Corps with its Tridentina, Julia and Cuneense divisions. The fascist militia was also represented, along with the Vicenza Infantry Division with its task of securing the rearward area. The CSIR would be assigned to the front as the third corps.

The troops led by 8th Army Headquarters numbered about 230,000 men and were armed with 250 light and 600 heavy artillery guns as well as 52 modern anti-aircraft and 54 German 75-mm anti-tank guns which Berlin had ultimately agreed to supply after all in the light of Italy's vulnerability to Soviet tank attacks. The army had about 23,000 motor vehicles at its disposal and almost as many riding, draught and pack animals, but only 19 light armoured cars. The Italians' heavier tanks were reserved for North Africa; the Germans would fight the tank war in the East. Considering that Mussolini had mobilized seven divisions against the British in North Africa, it was apparent that the 8th Army, despite its shortcomings, was the maximum he could assemble for the war on the Eastern Front.

Transport to the East was delayed several times. The German summer offensive had long since begun by the time Italian reinforcements arrived. The 8th Army was not actually fully deployed until October 1942, just before their tragic fate set in.[12] Up until that point, German liaison officers had gained a positive impression of the Italians, appraising them as disciplined and eager to fight despite the long foot-marches they had to undergo. They were 'especially good human material' since most of the soldiers came from northern Italy.[13] The units were certainly useful for basic and intermediate tasks.

Plans for Operation Blue had assumed that the mass of Army Group South would lead the thrust towards the Caucasus, forming a long secondary front on the Don. The latter was to be secured by German allies: the Hungarians to the north, then the Italians, and finally the Romanians to the south. A task like this was only feasible assuming the Red Army would be weakened to such an extent by its losses in the summer offensive that it would not be in a position to launch a significant counter-offensive. The OKH was well aware of the risks involved, and therefore endeavoured to move in German 'stays' so as not to leave allied armies to their own devices.

But with the German offensive divided and the Don Front thinning out, the Italians were faced with the task of taking on a front sector 270 kilometres long. Repeated enemy attacks were designed to put the Italians to the test. The strong German reserves they requested failed to materialize. In early November 1942, the 8th Army went into its winter positions. It was lucky that the Germans did not request the services of the Alpini Corps earmarked for the Caucasus. From a military perspective it might have seemed like madness to leave these highly trained mountain troops in the steppe, but for Colonel General Italo Gariboldi, supreme commander of the army, it was a welcome reinforcement.

His Alpini Corps were to the north in the Pavlovsk sector and maintained communication with the Hungarians. The II Army Corps joined forces with two divisions near the particularly threatened sector by Verkh, where the Red Army had managed at a bend in the river to maintain and fortify a bridgehead on the western bank. From there an enemy advance towards

Rostov was possible, followed by the encirclement of the entire German Army Group South. It was precisely at this spot that the Red Army later launched its offensive to crush the 8th Army. The XXXV Army Corps (previously the CSIR) was adjoined on the right by a German (298th) and an Italian (Pasubio) infantry division. The right wing of the ARMIR was comprised of the XXIX Army Corps with its Torino and – quite battered – Sforzesca divisions as well as the German 62nd Infantry Divison. They had to maintain communication with the Romanian 3rd Army from here.

Along with the reserve troops of the Italian 8th Army (the German 294th Infantry Division and the 22nd Panzer Division, as well as the Italian 3rd Mobile Division – essentially a cavalry brigade) an apprehensive Hitler had stationed considerable units of his own in the sector. If Stalingrad had fallen in September–October 1942, freed-up units could have helped reinforce allied forces even more. As it was, however, the urban 'rat war' ate away at German forces, who also had to concentrate on consolidating their winter positions. Once again, the Italians were disadvantaged in the allocation of scarce means of transport, fuel and building materials.

The mood between Germans and Italians rapidly worsened. The ARMIR had other ideas of how to organize defensively. Hitler's orders to build up a massive and continuous defensive line directly on the Don was at odds with Italian principles. The Italians preferred to set up a system of bases somewhat removed from the front line, each of which would be manned by a second lieutenant and an infantry platoon. Should the enemy succeed in taking such a base and infiltrating the system, powerful reserves would remedy the situation with a counter-attack. The Italians largely ignored the German call to concentrate all forces on a main line of resistance and to hold it at all costs.

The ARMIR was of course also responsible for securing and administering its rearward area. This comprised about 265 villages and towns with nearly half a million inhabitants. True, their scope of action was limited here, as the Italians were essentially bound to German regulations, but they were able to set their own accents in dealing with the Russian population. Italian veterans later described this behaviour using the cliché of the 'noble Italian', an image which has held fast in their homeland down to the present.[14] And yet there was no lack of effort on the part of fascist propaganda to motivate them for a 'crusade' against atheism and Communism. There is plenty of evidence of the effect it had:

I think it would be our downfall if our leaders weren't conducting this war. I imagine this mixture of peoples from all the depraved and barbaric races invading our continent …, killing our little son, raping you and our Italian women – and already I turn into a lion. The war has surely been won, but remember that I would rather be hacked into pieces than witness something like this should we lose. – Religion and the Christian civilization must triumph over Russian barbarism and the treacherous Jewish-Hebrew-Free Mason minorities. (From the letter of an Italian soldier to his wife, July 1942)[15]

It is hard, of course, to generalize from such statements. The mostly young and uneducated soldiers surely had a hard time expressing their varied motives in letters from the front, so the mere fact that they regurgitate chunks of propaganda perhaps has little bearing. And their attitudes surely changed after being confronted with the realities of a country and its people, with the increasing severity of the fighting and the dwindling prospects of victory.

The transfer of the 8th Army to the Eastern Front in the summer of 1942 resulted – at the express request of the High Command of the Wehrmacht (OKW) – in a considerable strengthening of Italian security units. It was they who ran the risk of overstepping the bounds of conventional warfare and committing war crimes during mop-up operations, while combating partisans or in the wake of reprisals. As early as 1941, the Italians could not fail to notice that the Germans were proceeding with extreme brutality and resolution in this theatre of war. German orders to nip the resistance of civilians in the bud and hand over political commissars and other political opponents to German collecting points met with a widespread willingness to conform. There was no official opposition.

The shooting of spies and members of the Soviet secret police by Bersaglieri in November 1941 can still be considered to be within the bounds of conventional warfare. Army soldiers handing over Jews to German special units, on the other hand, or Carabinieri hunting down not only political activists in occupied cities and villages but also Soviet Jews were perhaps just following orders, but not without adopting the perverted German notion of security.

The hanging of Jews has become so commonplace here that a news brief will suffice. They've got their just deserts – no mercy for these satellites of a race that has accomplished nothing for the whole of humanity but evil. They are marked with a round piece of yellow fabric, sewn onto their chest or left shoulder. That is to say, one on the front and one on the back. They are there for everyone to see, these notorious cutthroats who have starved out all of humanity. On the night of the 22nd, the German authorities strung up two of them and shot two more; they were rabble-rousers. (From the diary of Francesco Zito, sergeant in the 6th Bersaglieri Regiment, 25 February 1942)[16]

This is nowhere clearer than in the struggle against partisans. The more they felt threatened, the more brutal the reprisals were, despite claims of treating the civilian population humanely. Thus, in February 1943, a Bersaglieri regiment viciously crushed a revolt in Pavlovsk and, with German assistance, carried out reprisals against entire villages following the death of two Italian officers.[17]

Bersaglieri fraternize with German soldiers.

For the most part, however, German-Italian military relations on the Eastern Front were superficial and fleeting. Most soldiers barely noticed their allies. Exchanges were limited to brief meetings and a few friendly words. Even playing football together did not result in any lasting sense of unity. On the contrary, language barriers and a different way of life led to numerous misunderstandings. The Italian officer corps was marked by an unusually strong prestige-awareness which inevitably led to friction with their German allies. There was deep-seated resentment among leaders on both sides, however much they endeavoured to hide it through symbolic forms of camaraderie and loyalty as allies.

Relations had developed amicably on the whole by September 1942. In areas of close co-operation there was even a sense of mutual respect and admiration. Growing tensions essentially resulted from an increasingly critical military situation. German liaison officers were powerless to check this development. In deploying the 8th Army, the OKW installed a bigger 'German liaison staff' under the leadership of General Enno von Rintelen. He not only supplied more intelligence and information but also exercised a certain control function which the Italians, feeling patronized, interpreted as a lack of confidence. Assigning liaison officers to the Italian divisions who came from South Tyrol and had served in the Italian Army until 1939 may have seemed like a practical move, but it ultimately ignored the Italians' sensibilities.

Tensions were easy to diffuse once an offensive got underway. The first real test came in late August 1942, during the first battle on the Don, when the Red Army attacked the Sforzesca Division from its bridgehead and nearly toppled it. The inexperienced Italians had to defend a front sector of 30 kilometres, more than double what was considered reasonable according to German standards. When the Italian general command, after deploying all available reserves, decided to pull back the rest of the division to two rearward bases so as to prevent the front from rolling up, a wide gap temporarily emerged which had to be patrolled by cavalry units – a precarious situation. The infantry held on valiantly in its positions, but disengagement put some troops virtually on the run, activating deep-seated prejudices on the part of the Germans.

On 20 Aug., the Spighi Batallion defended its position valiantly and tenaciously, but eventually had to fall back. A Russian flank attack caused a panic while retreating. When the counter-attack of 3 other battalions began at 16:00, I observed along with the divisional commander the scattered remains of the Spighi Battalion. Some of them arrived with no rifles or equipment. The mass of the infantry's heavy weapons had been lost. Their morale was badly shaken. … They tried not to let on at first, when the situation became critical the next day following an attack in the centre. Parts of the division swept back and were absorbed either by the division command post or in Gorbatovo. They were repeatedly sent to the front in squad and platoon strength. Only some of them had their weapons, and would only go after much persuasion. Some of them were driven on lorries. According to some officers, the men hopped off in the middle of the journey. Some even arrived without shoes. (From the report of the German liaison officer at the Sforzesca Division, 25 August 1942)[18]

The German High Command of Army Group B was unable to provide reserves of its own to help the Italians at this threatened position, but decided instead to put Italian troops in this sector under the temporary command of a German general. This decision severely strained relations with their Italian ally; it was the first visible crack in the 'Axis'. The Germans acted accordingly and considerably expanded their liaison staff, dispatching a high-ranking expert in the person of Infantry General Kurt von Tippelskirch. As a 'German general in the Italian 8th Army' he had his own, parallel general staff at his disposal which could take command in a future crisis situation. His ambitiousness often made him blind to the Italian officers' delicate sense of honour. The clashes became more frequent. 'A hypersensitive resistance to advice and arrogant pedantry'[19] were incompatible traits – a bad omen for the crisis looming ahead.

The Soviet winter offensive launched on 19 November 1942 bypassed the Italians at first and mainly hit the Romanians in its initial phase. The ARMIR was fortunate to watch from a distance as the German 6th Army was subsequently encircled. But the outcome of this battle decided the fate of the 8th Italian Army as well. It successively lost nearly all of its major German formations which had been provided as 'stays' and were now being withdrawn to shore up the Romanians. Only the 298th Infantry Division remained in the XXXV Italian Army Corps. The latter was at least well equipped with heavy anti-tank guns, whereas Gariboldi ultimately had no reserves left.

While the newly formed Army Group Don fought a pitched battle with Soviet forces who had broken through, Stalin was preparing the decisive blow on the central Don, Operation Saturn. The offensive against the Italians and a deep thrust were to set the stage for destroying the entire southern flank of the German Eastern Front. Despite concerns about the

Sforzesca infantrymen destroying Soviet symbols in Krasnyi, August 1942.

vulnerability of this exposed front sector, even Tippelskirch did not realize the full extent of the impending danger, though there were some efforts as of early December to bring up new forces, especially anti-tank units, in the area of the 8th Italian Army.

But the Red Army was launching its offensive simultaneously, repeatedly attacking the Italian centre in battalion strength. A war of attrition ensued which particularly affected the II Corps with its Cosseria and Ravenna divisions as well as the German 318th Grenadier Regiment. Repeated breaches were sealed by counter-attacks incurring heavy losses. The Russians hammered away at Italian bases with artillery fire and weakened their mobile reserves. During this phase, the Germans praised the steadfastness of Italian infantry, who held out tenaciously even in isolated strongpoints but eventually reached their breaking-point under this constant pressure.

The Red Army, to be sure, had not even deployed its superior tank forces yet. Reinforced by the 3rd Soviet Tank Army, the 6th Army launched its main attack from the bridgehead at Verkhni Mamon on 16 December. The hopelessly outmatched Italians were faced by the 1st Guards Army together with a total of 10 rifle corps, 13 tank brigades, 2 tank regiments and 10 independent rifle brigades. With the simultaneous attack of the 3rd Guards Army, the Soviets planned to envelop the Italians in a broad southern sweep.

The attack at dawn failed to penetrate fully at first and developed into a grim struggle with Italian strongpoints, lasting for hours. The Ravenna Division was the first to be overrun. A gap emerged that was hard to close, and there was no holding back the Red Army when it deployed the mass of its tank forces the following day. German reinforcements came too late in the breakthrough battle. Some of the Italians panicked, and the disorderly retreat of entire units swept up German troops as well. The staff officers had lost control of the situation. Experience showed once again that Italian soldiers fought bravely and doggedly as long as they were in their familiar positions. When retreating, the young and poorly trained line officers lost their orientation and initiative. Their supreme commander noticed that the second lieutenants knew how 'to get themselves killed, but had neither the skill nor the vigour to give orders'.[20]

Since the most capable and committed commanders were the first to fall, the lower levels of command were often left to their own devices. The soldiers did not fail to notice their officers' lack of professionalism either, and in critical situations some preferred to turn to the Germans. Most of them, however, opted to fend for themselves, not least of all out of fear of being captured. An Italian officer, asked by his Soviet interpreter why his battalion surrendered without firing a single shot, replied with astonishing logic: 'We didn't shoot back because we thought it would be a mistake.'[21]

Despite numerous examples of death-defying gallantry, it was in this way that Italian units broke down. The intervention and coercion of German liaison officers were unable to halt the inevitable collapse. Their invectives and the sometimes ruthless behaviour of German units invariably upset the German-Italian brotherhood-in-arms.

At Kantemirovka, the mere sight of attacking tanks drove thousands of Italians into headlong flight, which only confirmed German biases, as well as the fact that the Italians usually discarded their weapons so as not to be sent back to the front immediately. Even within the ranks of the ARMIR, many officers felt shamed and embittered by this state of affairs.

> It breaks my heart to see them move up. What can we hope for from soldiers like these? They scatter or surrender at the very first shot. Although there are good men among them, they are swept along by the masses. I could howl with rage and shame. This is the Italian soldier? What has become of our nation? The most shameful thing of all is to compare us to people we always thought were below us. A few Romanians walked past us. They all have decent uniforms and all of them are armed, even the ones with frostbitten feet wrapped in blankets, slowly dragging themselves behind the others. The blame is all our own. We haven't given any spirit to our subaltern officers and we haven't been energetic enough to take immediate action against the disorderly and shameful habit of abandoning our weapons. All we can do now is suffer. (From the notes of Major Domenico Lo Faso, Sforzesca Division headquarters)[22]

Every attempt to set up new lines of defence failed. Two march columns were formed from the remnants of both southern corps, which under hazardous conditions in the icy steppe worked their way to their own front lines on sometimes week-long foot marches. Under incredible circumstances, Germans and Italians fought for food, vehicles and accommodation, quite often with force of arms. Whereas German command posts were focused on using all available forces to stabilize the situation, Gariboldi was concerned with saving his army. That is why he ordered that property of the Royal Army was to be 'defended with all means'.

The Alpini Corps deployed north of them were able to hold their positions on the Don until mid-January 1943 when another major Soviet offensive drew them into the maelstrom of destruction. With Hungarian positions penetrated on 14 January, followed by German positions, the Alpini ended up with Soviet armoured forces at their back. Though they did stave off the surprising advance on headquarters and a supply base in Rossosh, the order to retreat was inevitable. Four Italian and two German divisions had to fight their way back west together. And yet the bulk of them literally fell by the wayside and were captured or killed.

When the Italians switched
sides, the Germans took most
of the Italian Army prisoner and
occupied Rome on 10 September
1943.

The rest of the ARMIR was eventually massed in the Gomel area to gather their strength. Reports began to spread among survivors that the arrogant Germans had left their Italian comrades in the lurch, giving them up to the enemy. It even came to blows between them, though these were often grossly exaggerated. Both sides tended to blame the other for the disaster, the Germans, for their part, trying to pour oil on troubled waters whereas the Italians made a point of documenting and underscoring their self-sacrifice. German officers were justified, however, in complaining about the Italians' attitude and lack of discipline. They found it unpleasant, for example, that the rank and file were quite uninhibited when it came to playing music and then begging for money or making 'corrosive' comments to the Russian population. The soldiers, for example, supposedly declared at public markets that, 'The Italians and Romanians have gone home, the war is over. At home they will rest then go back to war against the Germans. ... They didn't want war with the Russians; Hitler and Mussolini wanted it'.[23]

ARMIR losses alone made it apparent that the 'Campagna di Russia' had deeply shaken the German-Italian alliance and made it hard to continue. With his victory over the 8th Italian Army, Stalin scored a far-reaching strategic success, facilitating the Allies' subsequent landing in Sicily and decisively contributing to Hitler's biggest European ally exiting the war in the summer of 1943.

Almost the entire artillery, the pride of the Royal Army, was lost, and nearly 80 per cent of all motor vehicles. No less dramatic and equally irreplaceable was the loss of soldiers. When the call came to march home, 37 per cent of NCOs and enlisted men as well as 42 per cent of officers were missing. The Royal Army had lost a total of 84,830 killed and missing in action in Russia; an additional 30,000 suffered from wounds, sickness or exposure. This accounts for around one-third of Fascist Italy's total military casualties before exiting the war.[24]

An exact breakdown is still impossible. It is estimated that about 25,000 men died or were killed while retreating. Another 70,000 Italians had been captured by the Russians. As with the German soldiers at Stalingrad, the majority of them did not survive. Around 22,000 of them did not even make it to a camp, but died from the strain of marching, from hunger, the extreme winter or the despotism of guards. Another 38,000 died from sickness in the camps. Only 10,032 former members of the ARMIR were allowed to go back home after years in Soviet captivity.

Their army – that is to say the staff of Gariboldi and the rest of the Alpini, the XXXV Army Corps as well as the Sforzesca – was brought back to Italy in March of 1943. The soldiers, a German liaison officer noted, went 'back home disappointed for the most part ... having often been treated by the German soldier in anything but a comradely way'.[25]

The II Army Corps (Ravenna and Cosseria) was actually supposed to be newly formed and sent back to the Eastern Front, but operations staff on both sides could no longer reach an agreement regarding equipment and deployment. Fascist Italy itself was facing its imminent demise and could no longer provide any notable equipment for Hitler's war in the East. Thus, this corps too returned to Italy in May 1943, only to fall prey to the Wehrmacht just a few weeks later. When Mussolini was suddenly deposed and arrested following the Allied landing on the Italian peninsula and the government of the king asked for an armistice, Hitler was eager to grab what he could. Gariboldi's 8th Army was stationed in north-east Italy when, on 8 September 1943, it was disarmed by Germany's Army Group B in the course of Operation Axis. The erstwhile allies suddenly became prisoners of war, actually mere 'military internees' – slave labourers no better off than Soviet prisoners of war, their former enemies.

All that was left on the Eastern Front after Italy's about-face were a few Italian rearward commandos, and a few hundred lorry drivers with their vehicles, who ended up joining forces with the Romanians. This saved them from being handed over to German prisoner-of-war camps.[26] German special units freed Mussolini on 12 September 1943, and after the royal government's declaration of war on 13 October 1943 installed a new Fascist regime in northern Italy under Mussolini's leadership. Their militias and military units were mainly used to combat partisans. The Wehrmacht and Waffen SS units, some of which were withdrawn from the Eastern Front, put up a fierce defence against the Allies in Italy and fought the local resistance with the harshest of methods. World War II ended in Italy on 2 May 1945. The country lost its colonies and its status as a great power, but found a future in the emerging European community.

5

Slovakia

Alongside the larger nation-states in Hitler's anti-Bolshevist alliance were a number of smaller states which owed their existence to German expansionist policy as of 1939 and which today would be termed satellite states. Their military contribution on the Eastern Front was more the result of their dependency on the Reich than their own national interests. That is why anti-Bolshevist slogans figured so prominently here.

Hitler's policy of force against Czechoslovakia led to the formation of a Slovak state in the spring of 1939, which put itself under the Reich's 'protection' and exercised a very limited sovereignty. With its approximately 2.6 million inhabitants, 130,000 of them ethnic Germans, the small state in the heart of Europe quickly developed a powerful national consciousness with a sense of responsibility for the large Slovakian minority in Hungary as well. The authoritarian regime of Josef Tiso had its base in the People's Party, the right-wing extremist Hlinka Guard and the Catholic Church.

After the fall of France, Bratislava put all its energy into building up relations with the Reich and joined the Tripartite Pact on 15 June 1941, just before Germany's invasion of the USSR. As in Romania, Hitler was unwilling to put up with a putsch by fascist extremists in Slovakia. He was counting on the co-operation of conservative elites to exploit the countries in his sphere of power entirely for German purposes. It is not far-fetched to say that the largely rural country of Slovakia was the 'only Catholic clerical state under the dominion of National Socialism'.[1] The papal nuncio, when blessing and seeing off troops for the Eastern Front, was later to declare: 'I am pleased to report to the Holy Father only the best from the exemplary Slovak State, which is steadily implementing its Christian, national programme expressed in the slogan "For God and the Nation".'[2]

A Slovak National Army comprising two infantry divisions with GHQ troops (about 28,000 men) had been formed from remnants of the Czechoslovak National Army. Defence Minister General Ferdinand Čatloš did not count on their rapid deployment and for the most part had to fall back on older reserve officers. The Slovaks were to switch to German armaments after the war. Indeed, the small German military mission took this into consideration while providing training assistance.[3]

Hitler refused to include the Slovaks in his preparations for Operation Barbarossa,[4] deeming them unreliable and fearing the possibility of Slavic fraternization. The OKH, of course, was keen to use these forces, at the very least for occupation and security tasks. The amassing of German troops on the Soviet border was no secret to Slovak leaders. Hence, as early as May 1941 Čatloš was offering the German military attaché troops for the fight against the USSR, provided the Hungarians also took part – Hungary's rivalry with its larger neighbour apparently urged them to act – requesting, in return, to be not 'entirely forgotten when the Balkans are redivided'.[5] Two days after a visit by Halder to Bratislava on 19 June 1941, Slovak leaders declared their willingness to participate in the operation.

The Slovak Mobile Brigade with antiquated armoured cars in Galicia.

On 22 June 1941, Slovakia broke off relations with the Soviet Union and mobilized its troops. Čatloš conjured up the 'mortal danger' of Bolshevism in an order of the day, but emphasized that the Slovak Army was not fighting 'the great Russian people or Slavdom'. The elite unit of the Mobile

Brigade with its approximately 3,500 men was immediately deployed. Equipped with antiquated, light, Czech tanks, the brigade saw combat on 22 July 1941 near Lipowiec, to the rear of the German 17th Army in its pursuit of the enemy. With stronger enemy resistance, however, the poorly trained and commanded infantry quickly retreated to its starting positions. The loss of tanks was considerable. The German liaison officer reported that the brigade staff's working methods were 'outrageous', and he was happy not to have been wounded yet, because Slovak medical facilities were virtually from the Maria Theresa era.[6] The Germans, careful not to offend, politely declined another Slovak deployment at the front. The brigade was sent into reserve and equipped with German gear. Only Slovak artillery and planes continued to accompany the German advance in the southern Ukraine.

Germans inspect Slovak tanks.

The small Slovak Air Force, fitted out with Czech equipment, dispatched a fighter group with an observation group and a liaison squadron to the Eastern Front. The vulnerability of these aircraft quickly diminished willingness for combat, however, and by October 1941, the deployment of Slovak planes had ceased. Meanwhile, the Slovak Army Corps, with two infantry divisions and corps troops (about 45,000 men in total) under the personal command of General Čatloš, had moved into the Ukraine. The insufficiently motorized corps with a total of 35 Czech tanks was considered of little value by the Germans. With officers in over their heads, it seemed sensible to reorganize Slovak troops from the bottom up. Thus, after only two months, Čatloš returned home with the bulk of his men, having accomplished nothing. The only troops to stay behind were the former Mobile Brigade, brought up to division strength with about 10,000 men, and a lightly armed security division of 8,500 men which fought partisans near Zhitomir and, later on, in the Minsk area, as well as assuming guard duties.

The Mobile Divison was responsible for security tasks on the Sea of Azov. With the Soviet counter-offensive on the Mius, the Slovaks found themselves in the midst of battle again. During Christmas of 1941, they took on a manageable sector of 10 kilometres, flanked by a German mountain corps and a Waffen SS unit. The division, now under the command of Major-General August Malar, was able to defend itself well under these circumstances, holding its positions until July of 1942. The Slovaks then took part in the 4th Panzer Army's advance on Rostov. They crossed the Kuban and were involved in capturing the oil region of Maykop.

Parade of Slovak soldiers in the Ukraine, 1941.

High casualties were less the result of fighting than of epidemics and malnutrition. The poorly commanded peasant soldiers suffered severe hardship and found little sympathy among their German allies. In late August 1942, the division set up defensive positions near Tuapse once the advance in the Caucasus had come to a standstill due to a lack of deployable forces. With the Stalingrad catastrophe at the end of the year causing a hasty retreat from the Caucasus, the Mobile Division was pushed back to the Sea of Azov along with German troops. The Slovaks barely managed to escape across the Strait of Kerch using all manner of amphibian vehicles. Their lorries and all of their artillery had to be left behind.

Reorganized into the 1st Slovak Infantry Division with about 5,000 men, the unit was evacuated to the Crimea in March 1943, where it was supposed to secure 250 kilometres of coastline. Months of calm were interrupted only by punitive actions against partisans and by field exercises. Few additional weapons and reinforcements arrived. Though morale was poor in the division, President Tiso was determined to uphold Slovakia's contingent on the Eastern Front in the hope that a grateful Hitler would protect Slovakia against Hungarian demands.

In August 1943, Hitler ordered the construction of a line of fortifications around the Crimea in order to defend the peninsula. The Slovaks, too, were to help defend this line. The division was divided at Perekop, however. One regiment stayed on in the Crimea, whereas the greater part of the division took up positions near Kakhovka and were soon caught in a major Soviet offensive. The division was smashed within a day in this Stalingrad of Slovakia. Despite occasional pockets of resistance, entire Slovak units defected to the Red Army, a changing of sides in part prepared by activities of the Czechoslovak communists on the Soviet side.

Remnants of the division, about 5,000 men under Colonel Karl Peknik, assumed security functions at the confluence of the Bug and Dnieper. Desertion was a daily occurrence. A number of officers and numerous soldiers went to the other side and reported for duty in the 1st Czechoslovak Brigade of the Red Army. The same thing was happening at the same time in the security division around Minsk. Slovaks were deserting to the partisans by the hundreds. The Germans saw to it that the remnants of the division were transferred to Italy, where it was used as a 'labour division'. A similar solution was found for the 1st Infantry Division, whose demoralized remains were put to work as a construction detail behind the front, first in Romania, then in Hungary.

But the fate of the Slovak Army was not yet sealed. In the autumn of 1944, military installations and forces in the homeland were faced with the decision of either defending the Beskids line together with the Germans against the advancing Red Army or, like the other German allies, trying to 'cut their losses' and getting out of a lost war.[7] Preparations for an open revolt had been under way in the Slovak National Council since July – parallel to conspirative efforts in the Balkan countries, which were likewise gearing up to switch sides. The government of Tiso would have to be taken down in the process. The *coup d'état* would be backed by the army, relying on an army corps stationed in eastern Slovakia which, with 24,000 well-trained and well-equipped men, was its strongest element. It would occupy the ridge of the Beskids, to the rear of Army Group Heinrici, and open the gates, as it were, for Soviet troops under Marshal Konyev. Another 14,000 men in training and replacement units were available in central Slovakia in order to build up a centre of resistance in the area of Banská Bystrica. The Germans were prepared, however, tipped off as they were by the increasing activities of communist partisans.

The murder of 22 German officers passing through Martin train station on 27 August 1944 by mutinous Slovak soldiers triggered off violent counter-reactions. Improvised German units moved into the country from multiple sides and disarmed regular Slovak troops in the east. In central Slovakia, however, the insurgents succeeded in augmenting their forces to 47,000 men and began the struggle for liberation. Under the leadership of SS Obergruppenführer Berger, German combat groups with a combined force of 10,000 men attempted to eliminate the threat to the rear of the Eastern Front, an area that seemed indispensable in terms of the war economy. The Slovak National Uprising was able to hold its ground for nearly two months on terrain conducive to defence. Only where Soviet troops failed to take the strategically vital Dukla Pass in the face of fierce resistance by the German 1st Panzer Army did it run into difficulties.

The final operation began on 18 October 1944, with the provision of three additional German divisions. It ended in the capture of Banská Bystrica and the suppression of the revolt. Hlinka Guardsmen as well as units of the Carpathian German 'Heimatschutz' were deployed in the operation, which later led to acts of revenge against the circa 135,000 ethnic Germans in Slovakia. Nearly 25,000 Slovaks died in the battles and as a result of German retaliatory measures. About one-third of Slovak soldiers went into hiding and headed home when the fighting ended; about 40 per cent went into German captivity. A small number of them continued to fight as partisans.[8] It was the Wehrmacht's last victory against a foreign army and the end of the first Slovak Republic. Becoming part of Czechoslovakia and the Soviet Empire after 1945, the country did not achieve full independence until 1993.

6

Croatia

In the wake of the German invasion of Yugoslavia on 6 April 1941, the Croatian part of the multi-ethnic republic declared its independence and was recognized by the Tripartite Pact states. Italy, in addition to occupying the Dalmatian coast and the area around Ljubljana, claimed Croatia as its 'sphere of influence'. Rome envisioned the formation of a Croatian kingdom ruled by Italian princes. Croatian exiles in Italy had long been preparing for this opportunity. The new state with around 6 million inhabitants was led by Ante Pavelić, head of the right-wing extremist and militant Ustaša movement. As 'Poglavnik' (head of state) he set up an authoritarian dictatorship there. The latter unfolded a campaign of unbridled terror against the Serbian minority. The mass murder and deportations it organized were even too much for the Germans, who endeavoured to keep it under control. It controlled ex-Yugoslavia from Belgrade, set up a military administration for Serbia, and was trying to keep an escalating civil war in check.[1] Its failure to prevent Yugoslavia from becoming a bloody battlefield was due in large part to the policies of the Ustaša.

In 1941, Italy secured a right of co-determination over the Croatian Army that was about to be activated. The army, along with a small air force, was trained and equipped in the Italian style. By the end of 1941, an army more than sufficient for national defence (46 battalions with 55,000 men) had been created and placed under the command of Slavko Kvaternik, a former Austro-Hungarian colonel, now defence minister and Marshal of Croatia. A navy was out of the question, as the Italians viewed the Adriatic as their exclusive domain. The Croatian officer corps was predominantly derived from the old Austro-Hungarian Army and considered the Wehrmacht its role model. Conversely, the high military esteem accorded to the Croatians by the

Germans existed thanks to a tradition going back four centuries and which held strong even in World War I against their erstwhile Italian foe. Despite their orientation towards Rome, Croatian political leaders clearly recognized the opportunity to acquire more leeway by granting the Germans greater political and economic influence.

The Croats played no role at all in plans for Barbarossa. Their job would be to pacify the Yugoslavian hinterland of the future Eastern Front, especially in the light of the resistance movement which developed once Barbarossa began, but also given the partisan war waged by Tito's communist forces. These tasks notwithstanding, Pavelić saw the start of Germany's Russian campaign as a chance to strengthen his country's position *vis-à-vis* the hegemonic Italians by offering a volunteer formation under German command. Hitler gratefully accepted this offer, deploying them as a unifed national formation within the Wehrmacht. For Zagreb this surprising concession was an added opportunity to organize its military after the German model.

Head of State Ante Pavelić (right) and Defence Minister Slavko Kvaternik.

Within a matter of days, 5,000 volunteers were fitted out first with old Yugoslavian uniforms then, at the Austrian troop training grounds in Döllersheim, with Wehrmacht uniforms. Arms and equipment were likewise issued according to German norms. Though not officially a part of the Wehrmacht, the men formed the 369th Reinforced Croatian Infantry

Regiment (with an additional artillery battalion of light howitzers) within the Austrian 100th Light Infantry Division. Zagreb retained its staffing rights, otherwise its soldiers had to swear an oath to Hitler and commit themselves to fight against Bolshevism 'fearlessly and valiantly'. From a German perspective, the significance of the Croatian deployment was not so much the military support it provided on the Eastern Front as the implicit political choice over allied Italy with the latter's competing claims to the Balkans. Thus, apart from supplying two air-force squadrons, Zagreb could also provide a navy contingent which, though intended for the Black Sea and not having any ships at first, still represented a circumvention of Italian arms prohibitions.

The Croatian regiment destined for the Eastern Front was led by Colonel Ivan Merkulj and embarked on 21 August 1941. From Romania it was still several weeks of marching on foot before it reached the front line and the 17th Army's 100th Division. Along with the Italian Mobile Corps likewise marching to the front, it was among the reinforcements used to fill up the Dnieper line. The Croats met up with their division on 10 October and took part in the capture of Kharkov. The regiment was not initially deployed as a single unit. Rather, the sub-units were distributed among neighbouring regiments in order to ease their transition and further their training. The troops apparently did not make a good impression after their long and exhausting march. Thus the training goals ordered for them were: 'Improved discipline. Strict handling of barracks duty. Elevated discipline while marching and resting.' The divisional chronicle went on: 'The Croats slowly got accustomed to the division. Despite the language barrier, communication was working at the lower level already. Those quartered in houses behind the front were extremely hospitable, and many a shot of slivovitz flowed down the thirsty throats of privates.'[2]

The Croats did not have an easy time of it with the Germans' strict regulations. The division's field court-martial did not shrink from applying the same standards in the case of violations of discipline. Behaviour that Croats considered 'harmless' led to a number of death sentences. 'Absence without leave' in order, for example, to roam the countryside and meet Russian women was a serious offence in the eyes of the divisional commander, whereas the Croats viewed punishment by the death penalty as murder. Even though they reached an agreement after some months that the Croatian regimental commander would act as 'justiciary' in future cases, discipline among soldiers was nonetheless shaky.

It was not only the attacks and assassination attempts of partisans that precluded peaceful garrison duty and their spending the winter in the city of Kharkov. A Soviet counter-offensive forced the Germans to abandon the strategically vital seaport of Rostov and Croats had to be called in from Kharkov to help stabilize the front. With marching orders on 22 November 1941, the soldiers began their arduous trek to the south, with temperatures of –18 degrees centigrade and no winter clothing. On the Mius they took on a defensive sector. The division, whose Croats were divided into different battalions, dug itself into the frozen earth. Its neighbours included the Slovak Mobile Brigade and the SS Wiking Division with volunteers from Western and Northern Europe.

In mid-January 1942, the Croats along with the 100th Division were called in from the Mius Front in order to relieve a precarious situation in the Stalino area fending off Soviet cavalry corps who had broken through. With sometimes heavy fighting on the Samara River, they succeeded in holding a new position over the winter. There was no support from their own air force, as both Croatian squadrons were fighting with Luftwaffe units in the north and south. Croatian bombers took part in raids over Moscow in the winter of 1941–2 and Hitler singled them out as a model for the other allies to follow.

Croats of the 369th Reinforced
Infantry Regiment near Stalino in
the autumn of 1941.

The Croatian Navy contingent kept an eye out for suitable vessels upon reaching the Sea of Azov. They organized 47 damaged or neglected fishing cutters, mostly sailing vessels, to help form a new Croatian navy, and hired Russian and Ukrainian seamen. The Croats then secured the coast of the Sea of Azov with this improvised equipment.

The commander of the infantry regiment was concerned about reinforcements from home in the spring of 1942, as Mussolini was putting massive pressure on Zagreb to provide another unit for the Italian Eastern Army. A battalion of 800 men was eventually assembled and sent to the front with Italian arms.

As of mid-May 1942, the Croatian regiment was deployed as a unified formation, its division joining the final stages of the battle of encirclement at Kharkov. In June, it followed the 1st Panzer Army along the Don, via Voronezh, to Kalach, where the Croats suffered heavy losses trying to cross the river in the face of dogged Soviet resistance. It took part in mopping-up and defensive actions in the great Don bend. In early September, the division was given a rest, which the new Croatian regimental commander, Colonel Viktor Pavecič, used to form a serviceable battalion out of his badly shaken unit. While the soldiers were hoping for a quick return home, an 800-man replacement unit arrived, most of them totally inexperienced. They, too, as of 17 September, had orders to march with the 6th Army towards Stalingrad.

> A strange lot, indeed, the men from the 369th. Always cocky and 'ready and willing to commit any dirty deed', big on organization (that is to say, stealing), but comradely nonetheless. Good on the attack, provided their bellies are full and there's enough schnapps to go around. Not very steadfast in defence, with a tendency to react in a panic if attacked unexpectedly. Now things were moving forwards, however, the enemy was fleeing, and since the first villages were badly damaged there were no delays from looting. (Excerpt from the divisional history)[3]

On 24 September, Poglavnik Ante Pavelić appeared at the Army Headquarters of Colonel-General Paulus and awarded decorations and promotions to a detachment of his Croatian soldiers. After wishing them good luck, he paid a visit to his 'navy' on the Sea of Azov and reached an agreement with the Germans to train and equip a Croatian submarine fighter flotilla.

Two days later, the 369th Reinforced Croatian Infantry Regiment took on a combat sector in the centre of Stalingrad. The 100th Light Infantry Division was in the thick of the battle in the so-called 'rat war' for the notorious 'Red October' factory and Mamayev Hill. German forces were engaged in heavy fighting as well. Numerous attacks with heavy losses failed to gain any ground. The Croatian regiment shrank once again to battalion strength by early December, having lost two-thirds of its forces. Compared to their German comrades, its survivors could at least rely on a well-organized supply system, as they had brought their own baggage train to the city with them and were supplied from the air by Croatian planes when the 6th Army was encircled.

The Croats, in the Germans' estimation, demonstrated a 'proper and military bearing' in trying situations.[4] Unlike the allied armies of the Italians, Romanians and Hungarians, they formed a small, fully integrated company within a larger German formation. They did not face major Russian offensives with masses of tanks in the steppe, but held a small sector in the maze of urban ruins, where fighting had virtually frozen since the end of November. In early January 1943, the Croats were pulled out of their exposed position, but had to put up a bold front with the onset of fierce Soviet attacks in the city. By mid-January, the Croatian battalion had been reduced to a small combat group under the command of Lieutenant Colonel Marko Mesič. The former regimental commander took personal responsibility for evacuating the wounded. All in all more than 1,000 of them were able to be flown out.

About 900 Croatian soldiers were captured by the Soviets with the capitulation of the 6th Army. Their fates were lost among the innumerable deaths of POWs. With the obliteration of the 369th Reinforced Croatian Infantry Regiment, Croatia's contribution was limited to the deployment of a bomber formation in the south of Russia. In July 1944, these forces, too, were able to go home. The Croatian Army was meanwhile occupied in battling Tito's partisans. The army reached its peak in December 1944 with 70,000 soldiers (the Domobrani Home Guard), 76,000 Ustaša militiamen and 32,000 rural policemen. The formation of a Croatian navy in the Adriatic Sea after the disbanding of its naval detachment in the Black Sea and Italy's withdrawal from the war was little more than a symbolic gesture.

As of 1942, Croatia became a main theatre of war in the fight against partisans. An increasing number of German troops were deployed there

– 80,000 by 1943. The newly activated 100th Light Infantry Division was stationed in Albania. Hitler pressed for a general mobilization in Croatia to compensate for the loss of the Italians in the Balkans. Along with the regular Croatian Army and the militia, 75,000 Croatian soldiers were to be transferred to the Wehrmacht and Waffen SS. As a political concession, the legionnaire divisions were assured that they would only be deployed in Croatia.[5]

Croatian pilots on the Eastern Front.

When the onslaught of Soviet and Bulgarian troops as well as Tito's army threatened Croatia in the autumn of 1944, Hitler protected his vulnerable ally despite the strategic disadvantages it cost him. On the Syrmian Front against the Yugoslavian People's Liberation Army they succeeded unexpectedly in stabilizing their positions, enabling the withdrawal of the German army groups from Greece and southern Yugoslavia. It was only the start of Tito's spring offensive on 12 April 1945 that brought about the collapse of Croatia – one of the last bastions of the Third Reich – and likewise dashed the hopes of locals who, not sympathizing with the Communists, had been awaiting the advance of the Western Allies.

A body of battle-weary German-Croatian soldiers, including the three Croatian legionnaire divisions and a number of German-Croatian police battalions, was still available under the command of Colonel-General Alexander Löhr.[6] Löhr endeavoured to organize their inevitable retreat so that his army group could cross over into Austria and surrender to the Western Allies. Only vanguards managed to do so, however, before overall surrender on 8 May 1945. Thus around 100,000 German soldiers had to enter into the privations of capture by the Yugoslavians. Their Croatian allies suffered a much harsher fate: most of them were gunned down in a series of mass executions at the end of May. In terms of numbers, these victims were equal to Croatia's losses in the first four years of the war. The Croatian armed forces recorded about 65,000 soldiers killed and missing in action by May of 1945. An additional 60,000 became the victims of mass murder by Tito's People's Liberation Army. After more than four decades as an autonomous republic of communist Yugoslavia, Croatia finally achieved full independence in 1991.

Part II

THE VOLUNTEERS FROM NEUTRAL AND OCCUPIED TERRITORIES

Introduction

Hitler's allied troops fighting on the Eastern Front were almost exclusively comprised of recruits and career soldiers concentrated in regular troop units under the command of their respective governments. Only the small Croatian contingent was an exception to this rule. Their loyalty was to their respective national authorities and military leaders, each of which had their own, different interests for taking part in the war. The shared ideology of a 'Crusade against Bolshevism' or even a racial ideology such as an 'anti-Slav' orientation was never in the foreground however much official propaganda might have emphasized these slogans.

The allied troops made up the bulk of foreign soldiers on the Eastern Front, with army-size, unified formations under the command of their own officers. German liaison officers were not in a position to give direct orders, and intense co-operation with Wehrmacht soldiers was the exception. Official, staged meetings and the occasional combining of forces on the battlefield or behind the lines produced only a limited sense of 'cameraderie' or mutual understanding. National prejudices and clichés were covered up as much as possible but were nonetheless virulent, eventually erupting in crisis situations.

Compared to these circa 600,000 men (1941) from six nations, volunteers from neutral and occupied territories, initially numbering little more than 30,000, were quite a small and heterogeneous group. Their military value was less than their symbolic one: the political rejection of Soviet communism. They were useful for Hitler on the international stage as well as for his policies towards the volunteers' homelands. Though the 'glue of ideology' may have been stronger among the legionnaires than among the national armies of his allies, these groups were more than mere adherents of German National Socialism and its Führer. They were representatives of right-wing extremist and fascist movements in their home countries, each cast in a peculiar mould. More often than not they were small political minorities, social outsiders who by volunteering to fight the Red Army in German uniforms hoped to gain political capital and recognition. Each displayed a unique mixture of adventurousness, idealism and political ambition.

But this group also included volunteers from foreign regular armies (Spain, France) or from armies defeated by the Wehrmacht who either wanted to avoid becoming prisoners of war or – if discharged already – were trying to escape recruitment into forced labour in the Reich. They fought in small, unified contingents, generally of regimental strength, within German formations, wore German uniforms – either the Wehrmacht or Waffen SS – with respective national armbands, and usually had German equipment and training. This undoubtedly promoted a strong sense of integration and loyalty, presumably made even stronger by swearing a personal oath to the Führer. Despite training and equipment according to German standards, they held on for the most part to their national identities and mindsets. Their ties to their respective countries and thus the length of their tour of duty on the Eastern Front were essentially dependent on the status and political clout of their homeland. The vast majority stayed in the ranks of the Germans until the final hours of the Third Reich and – with the notable exception of the Spaniards – were ignored or ostracized in their homelands after the war. Many, therefore, chose to emigrate.

7

Spain

Italy was Hitler's first ally, as of 1935–6, and the one he expected to be most advantageous in the struggle for European hegemony. The German dictator did not expect a military commitment from Italy in his campaign against the USSR. The same, in another way, went for Spain, the other Mediterranean power. Madrid was an especially interesting partner on account of its geostrategic position *vis-à-vis* the French-British bloc, the influence of Spain outside Europe, and its benevolent neutrality in World War I. The erstwhile great power on the Iberian Peninsula had largely crippled itself, however, through its economic backwardness and internal weaknesses. Berlin had secretly supported the Spaniards in the 1920s in defending their positions in Northwest Africa and endeavoured with some success to expand economic and trade relations.

With the overthrow of the monarchy and a phase of increasing internal conflict beginning in the early 1930s, Spain lost even more strategic importance. Parts of the officer corps who planned a putsch against the Republican government in 1936 were able, thanks to Francisco Franco, to renew old contacts with Berlin as well as gaining the support of Fascist Italy. With German and Italian assistance, they ultimately prevailed in a bloody three-year civil war over a Republican alliance receiving military aid from the Soviet Union. The Spanish Civil War offered Hitler the opportunity to test new Wehrmacht weapons and tactical procedures – dive-bomber attacks, for instance – as well as the chance to make a name for himself as a champion of anti-Bolshevism.

Franco, though approaching his fascist role models as 'Caudillo' and head of state with his Falange Party and the creation of an authoritarian regime, was nonetheless concerned about upholding ties to the Western democracies.

The state of his country, ravaged by civil war, left him no other choice. Despite Spain's potential as a German ally at the start of World War II, Berlin was quite happy for the time being if the country of 25 million opted for benevolent neutrality as it did between 1914 and 1918. The situation changed after the French campaign. German generosity *vis-à-vis* Spanish debts of both the fiscal and moral variety would now pay off in the form of securing Hitler's sphere of influence in the West, enabling him to strike out eastwards.

His efforts to expand German-Spanish relations into a war alliance showed the Führer to be virtually helpless in the autumn of 1940; he was clearly unable to match the qualities of his role model, Bismarck, in diplomatic affairs. Franco, on the other hand, was refined and clever at dealing with the entanglement of international interests in the Mediterranean as well as with his own weaknesses.[1] Berlin felt unable to meet Spain's conditions, especially its material demands, for entering the war against Great Britain. As fascinating as the strategic gamble might have been in theory, Hitler thought it imperative to delay the struggle for this part of the continent until after Barbarossa. Plans for seizing Gibraltar (Operation Felix) with Spanish assistance had to be put on hold for now.

The cooling of Spanish-German relations was interrupted by the start of the German invasion of the USSR on 22 June 1941. That very same day, Madrid offered the assistance of volunteer Falangists as a gesture of solidarity. With a common enemy in the Bolshevists, the ideological thrust was now agreeable to Franco again. Contrary to German expectations, however, there was no formal war alliance, not even an official declaration of war, and thus no deployment of regular troops. But military strength was not the issue. Rather, Hitler thought that Spain's offer – which he accepted without hesitation – might eventually allow him to wheedle Franco into a war alliance against the West after all. That is why he pushed for a rapid deployment of the volunteers, to have a sure guarantee despite his expectations of a short campaign.

A competition developed in Spain between the army and the Falange over who would earn more glory on the Eastern Front. United by fervent anti-Communism, these two pillars of the regime saw a commitment to Hitler's 'crusade' as the chance to gain political traction at home at the other's expense. Army officers were willing to offer an entire army corps, whereas some of the old Falangists who were disappointed with Franco's 'New State' essentially wanted to 'emigrate' to the front. The OKW had no interest in a more or less motley legion. Hence Franco decided to a raise a conventional infantry division in the form of a national unit, comprised of volunteer soldiers and militiamen and commanded by regular officers. Only the NCOs and second lieutenants had one-third Falangists in their ranks.

Recruitment was public and conducted throughout the whole of Spain. There was no lack of volunteers. From a German point of view, there were too many officers and too few NCOs. The Spaniards had no motorized vehicles of their own. On 13 July 1941 the men were bid farewell and sent to a troop training camp at Grafenwöhr near Nuremberg to be trained and equipped in the German fashion. The formation was given the German numbering of 250th Infantry Division and comprised 17,909 volunteers divided into three infantry regiments, an artillery regiment and the 250th Mobile Reserve Battalion containing mainly civil war veterans and former Foreign Legionnaires. They swore the usual Wehrmacht oath of allegiance to Adolf Hitler, albeit with an added 'in the struggle against Communism'. This effectively excluded deployment against the Western Powers. The commander of the División Española de Voluntarios (DEV) was General Agustín Muñoz Grandes, a seasoned officer. They were also called the Blue Division (División Azul) because of the Falangists' blue shirts.

The Escuadrilla Azul, an elite of 17 fighter pilots with German Me 109 aeroplanes under Squadron Commander Ángel Salas Larrazábal (who later became head of the Spanish Air Force in 1956), was formed with volunteers from the Spanish Air Force. As part of the VIII Air Corps, the unit saw action at the heart of the German offensive against Moscow. To their chagrin, however, the highly motivated pilots were mostly used for strafing instead of 'free-hunting' in fighter sweeps. While these airmen were deployed with Army Group Centre, their comrades in the infantry were active in Army Group North.

Having only been briefly trained with their many teams of horses, Spanish soldiers, especially the artillery, were unpractised and careless when the time came to head to the front in mid-August 1941. Horses were procured at short notice from Serbia, as it was unclear who was responsible for equipment. The government in Madrid insisted on the division being deployed in key areas of fighting. The Germans, of course, could have sent them to the Ukraine, but it may have been political considerations that kept them from putting the Spaniards together with other Southern and Southeastern European allies. The division was sent to the zone of Army Group Centre and unloaded in the Grodno area. A strenuous, weeks-long march lay before them. Redirected to the north and transported briefly by rail, they took over a wide front sector on the Volkhov south of Leningrad.

German liaison officers encountered many prejudices in their own camp. Commander-in-chief of the 4th Army, Field Marshal Günther von Kluge, for example, refused to deploy the 250th Division in his Moscow zone, claiming that they were more 'Gypsies' than soldiers.[3] The supreme commander of Army Group Centre, Field Marshal Fedor von Bock, was displeased by the unaccustomed look and manner of the Spaniards, the poor state of their horses, and their tendency to view any woman as free game. In Grodno, according to Bock, they even had orgies with Jewish women.

The Spanish division was considered incapable of attacking, but showed an unexpectedly high combat morale on the defensive. In the war of position north of Lake Ilmen, the Spaniards, despite insufficient equipment and training, managed time and again through their courage and vigour to repel the frenzied attacks of the Red Army. The senior German commanding general, Friedrich-Wilhelm von Chappuis, initially demanded their removal from his corps – for Muñoz Grandes all the more reason to spur on his division as if they were defending their Spanish homeland. There were atrocities and high casualties on both sides during heavy fighting. Hitler, too, was impressed by reports that the Spaniards, though a 'degenerate formation' with miserable relations between their officers and troops, never surrendered an inch. 'More gutsy people are hard to imagine. They don't even take any cover, just let themselves be slain. But our men are happy to have the Spaniards in their neighbouring sector.'[4]

The failure of Operation Barbarossa in the winter of 1941–2 occasioned Franco to bring his decimated volunteers back home. The flight squadron began its journey back in January 1942. It was agreed that a rotational procedure would be applied to the infantry, exchanging and replenishing personnel in a quarterly fashion without pulling the division out of the front. In this manner a total of 47,000 Spaniards went to the Eastern Front.[5]

Muñoz Grandes, general secretary of the Falange since 1939, viewed his position as divisional commander in Russia as an opportunity to increase his prestige in Spain and initiate a change of policy at home. He advocated 'harsh' order in home affairs and Spain's entering the war on the side of Germany. But Franco sought to improve relations with the Western Powers once the USA entered the war, and was intent on relieving Muñoz Grandes of his duties in the East in April 1942. The general, however, was awarded the Oak Leaves to the Knight's Cross of the Iron Cross by Hitler for 'exceptional bravery', and Franco was pressured by the Germans to leave him in his post. But Madrid was at least able to install a reliable deputy on the Eastern Front in the person of Major-General Emilio Esteban Infantes.

Spanish soldiers heading to the Eastern Front, September 1941.

On 12 July 1942, Hitler received Muñoz Grandes at his 'Wolf's Lair' for secret talks, mainly to discuss the future of Spain. The German dictator saw the devoted Spanish general as a potential successor to Franco, a trump card if German plans to march through Spain and capture Gibraltar should materialize after all. Until that time they would redouble their military glory on the Eastern Front.

A second Spanish flight squadron had meanwhile arrived in the zone of Army Group Centre. With new armoured aircraft, they flew numerous missions from Orel to provide support for ground troops. By November 1942, they had shot down 13 enemy planes. They were then relieved by a third Spanish squadron. The Blue Division was transferred in August from the Volkhov Front to the blockade ring around Leningrad at Tsarskoyo Selo. Hitler was apparently interested in letting the Spaniards take part in the supposedly imminent seizure of the city. The advance had to be called off due to the Soviet holding attack on the Volkhov. But the Spaniards had a considerably wide sector to defend on the periphery of Leningrad – 29 kilometres – in a second winter unusually harsh for them.

Muñoz Grandes returned to Madrid in December 1942.[6] The Allies had meanwhile landed in Northwest Africa and Franco apparently thought it more prudent to control his ambitious general directly. He thus made him head of the Military Cabinet, a position without power of command but which nevertheless allowed him to continue his intrigues. Esteban Infantes took over the 250th Division. In mid-January 1943, the Red Army succeeded in opening a land bridge to Leningrad. In the attempt to widen this corridor near Krasny Bor, the Russians encountered a well-entrenched Blue Division. Few kilometres were surrendered in battles with high casualties. Then the relative peace of trench warfare set in again, punctuated by assault operations and local advances. The division's demands for the replacement of material losses were now met with even less understanding in the OKH. Indeed, Spanish demands exceeded replacements for the entire Eastern Front.[7]

General Esteban Infantes with his soldiers on the Leningrad Front, 1942–3.

General Esteban Infantes regarded the enemy soldiers as very good, 'loyal and obedient'. They are 'stubborn and tenacious', 'but feel no real connection to the comrades in their unit. When a given order comes to naught, they quickly lose their aggressive qualities and sink into nothingness. When the Russians are on their game, however, they're an opponent that's not to be sneezed at.[8] The third replacement squadron was fitted out with nine Fw 190 A-3 aeroplanes in April 1943. It fared well in the middle sector during Operation Citadel, providing fighter escorts for dive-bomber formations and scoring 29 air victories in the 51st Mölders Fighter Group. There were even dogfights with Spanish exiles in Soviet aircraft, a postlude, as it were, to the Spanish Civil War.[9]

With the Allied landing in Sicily and Italy's changing sides, Franco was forced to switch from 'non-belligerence' to neutrality. On 1 October 1943, he asked for the return of the Blue Division, which Hitler approved without delay, benevolent Spanish neutrality being more than welcome to him for economic reasons. The usefulness of Spanish troops on the Eastern Front for purposes of political propaganda had exhausted itself anyway. It was agreed militarily to remove the division from its positions rather quickly and bring them back home. The last transport, including General Esteban Infantes, arrived in Madrid on 18 December 1943. A newly formed Spanish Legion comprised of volunteers stayed behind on the Eastern Front. Stationed in the Narva area, its 2,133 men formed units in regiment strength. Its first deployment was against partisans, and then the legion was made subordinate to the German 121st Infantry Division.

Under strong pressure from the Allies, Franco was prompted to withdraw the legion from the front in February 1944. Then, in early April 1944, all remaining Spanish units were sent home, except for a few hundred volunteers who renounced their government out of political conviction and stayed on in battalion strength to continue fighting partisans in the Ukraine and the Balkans. In late 1944, they were combined into an SS formation with a number of Spaniards who had secretly crossed the Pyrenees into France. These two companies were to witness the end of the war in Berlin. Spain's contribution to the war on the Eastern Front was undoubtedly of mere symbolic importance. A total of 47,000 men served in the Blue Division. Upwards of 4,500 were killed, and 8,000 wounded; 321 were taken prisoner of war and proved to be 'tough' in the face of Soviet camp conditions. Most of the latter returned home in 1954. The last POW returned to Spain in 1956.

Apart from that of Spain, the Germans in 1941 were hoping for the involvement of fascist Portugal as well. Prime Minister Salazar felt no debt of gratitude to the Third Reich, however, and limited his support to public rallies declaring Portugal's stance against the 'mortal enemy, Bolshevism'. Berlin would have been happy to receive even nominal military support; the Portuguese Army, to be sure, had no lack of volunteers. But the country's exposed location, its traditionally pro-British orientation, and not least of all its colonial possessions prevented it from accommodating Hitler's wishes. In the summer of 1941, Portugal might still have been helpful in swinging Brazil and thus, indirectly, the United States.[10] The largest country in South America with its Portuguese-influenced culture was in any case one of Germany's best customers in the arms export business. The USA took care, however, in the autumn of 1941 that South America's neutrality followed the drift of its own foreign policy. Portugal, with its strategically important tungsten reserves, did supply Hitler's war economy until 1944, but it also supplied the other side in the struggle for scarce resources.

8

France

After centuries of 'hereditary enmity', a German-French brotherhood-in-arms was utterly unthinkable in the Third Reich. The German defeat in World War I and the harsh stance of victorious France towards the Weimar Republic left a deep impression on both the German population and the Wehrmacht. Though rejecting France's claims as a great power and dreaming about the restoration of old Imperial Germany, national conservative circles, and with them the higher officer corps, displayed a deep and widespread respect for French culture and past military achievements. Up until May of 1940, however, revenge for Versailles was the first priority. What mattered most was to surpass the then greatest military power and hence their rival France.

The planned campaign was envisioned as a 'normal' war and was carried out in accordance with the notion of 'chivalrous' warfare. This meant that the opponent was viewed as a 'comrade', to be 'pardoned' after his defeat. The unexpectedly rapid German victory in May 1940 precluded any further ideologizing of the war. Though generous in their triumph, they did not want to miss the opportunity of humiliating the enemy, just as the Germans had suffered from the 'disgrace' of Versailles in 1919. Thus, the signing of the armistice was staged in the Forest of Compiègne, in exactly the same railway car where the Germans had surrendered in 1918. The need to pay back the 42 million French 'in their own coin' was so great that they even created the same institutions and imposed the same conditions the Reichswehr was subject to in the 1920s: a permanent armistice commission to supervise everything, partial occupation of the country, reduction of the army to 100,000 men, and severe arms limitations.

The surprisingly minimal resistance put up by the French Army was easily explained by the country's inner debilitation and as being the result of bitter conflicts in domestic politics at the time of the Popular Front government in the mid-1930s. The anti-government campaign of French communists carried out under Moscow's command since the start of World War II undoubtedly influenced troop morale as well, strengthening anti-Communist sentiment in the government, bourgeoisie and army.

The government of national unity formed by Marshal Philippe Pétain, the 'Lion of Verdun', was willing to co-operate with Berlin. A German-French alliance was now at least conceivable once the British had sunk the French Navy and installed an exile government under the 'renegade' General Charles de Gaulle. The lifting of arms restrictions would enable the government residing in Vichy – widely supported by the French population in 1940–1 – to protect overseas colonies from British-Gaullist attacks.

From heir apparent of the French Communist Party to officer of the anti-Bolshevist Volunteer Legion: Jacques Doriot.

All attempts by national conservative forces in the Foreign Office, in the High Command of the Wehrmacht and other German leadership circles, to pave the way for such an alliance were vigorously boycotted by Hitler. His personal talks with Pétain on 24 October in Montoire did nothing to change his temporizing and dismissive stance. He was intent, no matter what, on maintaining his freedom of decision with regard to France's future, and steered clear of anything that might have strengthened France's position, which is why he gave no thought to including the French in his plans for Operation Barbarossa.

With the beginning of the German invasion of the USSR and the strident calls for a 'Crusade against Bolshevism', many proponents of German-French rapprochement felt heartened. Not until 30 June 1941 did the right-wing government of Pierre Laval in Vichy break off relations with Moscow – conspicuously late. The German ambassador in Paris, Otto Abetz, was already in contact with representatives of right-wing extremist fascist movements in the country, which scented the opportunity to gain political capital by adopting the 'crusade' slogan. Under an anti-Communist and anti-Semitic banner, they were prepared to join the Germans on the Eastern Front – and only there. From their point of view it was not just a matter of France's glory and honour, or of advantages at the negotiating table their government might derive from joining the war effort; rather it was about creating their own armed forces, very much in competition with the regular, conservative army. The estimation of Jacques Doriot, a former leading communist now at the helm of the right-wing, radical Parti Populaire Français, was symptomatic: 'If there's a war I like, it's this one!'[1] As in Germany, this attitude could also be found among members of influential circles of the Catholic Church who did not sympathize with Fascism.

Together with other French politicians such as Marcel Deat and Eugène Delonde, Doriot called upon the French to join the struggle against Bolshevism. Abetz obtained Hitler's approval in early July 1941, but the Führer was reluctant to accept the offer and was anxious to avoid any binding obligations for Germany. It is telling that the notorious meeting on 16 July 1941, at which he set down the future directives for Germany's policy in the East, began with a reference to France's offer. He spoke of the mention in a 'shameless Vichy newspaper' that 'the war against the Soviet Union is Europe's war, so it should be fought for all of Europe. Apparently the Vichy paper is claiming that the beneficiaries of this war should not be the Germans alone, but that all European states should reap the benefits of it'.[2]

A French volunteer legion was therefore to be formed in the occupied territory and not in dependence on Vichy. Vichy had already created the legal requirements for Frenchmen to serve in foreign armed forces, albeit in vain. It was the Germans who dictated the terms. Modelled on the French Foreign Legion, the legion was not to have more than 10,000 to 15,000 men, would be sworn in allegiance to Hitler and accept only Frenchmen of Aryan descent,

between the ages of 18 and 40 and in good physical condition. They also had
to have a clean criminal record and to have already completed their military
service. As an enticement the Germans offered to release two prisoners of war
for every volunteer. Attempts to form a fighter-pilot unit were hindered by the
Germans.[3]

With strict regulations like these, it is no wonder that only about half of
the volunteers (6,429) were accepted. Moreover, Hitler forbade the inclusion
of Russian *émigrés*, a great number of whom resided in France. It was best,
he thought, to avoid such political implications. As 'cannon fodder', however,
the French were more than welcome. They were put in German uniforms and
paid German salaries. It is curious to note that Berlin simultaneously urged
for Germans in the French Foreign Legion to be allowed to return home.
Once back home, they were put into probationary units and for the most part
redeployed in North Africa.[4]

Abetz succeeded in bringing together sometimes competing groups
in the occupied territory into an Action Committee for the Légion des
Volontaires Français contre le Bolchevisme (LVF). Doriot as its mastermind
won the support of career officer Colonel Roger Labonne in forming the
first units in barracks at Versailles. The Wehrmacht was scrupulous about
these foreigners conforming and being treated as equals. They formed the
638th Infantry Regiment and were attached to the 7th Infantry Division, an
old Bavarian division. In September 1941, they assembled at a training area
south of Warsaw where their training was intensified. Here they received
their first and only message of greeting from the president. Pétain called
upon them to uphold France's military honour. The volunteers would earn
'the world's gratitude' by taking part in the 'crusade' and thereby defending
their fatherland.[5]

As a priest and a Frenchman I dare say that these legionnaires rank
among the best sons of France. At the forefront of the decisive battle, our
Légion is the living image of Medieval France, our France of resurrected
cathedrals. And I underline, for I am quite sure of it, that these soldiers
are doing their part to prepare the great rebirth of France. In truth,
this legion in its own way constitutes a new chivalry. The Legionnaires
are Crusaders of the twentieth century. May their arms be blessed. The
tomb of Christ will be liberated! (Cardinal Baudrillart, director of the
Institut Catholique, about the legionnaires of the LVF)[6]

Swearing-in of the I Battalion of
the Légion des volontaires français
(LVF) in Demba, 5 October 1941.

In late October, the three battalions were moved to Smolensk. From there, at the start of winter, the Frenchmen marched towards Moscow – in the footsteps of Napoleon. Sixty kilometres away from the Russian capital, they reached their German formation. With an order of the day delivered in French, General of the Artillery Fahrmbacher greeted them on behalf of the VII Army Corps as comrades 'in life and death'. Two battalions were sent straight to the front by the Nara Strait as part of the 7th Division. German soldiers were sceptical: 'There are young idealists among them, adventurer types and old Foreign Legionnaires with twelve or more years of service under their belt.'[7]

They constituted the reinforcements that were to help break through the last Soviet defensive positions. The time had come on 1 December 1941. The I Battalion charged across the open field. A German artillery observer reported: 'A gutsy attack by French volunteers, but completely idiotic, like in the days of Frederick the Great!'[8] Though suffering high losses, they managed to penetrate the wooded positions. Several bunkers were taken in heavy fighting. Divisional Commander Freiherr von Gablenz was pleased. The Frenchmen had 'made a good showing'.[9] Just a few days later, however, a Soviet counter-offensive followed and the badly shaken French battalion had to fall back. There were mutinies, and individual soldiers fled westwards on their own, commandeering German lorries to make their way back home via Smolensk. The bulk of the legion turned up in military hospitals on Polish territory where they were gathered and reviewed.

Together with new recruits from France, they numbered 2,000 in early 1942. Two powerful battalions were formed from them. Hitler insisted the Frenchmen be sent to the front sector. In the light of conflicting experiences, however, the battalions were attached instead to two German security divisions deployed in the hinterland of Army Group Centre to combat partisans in the Smolensk area. Well-organized strongpoints had been set up in forest areas, which the Germans had considerable difficulty combating. Nowhere else were the partisans so active in 1942–3. The Frenchmen again 'made a good showing', as was often said in German reports, and took advantage of the liberties offered by this manner of fighting. The tricolour waved over command posts and they were happy to be without German supervision.[10] The troops proved particularly useful and motivated in mobile deployment. They were hated, however – the Germans noted – for 'their constant looting of the population',[11] whereas the Frenchmen thought themselves quite popular with the women. The legionnaires accepted no restrictions: 'Either you cut our balls off,' they said, 'or let us have our way!'[12]

The ruthlessness of the French towards the peasant population need not be taken as revenge for 1812; this form of warfare was quite simply brutal, and German soldiers acted no differently. In several large operations under the command of Higher SS and Police Leader of Central Russia Curt von Gottberg they tried over and over to gain control of these enormous territories. Brute force was used against the population, including the plundering and destruction of villages. Since the partisans generally avoided enemy contact, the frustrated troops took it out on civilians. The ratio of partisan deaths versus German losses was often ten to one, sometimes more extreme, as 'gang suspects' were shot without conscience, whereas any Jews picked up were murdered on principle.

Several lots of new volunteers arrived from France to fill up the regiment's losses, making personnel levels relatively constant (113 officers, 3,528 NCOs and enlisted men). The autumn of 1942 offered Hitler another occasion to take advantage of French military manpower. The occupation of the rest of France and the disbanding of the Vichy armed forces opened up the possibility of placing these troops at the service of the Germans. But with a few exceptions

A new contingent of French
volunteers marching to a Paris
railway station, 9 April 1942.

Recruitment office for the LVF in
France.

it did not succeed. The military situation had changed, the Germans were on the road to defeat and had made themselves so unpopular in France that volunteers were much harder to come by now, especially after the catastrophe of Stalingrad. In the Légion itself, internal political conflict had increased given the change in circumstances.[13]

Marshal Pétain, on the other hand, was now interested in his legion in Russia, seeing in them an element for rebuilding French armed forces. He told the Germans he would disband the LVF and create a larger formation in France proper, an unpolitical 'Légion tricolore' under the command of professional officers and destined not only for the Eastern Front. Berlin turned down the idea, because the LVF was a German regiment and the Germans were not willing to lose this political trump card.

In May 1943, the LVF contained 2,317 men fighting against partisans on the Desna as part of the 186th Security Division in a unified regiment with three battalions under Colonel Edgar Puaud. The attempt to fill up the unit with Turkestani 'willing helpers' (*Hilfswillige*, or *Hiwis* for short) failed, as the latter formed their own national unit under SS command.[14]

In late January 1944, the regiment was used in a large-scale deployment, which the commander had asked for several times as a chance to prove their merit. Operation Morocco, as the Germans called it in his honour, aimed at 'mopping up' a large forest area near Somry. Winter fighting met with little success since the partisans generally avoided contact. Nevertheless, the OKW reported having destroyed 41 partisan camps and 1,000 blockhouses, as well as tallying 1,118 dead and 1,346 prisoners.[15] The French were caught in an ambush, however, on their march back to the Desna and the I Battalion suffered heavy losses. The big test came in June 1944 when, following the Allied landing in Normandy, the Red Army launched its summer offensive in Byelorussia, which led to the collapse of Germany's Army Group Centre. The LVF had to form a single combat unit which, reinforced by a German tank company, was to intercept a Soviet tank division that had broken through and pushed deep into enemy territory. Four hundred Frenchmen fought for days against a vastly superior enemy and were able to halt its progress. Forty Soviet tanks were disabled, but the French, for their part, suffered 41 dead and 24 wounded. This was just the beginning, however. Colonel Puaud and his regiment were caught in the general withdrawal near Minsk, a trying moment for the French. They were lucky to reach Vilna unscathed and, surprisingly, were transferred to Pomerania.

Edgar Puaud in German uniform.

The LVF was to be disbanded and become part of a Waffen SS division along with other French units. The French, until then, had been deemed unworthy of the SS, but Himmler now abandoned his scruples. There was resistance against this decision among the legionnaires, and some are said to have been sent to concentration camps.[16] The new 33rd Panzer Grenadier Division of the Waffen SS, Charlemagne, was formed in August 1944 from the remains of the LVF, 1,500 militiamen of the Vichy government, a pre-existing French SS assault brigade as well as volunteers who had previously served in the German Navy (Kriegsmarine). Others served in units of 'Organisation Todt' as well in the transport units of Arms Minister Speer.

Puaud, in the rank of major-general in the Waffen SS, became commander of the division, with around 7,000 men. Charlemagne had its baptism of fire in late February 1945 while defending Pomerania. The bulk of the unit was encircled and annihilated. In March, the remaining troops were assembled in Neustrelitz into a reinforced combat group of about 1,000 who took part in the battle for Berlin. Some of the companies helped defend the Reich Chancellery.[17] Henri Fenet numbered among them. A former member of the Vichy militia, he received the Knight's Cross as late as 29 April 1945 for putting 62 Soviet tanks out of action in the streets of Berlin with the help of his men. Out of 300 French volunteers, only 10 per cent survived the fight for the German capital. Fenet was wounded and taken prisoner by the Soviets, fled from a hospital near Eberswalde and was sentenced to 20 years of hard labour in France, of which he served only four.

The casualty rate of French volunteers on the Eastern Front cannot be put into exact figures. Out of a total of probably 60,000 Frenchmen deployed in various German formations, not more than 10,000 fought on the Eastern Front. Several thousand casualties are likely, which is not forgetting the French citizens from annexed Alsace (about 52,000) who, as ethnic Germans, volunteered for the Wehrmacht or Waffen SS during the war or (the majority) were forced recruits, conscripted into compulsory military service.[18]

9

Belgium

In both world wars, this western neighbour of Germany tried in vain to oppose a German invasion aimed primarily at gaining a strategic advantage over the French Army. The Belgian Army was therefore not considered a serious foe by the Germans. The country with its 8.4 million inhabitants was of interest to German policy-makers not only during war, however, thanks to its raw materials and connections overseas. With its historical-political division and the deep-seated tensions between Dutch-speaking Flemings and French-speaking Walloons, Belgium was considered easy to rule. Though the king remained in the country as a symbol of national unity as of May 1940, the German military administration knew that, given a relatively moderate occupational policy, it could use these inner conflicts to its advantage.

Right-wing extremist forces in both camps curried the Germans' favour in the hope of achieving a 'New Order' in Belgium in line with their respective interests. Ideological and political motivations caused the new masters to lean in favour of the Flemings. But the latter's vision of a Greater Dutch nation-state including Wallonia in no way corresponded to the notions of Hitler, who preferred the eventual establishment of two 'Germanic' *Gaue* in the western part of the future 'Greater Germanic Reich of the German Nation'. Flemish nationalist groups joined together in the Flemish National Union (Vlaamsch Nationaal Verbond – VNV) under the leadership of Staf De Clercq, a member of parliament. Though modelled on the NSDAP, they were true to the national idea. In the 1939 elections they received 15 per cent of the Flemish vote. The organization was subject to increasing infighting throughout the war and was also opposed by the Belgian resistance.

The first volunteers had already signed up for German military service in the summer of 1940 when Hitler, just days after occupation, approved the formation of a Westland Regiment. Dutch and Flemish volunteers were to be brought together and trained in the Waffen SS. The SS Nordwest Regiment was formed on 3 April 1941 and had recruited a good 2,000 men by August 1941, including 108 Danes and 1,400 Dutchmen.

Departure of Flemish volunteers to
the Eastern Front.

The Flemings formed part of the Germania Regiment in the newly activated SS Wiking Division, a reservoir for 'Germanic' volunteers from all Western and Northern European countries. With the German invasion of the Soviet Union, Flemish nationalists abandoned their reservations against SS recruiting and put their mutual anti-Communism in the foreground. An appeal to Flemish youth by VNV member Reimond Tollenaere on 20 July 1941 went as follows: 'If we now prove in deed that we are prepared to take on the common European foe – Communism – we shall have our rightful say later in building a new Europe. ... It is a matter of our people. It is a matter of saving Europe. It is a matter of our right to have our say in this era'.[1]

Illusions of this sort – earning the 'right to have their say' in the future formation of their own nation – were common not only among the Flemings. VNV leader Staf de Clercq was able at any rate to negotiate with the Waffen SS about basic conditions of the Flanders Legion to ensure that the legion was under his leadership and was a purely Flemish affair. By October 1941, the unit had 1,000 trained soldiers. On 8 November 1941, the Flanders Legion took part in the assault on Tikhvin, the Soviet bulwark southeast of Leningrad on the railway line to Moscow. The exposed position had to be evacuated on 8 December due to Soviet pressure. The Flemings participated in heavy defensive battles in extreme winter weather conditions during the Wehrmacht's retreat behind the Volkhov River. A protracted war of position developed here on this marshy front. In 1942–3, the Flemings fought alongside the Spanish Blue Division and with Latvian units in the Pushkin-Tsarskoyo Selo area. In mid-January 1943, they were caught up in the second major battle on Lake Ladoga and after eight days of intense defensive fighting the Flanders Legion was practically wiped out. Only 45 men out of 500 remained. The survivors were transferred to the Polish training grounds of Dębica. The legion was disbanded and newly formed as the 6th SS Volunteer Assault Brigade Langemarck. In December 1943, it had around 2,000 soldiers.

Remy Schrijnen: Born on 24 December 1921 in Kumtich near Leuven. Last rank: Unterscharführer (Junior Squad Leader). Deployments: Russia, Poland, Eastern Germany. Only Flemish recipient of the Knight's Cross of the Iron Cross (1944)[2]

The brigade was attached to the 2nd SS Panzer Division Das Reich and was engaged in heavy defensive battles east of Zhitomir. The German elite unit suffered heavy losses in the Yampol area in the winter of 1943–4 and was repeatedly brought in as a 'fire department' by Field Marshal

Manstein, supreme commander of Army Group South, in his attempt to crush Soviet spearheads with mobile operations. After withdrawing to the Carpathian line and with the start of the Soviet summer offensive in 1944, the combat group was practically annihilated in August 1944. The survivors and replacement forces were formed into the 27th SS Volunteer Panzer Grenadier Division Langemarck. Their planned deployment in the Ardenne counter-offensive in December of 1944 was abandoned, as the Flemings refused to fight against their compatriots. Thus, the division was transferred to Farther Pomerania in January 1945. Here the Flemings fought with the III (Germanic) SS Panzer Corps defending Arnswalde, and went down with their division in the area of Stettin (Szczecin). Of the survivors able to return home, 30 former volunteers were sentenced to death and executed.

Unlike the Flemings – the preferred recruits of the SS – the 'non-Germanic' Walloon volunteers joined the Wehrmacht and were fighting on the Eastern Front as early as 1941. The nationalist Rexist movement under the leadership of Léon Degrelle had failed with its plan of a fascist Greater Belgium in the autumn of 1940. Placing the 'revolutionary' idea of National Socialism above its racial component was not the way the Germans imagined it, the Walloons in their eyes being practically Frenchmen. Degrelle recognized the start of the Eastern campaign as his chance to give the Walloons some political ammunition in their rivalry with the Flemings by latching onto the idea of the anti-Bolshevist 'crusade'. He and several hundred followers signed up as volunteers for the war in the East. The German military administration put them together in the Wallonia Legion. Right-wing extremist propaganda succeeded in recruiting 1,200 volunteers who were used to form the Wehrmacht's 373rd Infantry Battalion.

After training in Poland, in October 1941, the Walloons marched towards the front under their leader Captain Jacobs and were first deployed east of the Dnieper in the struggle against the partisans.[3] In early December, they reinforced the exhausted 97th Light Division fighting in the 17th Army on the southern flank of the Eastern Front. But first the circa 670 men were used to secure a strongpoint behind the lines on the Donets. Degrelle was itching for his troops to have their first engagement at the front, aware that his German superiors did not think them capable of much. 'Unknown and unappreciated, we meanwhile had to wear ourselves out in petty and bitter duties,' he wrote in his memoirs.[4]

German reservations were understandable given the internal factional disputes in the legion. The divisional commander, Major-General Maximilian Fretter-Pico, was asked to mediate between the Rexists and a stronger National Socialist movement.[5] The higher army corps judged the battalion – rather hastily it might be added – as 'militarily useless'. Degrelle went straight to the OKH and complained. The supreme commander of the 17th Army, wanting to avoid a foreign policy debacle, finally put the battalion directly under the command of another army corps, but sent six officers and 50 soldiers home for alleged incompetence and illness. In late January 1942, the battalion was shifted to the 100th Light Infantry Division where it replaced the French troops withdrawn there. Here, too, the Walloons were assigned to 'town and railway defence' in the hinterland, where they did in fact encounter heavy fighting against Soviet units that had broken through. By March 1942, the legion had only one-third of its original strength. Out of 22 officers only two were still on duty.[6]

After reorganization and intensified training in discipline and tactics, the Walloons, in the ranks of the 97th Light Infantry Division, joined up with the German summer offensive on the long march to the Caucasus.[7] The legion was now considered a battalion 'of equal rank', fighting at Maykop and surviving the retreat at the end of the year. In late January 1943, it was reassembled in Brussels. Despite Germany's difficult military situation, about 2,000 new volunteers had meanwhile been found, mostly miners who were tired of slaving away in the coal pits, along with numerous POWs from the former Belgian Army who wanted to escape the camps in Germany. Degrelle asked his followers to see the future of Belgium 'from a purely Germanic angle', a new way of thinking that pleased the 'Reichsführer SS'.[8]

Following an agreement between the Wehrmacht and Himmler, the Walloons were taken into the Waffen SS as of 1 June 1943. As 'non-Germanics', in other words, they were now deemed worthy of serving in the SS. The legion was turned into the SS Assault Brigade Wallonien, which was deployed in the Ukraine as part of the SS Panzer Division Wiking at the end of 1943. In January 1944, the brigade bore the brunt of the defensive battles in the Cherkasy pocket as well as the break-out, which only 632 men survived. After reassembling in July 1944, it saw action in the Battle of Narva in the Baltics, once again suffering heavy casualties. In October, after being replenished, it was refashioned into the 28th SS Volunteer Panzer Grenadier Division Wallonien. Degrelle had advanced from the rank and file to become a highly decorated divisional commander and SS Standartenführer.

Awarding the Iron Cross to Walloon volunteers on the Eastern Front in March 1942.

In 1945, the unit returned to the Eastern Front and fought in the ranks of Army Group Vistula in the Pomerania region under the command of Himmler. In the end it had 700 men, some of whom escaped to Denmark. Degrelle fled via Norway to Spain. There he went into hiding and died in 1994 in Málaga. A total of about 6,000 Walloon volunteers fought on the side of the Germans during the war, 2,500 of whom were killed in action. All in all 22,000 Flemings and 16,000 Walloons served in the Waffen SS throughout the course of World War II.[9] The inner division of Belgium, the country's negative historical heritage, was responsible for the fact that Belgian volunteers fought in two separate legions on the Eastern Front. The survivors were summarily sentenced to death after the war, but the sentence was only carried out against officers and holders of the Knight's Cross. The rank and file were let off with 10 to 20 years of hard labour. Legionnaires who had ended up in Soviet POW camps generally preferred to stay in West Germany after their release from years of captivity.

Léon Degrelle speaking in Berlin.

10

The Netherlands

The German Reich profited greatly from the neutrality of its western neighbour the Netherlands in World War I, a fact that was disregarded, however, in planning a new campaign to subjugate France in late 1939. Yet the Nazis still endeavoured to win over the circa 8.8 million Dutchmen after occupying the country in May 1940. This effort was partly fuelled by the illusion of 're-educating' the population during a transition period so that, through preferential and 'generous' treatment, they would eventually accept being absorbed in the future 'Greater Germanic Reich'. The Dutch were thus put under a civil German Reich commissioner (Arthur Seyss-Inquart), who relied on the Dutch right-wing radical National Socialist Movement in the Netherlands (NSB) under Anton Adriaan Mussert to help with their ideological orientation.[1] But the NSB did not toe the German line, holding firmly as it did to the idea of national autonomy within a 'Germanic' confederation of states.

Hence recruiting efforts for the Westland Regiment of the Waffen SS, formed in May 1940, lagged far behind Himmler's expectations, despite the fact that Dutch prisoners of war were 'magnanimously' allowed to go back home. Added to the reservedness of the Mussert movement was an occupation policy that quickly strayed from its 'good' intentions and gradually became more radical, including the country's increasing economic exploitation. The result was a disastrous deterioration of the general mood. The collapse corresponded more or less exactly with the start of the war in the East and was more economically than politically motivated. Occupied Holland, with its highly developed agriculture, was ruthlessly exploited by the Nazis.[2]

Yet the SS used the start of the war against the USSR for its anti-Communist propaganda, milking it for what it was worth. On 28 June 1941, Arnold Meijer, leader of the National Front, suggested the formation of a legion, an idea that Mussert was keen to adopt as he saw in it the chance to rebuild a Dutch army. Meijer eventually withdrew after failing to prevent its absorption in the Waffen SS and withdrew. On 26 July 1941, the Dutch volunteer unit in the Westland Regiment of the Waffen SS was reorganized into the Volunteer Legion Niederlande. This, parallel to the other legions, was to be a reservoir for the 'Crusade of Europe' against Bolshevism. The Germans succeeded in making the legion's affiliation to the SS invisible at first.

Lieutenant General Hendrik Alexander Seyffardt, chief-of-staff of the Dutch Army from 1929 to 1934, was persuaded to take command of the legion. The insignia he chose for their uniforms underlined their independence. The legionnaires wore the 'Prinsevlag', the Dutch coat of arms, and – instead of the traditional SS runes – the 'Wolf's Hook' in allusion to the NSB. The soldiers swore an oath not only to the Führer but also to the Prinsevlag. In composing a song for the legion, they endeavoured to create a special Dutch flavour to give the recruits the impression they were serving in an independent national formation in the fight against the Soviet Union. Most of them were unaware that they were in the clutches of the SS already. They did not officially become part of the Waffen SS until 1943.

Though General Seyffardt obviously had inside knowledge of these developments, the Germans ignored his objections to integrating the unit into the Waffen SS. He did not entirely share Nazi ideology either, and most likely served the Germans primarily as a figurehead. At the end of 1941, the Dutch with their 4,814 soldiers comprised the greatest share of 'Germanic volunteers of non-German nationality' in the Waffen SS.[3] Even Anton Mussert as the leader of the NSB tried to avoid the 'embrace' of the SS. The legion did in fact have a character all its own, and was different from regular Waffen SS units in terms of discipline and conduct.

Relations with German instructors were bad from the outset. After training in East Prussia, the legion was attached to Army Group North and was supposed to take part in the capture of Leningrad. It saw action at the end of 1941 on the Volkhov Front. The legionnaires held their own in hard-fought defensive battles, while mopping up forest areas as well as in combating partisans. In February 1942, Mussert paid a visit to the unit, now commanded by SS Brigadeführer Klingemann. The Dutch fought off repeated and massive Soviet attacks in the winter and spring battles of 1942. Despite suffering heavy losses, they took part in a German assault in the summer and

succeeded in taking 3,500 prisoners, including Andrey Vlasov, the famous
Soviet general who was later to command the pro-German Vlasov Army.

In July 1942, the legion was transferred to the Leningrad Front and,
joining up with the 2nd SS Infantry Brigade, took part in besieging the
city. It again suffered heavy losses, losing half of its original strength. Now
under the command of SS Obersturmbannführer Josef Fitzthum, the unit
was able to gather strength thanks to relative calm on the battlefront. But
already in July, the legion again saw heavy fighting in renewed attempts
to take the city as part of Operation Northern Light. The insufficiently
prepared and poorly supplied legion ran into trouble in the Krasnoye Selo
area when Soviet counter-offensives repelled German forces back to their
starting position. But Soviet attacks on the German defensive front in
the course of this first Battle of Ladoga ultimately failed as well. In mid-
January 1943, the Red Army renewed its attack with massive tank forces.
Together with the neighbouring Norwegian legion, the Dutch held their
ground. Gerardus Mooyman received the Knight's Cross for destroying
13 Soviet armoured cars. In April, Himmler withdrew the Dutch legion

Decoration of Dutch soldiers in Selo
Gora, February 1942.

from the Leningrad Front, reorganizing it into the independent 4th SS Volunteer Panzer Grenadier Brigade Nederland. The politically motivated game of hide and seek with the SS was now over. The Dutch resistance's assassination of Lieutenant General Hendrik Seyffardt, who as 'commander' of the legion had long since lost his influence, clarified the political front back home.

Equally unmasking was the internment of formerly released Dutch prisoners of war who now, in April 1943, had to work as forced labourers for the Germans, giving rise to considerable protest. A large number of demonstrators were gunned down during the ensuing mass strike. With that, another chapter of collaboration on the Eastern Front was nearing its end. German settlement plans for its future colonies in the East included the use of foreign 'Germanic' administrators. As early as 1941, its civil administration had appointed 416 Dutchmen as economic experts in Lithuania and Byelorussia. Alfred Rosenberg, Hitler's Reich minister for the occupied eastern territories, was hoping to offer the racially desirable Dutch an alternative to their lost overseas colonies. In June 1942, the partly state-run Nederlandse Oostcompagnie (NOC) was founded. The company recruited hundreds of agronomists, manual labourers, technicians and businessmen to take on functions in the occupied Soviet territories. They performed valuable tasks, in commerce as well as in agriculture, in peat extraction and the fisheries on Lake Peipus.[4] In the summer of 1943, 365 Dutch farmers were employed in the Ukraine alone. They were armed on account of the partisan threat, and many of them lost their lives.

By placing them together with its Norwegian and Danish units, the SS wanted to create a greater European volunteer army of preferred 'Germanic countries'. Despite Mussert's objections, the division was named Nordland; the Dutch, though the largest contingent, were still not enough to form a complete division with up to 20,000 men. During its reorganization and merging with the approximately 1,500 Dutch volunteers from the Wiking Division, the brigade was stationed in Croatia where in the summer of 1943 it was deployed with other units of the III (Germanic) SS Panzer Corps against Tito partisans. At the end of the year, it was sent back to the Leningrad Front together with two Dutch regiments (No. 1 General Seyffardt and No. 2 De Ruyter).

There it was caught in the midst of heavy fighting in the vicinity of Oranienbaum, where, in February of 1944, the Red Army had launched a new

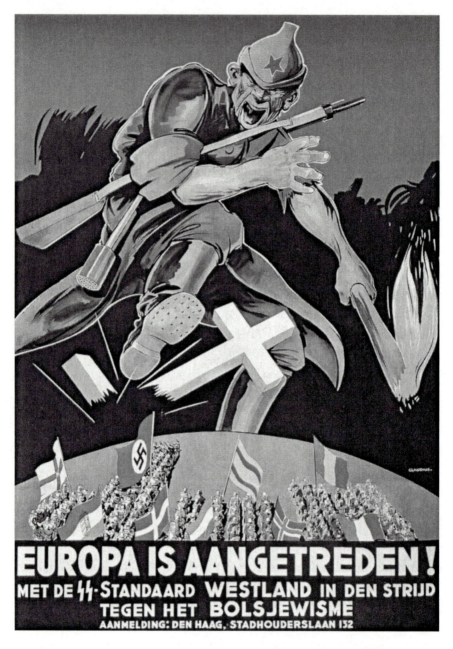

Propaganda poster of the
Reich Commissariat Westland,
proclaiming the European struggle
against Bolshevism.

Members of the 23rd SS
Nederland Division.

offensive to end the siege of Leningrad definitively. Following a breakthrough in the neighbouring Luftwaffe field division, the Dutch brigade had to fight its way back to the western bank of the Narva to avoid being encircled. As part of the newly created Army Group Narva, along with four German infantry divisions and the Estonian 20th SS Volunteer Panzer Grenadier Division, it defended this vital position against fierce Soviet frontal attacks in the spring of 1944. The brigade suffered heavy losses. From January to April 1944, it lost 87 officers, 502 NCOs and 3,139 enlisted men.

The collapse of Army Group Centre in the summer of 1944 put the Dutch at 'fortress' Narva in a precarious situation as well. The Dutch held their ground, despite high losses and without any supplies or reinforcements. The brigade was praised on multiple occasions for its commitment. In late July 1944, it was supposed to retreat to the Tannenberg Line together with Army Group North. Command errors led to a catastrophe. The General Seyffardt Regiment missed the route of retreat, was discovered by the Soviet Air Force and completely destroyed in relentless air attacks in the forests outside Narva. Only a handful of survivors caught up with the rest of the brigade.

The political morale of the Dutch remained high, but their fighting power was diminished due to the lack of munitions and fuel. Following a phase of relative calm, the brigade was reinforced with a Walloon battalion and was supposed to defend the strategically vital town of Pernau (Pärnu) against Soviet attacks. With the Soviet breakthrough on the Baltic Sea near Riga, however, the front was jeopardized once again. The retreat to Kurland (Kurzeme) was inevitable, where, after heavy losses the brigade was forced to dig itself in again in mid-October 1944. In the first Battle of Kurland, it successfully defended the important seaport of Libau (Liepāja). The Dutch fought off fierce partisan attacks in the hinterland, and did not shy away from shooting civilians in the course of retaliatory measures.

In the second Battle of Kurland in late October, a battalion of the De Ruyter Regiment was hit hard by a Red Army frontal attack. The volunteers held their ground at the Krimhilde defensive position. In the third Battle of Kurland, beginning on 21 December 1944, Libau, too, became a main point of attack. The Dutch repelled every Soviet attack there.

Back home, the southern part of their country had already been liberated by the Allies. As a result of extensive German defence measures, including the flooding of large tracts of land, and due to a ruthless occupation policy, about 20,000 people perished in the northern Netherlands during the Dutch famine of 1944–5.[5]

In late January 1945, the III (Germanic) SS Panzer Corps with the Dutch brigade was to reinforce the imperilled Vistula Front. The front had already been penetrated, however, by the time the brigade was unloaded in Swinemünde (Świnoujście) in early February. Though insufficient in terms of numbers, the Dutchmen were now elevated to the status of a division (23rd SS Volunteer Panzer Grenadier Division). Among its 6,000 troops were a large number of Romanian-German recruits.

Together with the SS Wallonien, Langemarck and Nordland divisions, they comprised Himmler's elite for defending Pomerania, the Reichsführer SS assuming personal responsibility for them. But defence efforts failed in March 1945 due to fierce Soviet attacks and the lack of fuel. The Nederland Division was divided and the De Ruyter Regiment was captured by the Americans near Parchim, whereas the General Seyffardt Regiment was crushed by the Red Army further south near Hammerstein. Those taken captive were shot.

In the course of World War II, about 40,000 Dutchmen served in the Waffen SS, forming its largest non-German contingent. These considerable figures were achieved despite the reluctant attitude of Mussert and a stiffening resistance among the majority of the population. Nevertheless, they were a minority whose collaboration was severely punished at war's end. In soldierly terms, the Dutch volunteers were hardly distinguishable from their German counterparts on the Eastern Front. Their actual military contribution as a brigade-sized unit of 3,000 to 6,000 men on average was less significant than the usefulness Hitler derived from them for propaganda purposes.

11

Denmark

This northern neighbour of the German Reich was able to remain neutral in World War I. Its agricultural products were much in demand between the wars and an important object of German trade policy. Yet its occupation was not in Hitler's original plans and resulted instead from the unexpected course of conflict with the Western Powers. The invasion of 10 April 1940 was primarily motivated by military-strategic concerns. Denmark was a springboard to Norway and was an important Baltic Sea outlet. Officially the Germans were merely concerned with ensuring the country's neutrality. It was therefore essential that the invasion of Wehrmacht troops go off without a hitch.

The plan succeeded in the case of Denmark. Unlike the Netherlands and Norway, its army of 14,000 men did not put up a fight. King and government stayed in office and the Germans limited themselves to supervisory administration. Despite a host of promises to the contrary, there was no question of Denmark's inclusion in the 'Greater German sphere', the country being a 'militarily indispensable bridge to the Norwegian Atlantic position so vital to Germany'.[1] Though no formal annexation was planned, the country had no choice but to form a close reliance on the Third Reich with satellite status.

Its 3.8 million inhabitants were considered 'blood relatives' and thus attracted the attention of the SS. As early as May 1940, the first volunteers were accepted into the SS Nordland Regiment. Apart from members of the German minority in southern Denmark (almost 25 per cent of the Danish volunteers), they were mainly adherents of the National Socialist Workers' Party of Denmark (DNSAP) as well as former legionnaires who had originally signed up to fight the Red Army on the side of the Finns and had now returned home.[2] The Germans also hoped to recruit soldiers discharged from the Danish Army, though recruitment into foreign armies was actually prohibited according to the laws of the land. The SS was disappointed, as its Danish contingent amounted to a mere 216 men by the summer of 1941. Only about half the Danish volunteers passed muster. As part of the SS Wiking Division, they joined the advance in the Ukraine and were pushed back from Rostov in December 1941. They took part in the summer campaign of 1942, advancing deep into the Caucasus, but had to retreat in December. About 170 Danes stayed on in the Wiking Division after Nordland was formed and saw action on the Eastern Front until surrendering to US troops in Austria.

Outside a recruiting office of the Freikorps Danmark.

More important than the Wiking volunteers were the members of a new volunteer corps formed after the invasion of the USSR with the considerable support of the Foreign Office. The Danish government turned down the suggestion of the High Command of the Wehrmacht that the Danish Army provide a regiment for the Eastern Front. Thus, the search for volunteers began in the war against Bolshevism. The Germans were not pleased that the first volunteers to sign up had wanted to fight on the side of Finland, and were happy when Helsinki flat out denied these reports.[3] The government in

Copenhagen received promises that the new Freikorps Danmark, deployed in the Waffen SS as a unified Danish formation, would only fight against the Soviet Union. Explicit reference was made to the 'struggle against Bolshevism' when swearing their allegiance to Hitler.[4]

Members of the Danish armed forces, meanwhile reduced to 2,200 men, were eventually allowed to join, and, in late June 1941, about 600 volunteers were transferred to Germany for training. Among them was a handful of pilots who were absorbed into Göring's Luftwaffe.[5] The Volunteer Corps was awarded a flag from the Danish defence minister on behalf of King Christian X, thus lending the unit a quasi-official character. After the war, of course, no one from the state was willing to recognize this act as such.

Christian Frederik von Schalburg
with his wife.

By the end of the year the unit had grown to over 1,000 men and, in May 1942, it went into battle as a reinforced infantry battalion of the SS Totenkopf Division at the Oranienburg pocket outside Leningrad. It was led by Christian Frederik von Schalburg, a former captain in the Royal Guard who had already fought as a volunteer in the Finnish Winter War of 1939–40.[6] Killed in action on 2 June 1942, he became an almost mythical hero:

He entered our ranks ... filled with the greatness of the Germanic idea of community. ... He was the model of a duty-bound, courageous and enthusiastic soldier. As a champion of our shared Germanic cause, he was at the fore of the Germanic volunteers of his country. He is a model for us of the heroic, selfless, loyal, Germanic man. ... Christian von Schalburg shall always be bound to the fate of our division. (From an order of the day by SS General Felix Steiner on the death of von Schalburg)[7]

After heavy losses in the Demyansk pocket, the unit was pulled out in August and sent home on furlough to Denmark. Propaganda campaigns of the DNSAP failed to recruit any notable number of new volunteers. A relatively unified Danish resistance succeeded in foiling recruiting efforts.

Recruiting among ethnic Germans in North Schleswig as well yielded only about 1,000 volunteers for the Wehrmacht and Waffen SS in 1942. These recruits did not want to be part of the Volunteer Corps with their Danish compatriots but were assigned – after considerable protests – to the SS Totenkopf Division. With a fighting strength of around 500 to 650 men, the Freikorps was sent back to the front in northern Russia in mid-October.[8] There the Danes successfully defended a line of strongpoints near Nevel during the winter before being pulled out again in March 1943. In May, at the Grafenwöhr training grounds near Nuremberg, they received the unexpected news that the Germans had decided to disband the corps.

Resistance in the country was intensifying, and when the Danish National Socialists won a mere 2.1 per cent of the vote at elections on 5 May 1943, the Germans proclaimed a state of emergency. A 'Second Occupation' ensued. Danish armed forces were disbanded and its soldiers arrested. Some of them managed to escape abroad (about 1,000 Danes eventually served in the British armed forces). Of the 10,000 active and former Danish soldiers placed under arrest, the SS hoped to win about 4,000 volunteers for the Eastern Front. When these expectations failed to materialize, all but 1,300 of them were released in December 1943.[9]

Danish volunteers from the disbanded Freikorps Danmark and the Wiking Division were used to form the 24th SS Panzer Grenadier Regiment Danmark in the new Nordland Division. In the autumn of 1943, it was deployed in the III (Germanic) SS Panzer Corps to combat partisans in

Croatia. There they participated in burning down villages and in executions. They were then transferred north in the winter of 1943–4, this time to the Narva Front, where they held their ground in a war of position while suffering high casualties. Their route led through the Kurland pocket, where again they suffered heavy losses during fierce fighting in late 1944. A number of Danish officers commanded other foreign SS units. Among them was Obersturmführer Johannes Hellmers, who led a Dutch company of the Nederland Division:

> On the morning of 25 January, the Russians attacked from the near-by forest with tanks and 200 men. They succeeded in penetrating the piece of trench, rolling up half the trench. In this seemingly hopeless situation, SS Obersturmführer Hellmers decided to launch a counter-attack with the few men at his disposal. Taking the lead with a submachine gun in hand, he charged ahead and drove them out of their trenches with heavy losses and much bloodshed. Though wounded twice himself in the process, he remained in the main line of resistance and, together with his men, fought off amidst infantry gunfire all subsequent attempts of the enemy to take the main line of resistance. It is thanks to his decisiveness and exceptional personal bravery that the main line of resistance in the Kaleti area was held completely on 25 January and the enemy was hindered from breaking through at Kaleti. The resistance he put up was instrumental for the entire sector between Purmasati and Skuoda. (From the proposal to award the Knight's Cross to Johannes Hellmers on 8 February 1945)[10]

In late January 1945, the remaining troops – some of the companies had a mere ten men left – were transferred to Pomerania. With German navy men filling up their ranks, they were supposed to support Himmler's counter-attack against the Red Army. Operation Solstice broke down near Arnswalde (Choszczno). Then, in April, the Danmark Regiment was ordered to Berlin to help defend the capital of the Reich. Many Danes fought fanatically, despite their hopeless situation. Some, when defeated, were able to flee to the British; most of them lost their lives, however. In the final stages of the war, Denmark was a safe haven for many German refugees from the eastern territories, who escaped across the Baltic Sea and ultimately found asylum there. A total of 186,000 German soldiers were stationed in the country under nearly peacelike circumstances. Wehrmacht leaders could count on the fact that the British would not let this strategically vital position fall into Soviet hands.

Danish volunteers after a counter-attack, spring 1944.

With partial capitulation in Northern Europe on 4 May 1945, the hour of liberation had come for Denmark as well. The Danish liberation movement took power and oversaw the withdrawal of armed German units to the south. The sick and wounded, 'willing helpers', POWs and refugees were allowed to remain in Denmark for the time being.

A total of 6,015 Danes supposedly signed up voluntarily to serve in the Wehrmacht and Waffen SS. Just as many were carried off to German concentration camps. Added to this were 2,000 ethnic Germans in North Schleswig. About half of the Danish soldiers on the Eastern Front (3,890) were killed; 400 are considered missing in action. Though promised by their government that they could return to the Danish Army after the war, Danish career soldiers were punished instead. A total of 34,000 collaborators were sentenced after 1945.

12

Norway

Like Denmark, Norway was also able to preserve its neutrality in World War I. The country with the longest coastline in Europe and around 3 million inhabitants was hoping to remain neutral at the start of World War II, too, though the sympathies of this stable democratic society and monarchy clearly lay with the Western Powers. British attempts to block the strategically vital transport of ore from Sweden via the Norwegian seaport of Narvik forced the Wehrmacht to engage in a daring sea-air operation in April 1940 which, due to unexpected Norwegian resistance and the intervention of the Western Powers, nearly ended in disaster. The sparsely settled country was not a serious military opponent, and thanks to its geographical location offered important strategic advantages to the Germans in their fight against Great Britain. With the capitulation of the Norwegian Army and the surrendering of its arms, Norwegian prisoners of war were 'magnanimously' allowed to return home. Norway's greatest resource, its merchant fleet, had found refuge in Western ports and was being used by the British. King Haakon VII and his government organized the resistance movement from English exile.

Hence the Germans transferred governmental power to Vidkun Quisling, the 'Fører' of the right-wing radical splinter group National Unification (NS). Quisling was under the supervision of Josef Terboven, Gauleiter of Essen and Reich commissioner for the occupied Norwegian territories. The population rejected him, considering him a traitor. But the Norwegians ultimately had no choice and were forced to come to terms with a German occupation army of 300,000 men. To Hitler's mind, Norway would remain an independent state, but would definitely be part of the future 'Greater Germanic Reich of the German Nation'.[1]

From a racial-ideological point of view, the Norwegians were a favoured nation, albeit politically unreliable, being considered 'notorious' democrats. The SS nevertheless began recruiting for the Nordland Regiment immediately after invading the country. The results were not particularly impressive. By the end of 1941, 1,883 volunteers had signed up for the Waffen SS.[2] In August 1941, 294 Norwegians belonged to the SS Wiking Division.

In the preparations for Operation Barbarossa, the North Cape became a deployment zone for the German Mountain Corps Norway under the command of Mountain Troop General Eduard Dietl. Two reinforced German mountain divisions and subordinate Finnish border troops were to take the strategically important seaport of Murmansk in Operation Platinum Fox. German troops turned out to be much too weak, however, to overcome powerful Soviet defensive positions. A three-year war of position ensued, characterized by unfavourable terrain and weather conditions. Northern Norway, moreover, became the basis for deploying the German Navy and Luftwaffe against British convoys to Murmansk, which were supplying aid to the USSR.

Recruiting poster for the Norwegian Legion.

German occupying forces in Norway had fewer problems with local resistance than with securing reinforcements and protecting a long and unmanageable coastline from attempted enemy landings. The notorious shortage of German troops on the Arctic Front led to intensified recruiting efforts among the Norwegians. The recruits were assembled in the Norwegian Legion. Under its first commander Jø Bakke, the unit was trained at Fallingbostel and was flown close to the Leningrad Front in January 1942. The legionnaires signed up for six months and were later replaced. German soldiers considered them calm and level-headed people, though allergic to master-race arrogance. One volunteer reported: 'I had a good fellow officer who was so put off by German mouthiness that he deserted while passing through Sweden. In 1944 four Norwegian officers were sent to delinquent companies for aiming at Hitler portraits one evening. This shooting at portraits was a reaction.'[3]

The Norway Legion was disbanded in the wake of Himmler's change of policy, and the SS Panzer Grenadier Regiment Norge became part of the SS Nordland Division in the summer of 1943. With the activation of the 6th SS Mountain Division Nord in the winter of 1943–4, volunteers signed up for the division's Norwegian Ski Battalion and ultimately fought on the Kandalaksha Front in northern Finland. The battalion was virtually destroyed, down to the last man, in the fight for Kaprolat Hill. Only a few of the soldiers returned home.

Individual groups of Norwegian officers were being arrested as of early 1941, and, in July 1943, Hitler recalled all officers and ordered them to be taken captive.[4] This action was part of a tightening of occupation policy. As of the spring of 1944, emplacements were built at Lyngenfjord, where the Wehrmacht eventually retreated in October 1944 under pressure from the Red Army. The 20th Mountain Army under Colonel-General Lothar Rendulic left a trail of scorched earth in Finland and northern Norway. Along with the destruction of towns and infrastructure, about 40,000 Norwegians were forcibly transported to the south.[5] They waited here until May 1945 to be liberated by the British, who occupied the country without a fight once the Germans had surrendered. At last count, the Wehrmacht commander of Norway had nearly 400,000 men at his disposal and 77,300 prisoners of war. German expectations of continuing the fight from here even after Berlin had fallen never materialized. They did succeed, however, in pulling out the bulk of Wehrmacht units from northern Norway and moving them to the south.

Norwegian ski trooper.

After capitulation on 8 May 1945, Norwegian resistance fighters used the threat of force to snatch from a German military hospital in Oslo 32 of their compatriots who had fought against the Soviet Union. All collaborators faced harsh sentences. Quisling was executed. More than 14,000 received prison sentences, and the death penalty was carried out in 25 instances. Others were lucky to get off lightly. About 15,000 Poles, most of whom had served in the Wehrmacht, were allowed to go home unmolested; about 4,000 of them preferred, for political reasons, to stay in the West or were rejected by the Polish authorities for being ethnic Germans. The circa 6,000 Norwegians who fought against the Red Army – first with the Finnish Army, then on the side of the Germans – were an ostracized or forgotten minority, unlike the majority, who had joined the Allied struggle against Nazi rule.

Norway, Denmark, the Netherlands and Belgium were constitutional monarchies and neutral states invaded by the Wehrmacht in 1940 and forced by an occupying power to fight against a distant USSR. The situation was quite different, however, in the Baltic republics of Estonia, Latvia and Lithuania. These became Soviet zones of occupation in 1940, were ostensibly liberated by the Wehrmacht in 1941, and thus had their own reasons to take up arms against Stalinism, as did other Eastern European nations and parts of the Russian population.

Part III

THE EASTERN EUROPEAN NATIONS IN THE STRUGGLE AGAINST STALINISM

Introduction

On 22 June 1941, Hitler's Wehrmacht began fighting on the western fringes of the Soviet multi-ethnic state. The Germans, for various reasons, could count on considerable support here, even the willingness to fight alongside them in their Eastern campaign against Russia. The centuries of Tsarist rule in East-Central Europe, though varied in degree, had indeed been experienced as oppressive. Cultural and linguistic peculiarities had been preserved in the region despite massive Russification. In the nineteenth century, national movements emerged that aimed at greater autonomy or independence. Pan-Slavism as Moscow's ideological counter-movement had little chance of taking root here, if only for the virulent conflict between the state-sponsored Russian Orthodox Church and the Catholicism of the western border areas.

At the same time, a strong German influence had spread from the Baltics to eastern Poland and western Ukraine. In the Baltics, this influence went back to the Teutonic Knights and Hanseatic merchants who maintained their role as leading citizens even under later Russian rule. Colonization of the East by German farmers and craftsmen likewise gained a foothold in eastern Poland and western Ukraine. Advancing into this region in 1915, the German Army encountered a hotchpotch of conflicting national interests that they were able to turn to their advantage. The Germans promoted nation-state-building in East-Central Europe as part of a future German Empire. Thus the period of German occupation left a thoroughly positive impression on the locals.

In 1919–20, the largely unstable fledgling states in this in-between zone were able to ward off the threat of the Russian revolutionary army, partly with German assistance, partly with the help of the Western Entente Powers. They turned into front-line states in the European 'civil war'. By the 1930s, the persistent 'Bolshevist threat' seemed to have been banished thanks to German rearmament and Hitler's claim to be a 'bulwark' against Bolshevism.

Pronounced ideological differences between the two great powers seemed to prevent the Baltic states and Poland from becoming caught between the 'hammer and anvil'. If push came to shove, however, the people's sympathies lay more with the German Reich, despite its aggressive foreign policy and the concomitant threat of war.

The shock of the Hitler–Stalin Pact changed this situation dramatically. Poland was torn asunder, and the Stalinization of eastern Poland was more brutal at first than German rule in the western half of the country. This confirmed deep-seated fears in the Baltic states, whose independence was spared only briefly before they, too, were overrun by Stalinism. Abandoned first by Germany then by the Western Powers, these peoples witnessed political repression, radical social changes and the deportation of their ruling elites in the first year of Soviet occupation. The departure of Baltic Germans as well as ethnic Germans in eastern Poland and Bessarabia 'back home to the Reich' destroyed neighbourhoods and social environments just as much as the political 'purges' conducted by the communists did.

When the Wehrmacht invaded the newly formed border provinces of the Soviet Empire soon afterwards, the majority of the population there greeted them as liberators. Local soldiers and officers were prepared to switch sides and once again join the Germans in the common front against Bolshevism that had protected their homeland in 1919–20, believing it would succeed again. Patriotism and anti-Communism united and divided them at the same time. Their new masters, however, were only superficially interested in carrying on the tradition of World War I. National Socialist war aims were not to re-establish independence and a brotherhood-in-arms. Rather, the East-Central European buffer zone was to form a kind of 'settlement bridge' in Germanizing the future Lebensraum in the East. This ultimately meant oppression, exploitation and expulsion, something these nations failed to realize at the time.

The Nazis thought it opportune to hide these aims in their wartime propaganda, at least for the duration of the war, while singing the song of the 'Crusade against Bolshevism' in every possible key. The people experienced a seemingly zigzag course under the Germans given the convoluted structures of the new occupying regime and the sometimes contrary interests of Wehrmacht, SS, civil and military administration, and the economy.

Having reached the Caucasus in 1942, the Germans reacted more positively to the willingness of these varied nations to collaborate, forming armed units out of them. In the case of Muslim communities, anti-Russian and religious impulses were a major factor, alongside the experience of Stalinist nationality policies, which resulted in the destruction of traditional ways of living. This applied to a certain extent to the southern Russian Cossack regions as well.

The greatest potential, however, was in the millions of Red Army members who had failed to become committed communists, among them many officers who had barely survived the Stalinist purges of the late 1930s. Stalin's proclamation of the 'Great Patriotic War' was hollow-sounding to them at first. The Germans, however – unlike during World War I – with their brutal occupying regime and with Soviet prisoners of war dying in masses, demonstrated their contempt for the Russians, who Hitler viewed as 'subhumans' and as slaves without rights. Even in the jaws of defeat, the German dictator clung tenaciously to this policy that was so counterproductive to the Reich, and this despite the fact that the Russians, alongside Hitler's allies, made up the largest contingent of foreign auxiliary troops on the German side with upwards of 1 million men.

13

Estonia

The German Empire forced Russia to give up the Baltic states in the Treaty of Brest-Litovsk in March 1918, a condition Lenin grudgingly accepted. During World War I, the idea increasingly took hold in Germany that the formation of independent border states would effectively weaken the Russian Empire. Apart from the strategic and economic benefits the Baltic region offered Germany as a future great or even global power, it also presented the opportunity for a German eastern settlement. This settlement was to be based on the Baltic German minority there, which had wielded significant cultural, economic and political influence ever since the Late Middle Ages and maintained it during Tsarist times.

With its approximately 1 million inhabitants, Estonia was the smallest Baltic state. Though bigger than Denmark or Belgium in terms of its territory, it was extremely sparsely settled and was a largely agricultural region in which 90 per cent of the population (in 1920) were ethnic Estonians, a nation related to the Finns on the opposite coast of the Baltic. Alongside this predominantly peasant population were Russian (8.2 per cent), Swedish (0.7 per cent) and Jewish (0.4 per cent) minorities, among which the Baltic Germans (1.7 per cent) were over-represented in the land-owning and urban middle classes. Estonian politicians had proclaimed independence on 24 February 1918, but were unable to put it into practice under German occupation.

The German withdrawal in late 1918 forced the provisional government of Estonia to assemble its own armed forces in order to hold the Narva Front against an approaching Red Army. Prime Minister Konstantin Päts, however, had to accept the fact that Estonian peasants were not willing to fight for urban dwellers and their national idea. Anti-Bolshevist Russian units (White Guardsmen), volunteers from Denmark and Sweden and about 3,500 Finns came to his aid instead. Promises of land reforms ultimately won over the peasants, too, although this collided with the interests of German Baltic landowners. The most effective deterrent, however, was a British squadron that turned up outside Tallinn and caused the Red Army to bypass Finland and march towards Latvia instead. Estonian troops took part in the defence of northern Latvia and even did battle with the German Baltic Landwehr in June 1919. After a number of defeats, Moscow finally yielded and in 1920 abandoned 'voluntarily and for all times' any territorial claims to Estonia.

In the 1920s, the Estonian government pursued a strictly anti-Bolshevist line and a liberal domestic nationality policy granting considerable autonomy in the cultural sphere. Its parliament was weakened by a plethora of political parties. The office of president was, after the Swiss fashion, entirely lacking. In the interwar period, Berlin endeavoured to strengthen the country by promoting the German Baltic influence.[1] Tallinn trusted in its neutrality throughout the 1930s and rejected any allegiance to one of the great power blocs. The Estonians were concerned about the growing threat posed by Stalinist foreign policy, the Latvians feared the Germans, whereas the Lithuanians were scared of the Poles. Stronger co-operation between the Baltic border states foundered on their conflict of interests.

Chief-of-Staff Halder (right) inspecting a company of the Estonian Defence Corps on 30 June 1939.

In 1934, Estonia averted a *coup d'état* by the so-called 'freedom fighters', a growing fascist movement. Konstantin Päts of the Peasant Party, the founder of the state of Estonia in 1918, pushed through a new presidential constitution with the help of the military. Thus, as of 1938, Estonia found its way back to democracy of its own accord. Given the tense foreign policy situation, the visit of German Chief-of-Staff Halder in late June 1939 was an important event. In all of the talks, the Germans noted, a 'strong hatred of Russia' surfaced. Only side by side with the Reich did the Estonians see a chance of defending their national sovereignty. With the importance of agrarian reform in Estonia's domestic politics, however, they rejected any involvement of Berlin on behalf of the Baltic Germans. The Estonians would fiercely resist any Soviet military attack and could apparently hold their own for some time.[2]

It was not until several days later that Hitler decided to give up Estonia and sacrifice it to his pact with Stalin. The Estonians were not aware at first of the extent to which the pact would affect them. Hitler's appeal to the Baltic Germans on 6 October 1939 – after the subjugation and division of Poland – to 'return to the Reich' was met in the Estonian press with rather unfriendly remarks about their fellow citizens of German descent. At this point in time the Red Army already had 160,000 troops and 600 tanks and aeroplanes amassed along the Estonian border. The Estonians, by contrast, had only 15,000 recruits and 16 tanks to defend themselves with. Moscow eventually demanded permission to set up bases and the signing of a mutual assistance pact.

The utterly isolated Estonians had to give in and watch as Soviet air attacks were launched against Finland from Estonian soil. Only a small number of volunteers succeeded in coming to the aid of their besieged sister nation. A total of 14,000 Germans left Estonia. In the spring of 1941, 7,000 people – half of them Estonians – followed, seeking refuge in Germany.

In the wake of Germany's victory over France, Stalin strove to keep his own prey on a tight leash. Estonia, after rigged elections, became a Soviet republic and part of the Russian empire in August 1940. The country's Sovietization reached its apex just before the German invasion. In the course of mass deportations on 14 June 1941, 11,000 'anti-Soviet elements' – that is, former politicians, officers, businessmen and landowners – were forcibly taken to the interior of the USSR. About 1,000 of them were murdered in the 'Baltic Katyn' near the city of Norilsk. Another 30,000 Estonians were forcibly recruited into the Red Army, but soon discharged once the war began and sent to labour camps. It is therefore no surprise that when German troops invaded Estonia two weeks after the start of Operation Barbarossa, many people there welcomed them as liberators.

A good number of Estonian soldiers had already deserted from the Red Army or defected to the Germans. In the Summer War of 1941, thousands of Estonians who had fled to the forests to escape deportation waged a guerrilla war against the extermination battalions of the Red Army, foiling the latter's scorched-earth strategy in Estonia. They organized their own administrations at the local level and helped the Wehrmacht in its advance on Leningrad. They were supported in this by volunteers recruited by German intelligence (Abwehr) in May 1941 from among the Estonian exile community. About 80 men were smuggled into Estonia at the start of the war. They established contact with the 'Forest Brothers' and conducted reconnaissance in the Soviet hinterland.[3]

Though zealously taking part in the pursuit and murder of communists after being liberated – upwards of 8,000 people are thought to have been killed, according to the latest figures – the Estonian Self-Defence, unlike similar groups in the other Baltic states, did not use the opportunity to carry out pogroms against their Jewish fellow-citizens. The majority of Estonian Jews were victims of Soviet deportations anyway – safe from persecution by the Germans, to be sure, but at the mercy of Stalinist terror. Many Estonians wrote petitions to the Germans asking them to spare the remaining Jews. Nevertheless, about 1,000 Jews had been murdered by the end of 1941, making the country – in Himmler's view – one of the first to be 'Jew-free' (*judenfrei*). In return, thousands of Jews from Eastern Europe were deported to Estonian camps and nearly 10,000 murdered there. Many Estonians worked in departments of the German security police in Estonia and played an important role in 'combating the enemy'.[4]

The country's last prime minister, Jüri Uluots, demanded in a memorandum to the supreme commander of German Army Group North, Wilhelm Ritter von Leeb, an independent role for Estonia if the latter made common cause with the Reich. An Estonian army was to join the Wehrmacht in battling the 'Communist peril' and liberate from the interior of the USSR the Estonians who had been deported there then forcibly recruited. The volunteer battalion Erna II was formed in August and took part in liberating the Estonian islands. By September 1941, 5,000 men had volunteered. Organized into six Estonian security departments within the 18th Army, they were predominantly used in the hinterland of Army Group North, where the willing support of Estonians was welcome.[5]

But winning back independence was out of the question. As the majority of Estonians were considered 'Germanizable' according to SS standards and counted among the 'best racial elements', annexation to the Reich was a foregone conclusion. Estonia was put under the military administration of the Wehrmacht. In September 1941, the commander of the rearward army area, General Franz von Roques, appointed Hjalmar Mäe 'first provincial director', replacing Prime Minister Uluots. Mäe, a former putschist among the 'freedom fighters' who found refuge in Germany after serving his prison sentence, was extremely unpopular in his country, being considered a henchman of the Germans.

In late 1941, the Berlin-based Reich Ministry for the Occupied Eastern Territories took over the General District of Estonia as part of the Reich Commissariat Ostland. SA Obergruppenführer Karl Litzmann as commissioner general had a co-operative relationship with the Estonian self-government. The Estonians adopted a wait-and-see attitude, reluctantly loyal without opening up to National Socialist ideology.[6] The German Security Service complained about widespread Anglophile tendencies in the population, the greatest fear of the people being the return of Baltic German landowners. That the Germans did not entirely break up the Soviet kolkhozy and give the land back to Estonian peasants only worsened these fears. This notwithstanding, the Estonian population had close relations with German soldiers, particularly near to the front. It was hard to turn down a German soldier proposing marriage to a local girl when the bride-to-be was quite possibly the sister of an Estonian volunteer in a German division. Thus the racial scruples of certain German authorities had to take a backseat when it came to political considerations and the sensibilities of the local population.

The six Estonian security divisions of the 18th Army, combined into three Eastern Battalions (Estonian), stood the test on the front, even during heavy fighting on the Volkhov.

Estonian volunteers! You can be proud to have played your part in this victory. You showed exemplary self-sacrifice and bravery in the battles you had to endure. You inflicted heavy losses on your arch enemy, who as so often in history was trying to rob and plunder your homeland. (From the order of the day of General Lindemann, supreme commander of the 18th Army, 4 July 1942)[7]

In the summer of 1942, the Germans were preparing a new assault on Leningrad in which the formation of an Estonian legion in the Waffen SS was expected to be a useful reinforcement. Hitler consented, and Commissioner General Litzmann publicly announced the legion's creation on 28 August 1942, the first anniversary of the German invasion of Tallinn. Originally organized as a motorized infantry regiment, the SS legion was reorganized into a brigade in May 1943 and was deployed in late 1943 in the Nevel area, at first to combat partisans in the hinterland of Army Group North, then to defend against Soviet penetration. Here, at least, the men were fighting close to home.

At the start of the campaign, 33 Estonians were serving in the SS Wiking Division. But there was little willingness among them to fight outside the homeland. Thus members of the Estonian security police and Schutzmannschaft (auxiliary police) battalions had to be assigned to the unit on detached duty. The Wiking Division took these 'volunteers' and formed the independent Narva Battalion, transporting it to the Ukraine, where the unit suffered heavy losses, especially in the battles around the Cherkasy pocket.

The Estonian division is deployed at the Heidelager training grounds near Dębica.

The German sphere of influence in the Baltics, 1941

GULF OF FINLAND

STOCKHOLM

Tallinn

Narva

ESTONIA

Pärnu

GULF OF
RIGA

BALTIC SEA

Riga

LATVIA

Liepāja

REICH COMMISSARIAT

Daugava

Klaipéda
(Memel)

LITHUANIA

Neman
(Memel)

Kaunas

OSTLAND

Königsburg
(Kaliningrad)

Vilnius

Danzig
(Gdańsk)

WHITE RUTHENIA

Min.

Toruń

Białystok

WARSAW

Brest-Litovsk

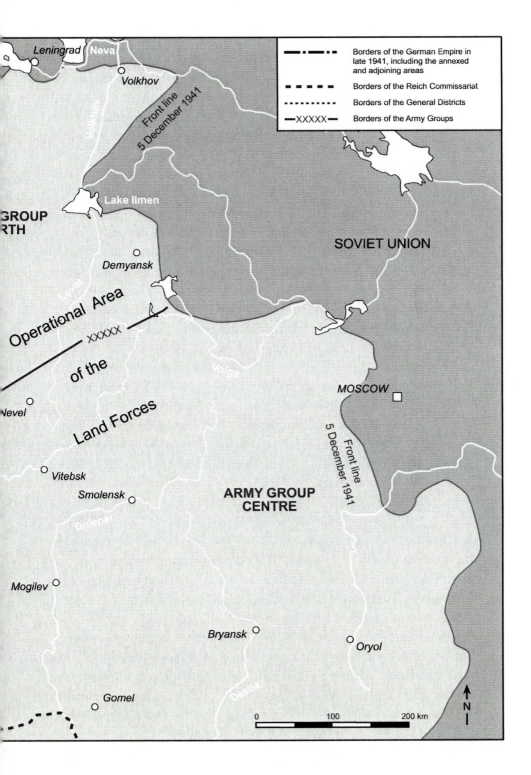

—··—··—	Borders of the German Empire in late 1941, including the annexed and adjoining areas
– – – – –	Borders of the Reich Commissariat
··········	Borders of the General Districts
—XXXXX—	Borders of the Army Groups

Leningrad
Neva
Volkhov
Volkhov
Front line 5 December 1941

Lake Ilmen

GROUP
RTH

SOVIET UNION

Demyansk

Lovat

Operational Area

XXXXX

of the

Volga

MOSCOW

Land Forces

Nevel

Front line 5 December 1941

Vitebsk

Smolensk

ARMY GROUP
CENTRE

Dniepr

Mogilev

Bryansk

Oryol

Desna

Gomel

0   100   200 km

N

Hauptsturmführer Puusepp gathered all the NARVA men around him.
He formed two companies, each 100-man strong, from the men who
were fit for action. From the rest of the walking wounded he formed
an additional company which he placed directly behind the other
companies. All walking NARVA men had returned to the battalion from
the hospital and field dressing station. Anything burdensome was left
behind; only handguns, ammunition and the remaining hand grenades
were taken along. The men were well aware how difficult the task would
be, but were glad to take a decisive step. These were the men who came
up with the saying: 'Death here or to Siberia'. ... Shortly afterwards
hundreds then thousands of men, as well as panje wagons and horse-
drawn carts, streamed into a hollow from the right. In no time at all
the battle group was torn apart. Communication with the next man
was lost. It was impossible to give orders in this chaos. On top of it, the
Russians on the hill were firing heavily into the throng of people. The
NARVA men turned to their left to seek cover from massive enemy fire.
Then they tried to head west again, *en masse*. It was getting light when
Russian tanks appeared on the scene and fired indiscriminately into
the mass of people or simply ran them over! ... No one dared leave the
hollow anymore. ... After being given rapid instructions, 60 NARVA
men were ready to go on the offensive. At Türk's signal, the men got
up all at once and ran with a loud hurrah towards the machine-gun
positions. (Excerpt from the veterans' report of the Estonian SS Panzer
Grenadier Battalion Narva on breaking out of the Cherkasy pocket on
16–17 February 1944)[8]

In the light of the failed attack on the Leningrad Front and Soviet victories in
the winter of 1942–3, Army Group North demanded the general mobilization
of Estonia.[9] As Berlin was still not willing to consider further political
concessions, forced recruitment was camouflaged as conscription into labour
service. The recruits could decide whether to do their compulsory service in
the SS legion, in auxiliary units of the Wehrmacht or as factory workers in
war-related industries. Those signing up for the legion were promised the
immediate return of their lands. From a German perspective, recruitment in
Estonia was a success. About 85 per cent of those called up, born between
1919 and 1924, showed up at the recruiting offices, so that 5,300 additional
men were assigned to the legion and 6,800 men to the Wehrmacht.[10] Given

these impressive results, the Germans opted not to send any forced labourers to the Reich.

The hopes of the Estonian self-government for greater autonomy were dashed once again. A strike at Tartu University in February 1943 and the demand of Estonian officers for the creation of their own army did little to alter the German course. The number of those seeking to evade forced recruitment by fleeing to the forest or to Finland was still relatively small. There was no small number of young men, however, who preferred to wear an 'honourable uniform' and fight with their Finnish brothers against the Red Army.[11] In the summer of 1944, an Estonian infantry regiment took part in the defence of Karelia. Helsinki did not comply with German demands to send back the 'refugees'. Relations between Estonians and Germans worsened. The Estonian population felt that they were in an occupied country and that they were not being taken seriously as a partner. According to an assessment of the country's mood by the High Command of Army Group North, their previous military commitment was not being honoured by the Germans.[12]

Lieutenant Harald Riipalu, leader of a combat group in the 20th Estonian Volunteer Division (Estonian No. 1).

At the second call-up in the autumn of 1943 for those born in 1925, only 70 per cent of the conscripts showed up. Of those deemed fit for service, 76 per cent reported for duty at their units (3,375).[13] Hitler's order to call up ten age groups in order to relieve an impasse at the front was supposed to yield another 10,000 men for the the SS and disregarded fears of the civil administration that mobilization of this magnitude would hinder the armaments industry. By late January 1944, the call-ups had yielded only 900 new recruits. Himmler responded by introducing compulsory military service for all officers and NCOs of the former Estonian Army along with the registration of all eligible men between the ages of 17 and 55.

In the face of the advancing Red Army, the Estonians' immediate concern was defending the homeland against re-Sovietization. Soviet partisan activities were limited to minor acts of sabotage and found little support among the population. The Estonians were counting on the support of the Western Allies, who did not recognize the Soviet annexation of 1940. Former Minister President Uluots was prepared to lend his public support to a call for general mobilization after discussing the matter with opposition groups. This yielded 30,000 new volunteers, twice as many as the Germans had expected.

Estonian soldiers in the Waffen SS were now combined in a larger national unit and saw action at the Narva Front as part of the III (Germanic) SS Panzer Corps in defensive battles with high casualties. The 20th Waffen Grenadier Division of the SS (Estonian No. 1), with a strength of 13,500 men, was complete by August 1944. Frontier guard regiments were also formed during general mobilization. A total of 60,000 Estonians were fighting in the ranks of the Germans in 1944 compared to about 30,000 on the Soviet side.[14]

The founding of a National Committee of the Republic of Estonia in early March 1944 marked a further step towards securing the country's independence, despite attempts of the German security police to weaken the national opposition through a series of arrests. A government was not set up, however, until just a few days before the withdrawal of the Wehrmacht, and had no opportunity to assert Estonia's independence. Whereas the auxiliary forces of the Wehrmacht went underground and sometimes continued the fight against the Red Army in the forests, volunteers in the Waffen SS were forced, under duress, to follow the German retreat. The 20th Waffen Grenadier Division was virtually annihilated in rearguard action and was newly formed in Silesia in early 1945. In April, the remnants of the unit assembled in the Goldberg (Złotoryja) area after heavy defensive fighting. Few of them managed after capitulation to make their way to the Western Allies.

Estonia lost about 25 per cent of its population as a result of World War II and was unable to defend its sovereignty against German and Soviet claims to hegemony. The country, about the size of Denmark, had the greatest percentage of foreign volunteers in Hitler's war in the East, with 60,000 soldiers out of a population of 1.2 million. About 5,000 Estonians fought in the Wehrmacht, 20,000 in the Waffen SS, another 20,000 in SS frontier guard regiments, 9,000 in Schutzmannschaft and police battalions, and several thousand in self-defence and other units – mostly with the aim in mind of winning back Estonian independence. About 15,000 Estonians were killed fighting on the side of the Germans. A comparable number of Estonian civilians were victims of partisan warfare. Another 30,000 people were executed or deported by the Soviets in 1944–5. Yet another 80,000 Estonians were deported between 1946 and 1953. Their place was taken by the 230,000 Russians, Byelorussians and Ukrainians who migrated to the country.[15]

Estonia did not achieve its independence until after the fall of the Soviet empire. The country now belongs to the European Union and NATO, and is the most Western-oriented and economically developed part of the former USSR. Historians in the country tend not to differentiate between collaborators and 'freedom fighters'. This has elicited protests by the Russian minority, especially Red Army veterans, who regard themselves as victors and patriots. The inauguration in 2004 of a monument to Waffen SS legionnaires outside the Museum of the Struggle for Estonian Liberation in Lagedi resulted in violent protests. The same occurred in 2007 (with support from Moscow) when a monument to Estonia's liberation by the Red Army was removed from the centre of the capital.

14

Latvia

The developments in Estonia's larger neighbour Latvia with its 1.9 million inhabitants (1935) were similar, albeit with a number of fundamental differences. The share of Baltic Germans in the population (3.3 per cent) was considerably higher thanks to a sizeable urban middle class, particularly in the capital of Riga. Added to this were a higher degree of industrialization and the existence of a working class strongly influenced by the Bolshevist movement even before World War I. At local elections the Bolsheviks received upwards of 70 per cent of the urban vote (compared to 35 per cent in Estonia).[1] As of 1915, Latvian rifle regiments with a combined strength of 130,000 men fought in the ranks of the Tsarist Army. Their anti-German sentiment was instrumental in awakening national consciousness. German troops captured Riga in September 1917 and encouraged Latvia's separation from the Russian Empire. The mass settlement of German peasants was envisioned as part of the process. The Baltic German ruling elite even hoped for a union with Prussia.

But a People's Council declared independence on 18 November 1918. The first cabinet was led by Kārlis Ulmanis and carried by the bourgeois parties. The Red Army's advance towards Riga united the divergent Baltic Germans and Latvian nationalist forces. The Latvian Territorial Army joined forces with the 'Iron Brigade' comprised of volunteers from the withdrawing German 8th Army. An attempted Baltic German putsch failed in April 1919 and seriously burdened subsequent Latvian-German relations. Military leaders in Berlin mourned the loss of the opportunity to influence developments in the Soviet Union through a bridgehead in the Baltics. Strategic interests had to be set aside for the time being due to conditions imposed by the Versailles Treaty, but at least economic exchange offered prospects of maintaining German influence.

Latvian democracy was shaky from the outset and was unable to overcome its party-political divisions. Agrarian reforms in favour of Latvian small farmers decisively weakened the influence of landed Baltic Germans with their large estates. In the interwar period, Latvia developed a strong agriculture and timber industry. The large-scale industry of former times could not be re-established if only for the loss of the Russian hinterland. As in Estonia, in the spring of 1934, Ulmanis was forced to resort to the army and declare martial law to ward off a potential *coup d'état* by extreme nationalist organizations. Unlike its neighbour, however, Latvia failed to find its way back to halfway democratic conditions. Ulmanis set up an authoritarian regime with the Führer principle of National Socialism. The ideal of a 'unified nation', however, was linked to pronounced anti-German and anti-Semitic tendencies.

With the start of World War II, the USSR forced Latvia, too, to sign a pact of mutual assistance and permit the establishment of Soviet bases. Around 51,000 Baltic Germans were 'resettled' in the Reich in early 1940. One year later another 10,000 followed, including Latvians who used the opportunity to escape Stalinist deportations, especially former members of the Latvian Army. The Sovietization of Latvia which began in August 1940 claimed 35,000 victims, murdered or deported, half of them in June 1941.

In preparing Operation Barbarossa, German intelligence recruited a group of Latvian exiles who established contacts with partisan groups in the Soviet hinterland and were to support the advancing Wehrmacht. Riga was an important strategic goal, but it was only a stop on the way to Leningrad. Thus, the Germans were planning to rely on the help of locals in capturing the Latvian capital, despite Hitler's rejection of governments being formed and troops being assembled in the Baltics. Army Group North was only authorized to allow self-defence police corps in Latvia,[2] because plans for settlement were still being considered and the country seemed the ideal location.

In the battle for Riga in late June 1941, former Lieutenant Colonel Voldemars Veiss called on his fellow countrymen to take up arms against the 'inner enemy'. Viktor Arajs, a former Latvian policeman, took the initiative and occupied police headquarters along with his men. The anti-Communist, anti-Russian and anti-Semitic nationalists unleashed a mob that launched the first pogroms, murdering Jews and Communist Party men alike. As auxiliary police in the service of the SS, thousands of young Latvians played an important role in carrying out the Holocaust, which affected a total of 60,000 Latvian Jews. Riga became a centre of Jewish extermination, though the Wehrmacht was more interested in ghettoization and forced labour with its numerous offices and workshops there. Yet neither the Wehrmacht nor the civil administration of the Reich Commissariat Ostland with its headquarters in Riga prevented the often unco-ordinated murder campaigns of the SS and Latvian police.

The General District of Latvia was entrusted to Dr Otto Drechsler, Mayor of Lübeck. 'Eastern Minister' Rosenberg made sure that Riga received a German city mayor (Hugo Wittrock). For him the Latvian capital was a German city anyway and the base for a future Germanization of the Baltics. As the local intelligentsia were considered anti-German, there were efforts to limit their administrative influence. Oskar Dankers, a retired general of the Latvian Army with no affiliation to any of the competing political parties, was appointed administrative chairman of Latvia.

Volunteers of the Latvian Self-Defence forming a police battalion, August 1941.

Even the fascist 'Thunder Cross' was viewed with suspicion by the Germans. The offer by their leader Gustav Celmiņš to raise a military legion from auxiliary police units and Schutzmannschaft battalions in the fight against Bolshevism was categorically refused by Himmler in autumn 1941, despite the fact that Army Group North was urging for the recruitment of local volunteers. Looking back in 1943, Commissioner General Drechsler considered it a grave political mistake not to have organized the Latvians into military units earlier.[3] But the Latvian police and Schutzmannschaft battalions of the German 'Ordnungspolizei' were, in fact, used abroad in the fight against partisans.

In June 1942, Higher SS and Police Leader in Ostland Friedrich Jeckeln adopted the idea of recruiting for a military SS legion among police and Schutzmannschaft volunteers whose tour of duty had expired, despite the fact that deployment abroad was unpopular. A subsequent idea was to man such a legion with young Latvians who had completed their compulsory labour service. It was only after the disaster of Stalingrad that Hitler approved such a formation. To this end, they took four Schutzmannschaft battalions that were already deployed in the 2nd SS Brigade and gave them the designation 'legion'. A considerable number of volunteers had to be recruited to form an entire Latvian division. In exchange for mobilizing entire age groups, Dankers demanded the restitution of Latvian independence, power of command for a Latvian senior officer, deployment only for home defence, and assignment of the legion to the Wehrmacht, which Hitler unconditionally refused.[4]

As in Estonia and Lithuania, recruiting goals were ultimately met through forced mobilization into labour service. Call-ups in Latvia turned out to be highly satisfactory. The Latvian legion gained about 17,900 new recruits, and 13,400 men signed up for other forms of military service. The ideological indoctrination and loyalty of Latvian units were quite limited, however, as the Germans were unwilling to make any tangible political concessions. German security police noted in August 1943 that 'anti-German' propaganda in the country had even infiltrated the SS legion.[5] Celmiņš, the leader of the Thunder Cross movement, was arrested in March 1944 by the Security Service of the Reichsführer SS. As a result, disappointed Latvian collaborators were no longer willing to co-operate with the now weakened Germans.

Latvian SS volunteer on the Eastern Front.

SS Gruppenführer Rūdolfs Bangerskis (left) during an interview in July 1944.

These were hardly favourable circumstances for meeting Himmler's demands for an additional 20,000 men for the legion. Subsequent call-ups were handled by the Latvian self-government in the hope of fulfilling its old political demands. The principle of hope was also evident in a speech given by General Dankers on 18 November 1943, Independence Day of the former Free State of Latvia. He spoke of the red-white-red flag, which had 'again, in battle, secured its place in the sun'. The legionnaires would march under this flag in the fight against Bolshevism 'in the firm belief in a free Latvia in the community of free nations'.[6] The Latvian SS legion was now under the general supervision of Rūdolfs Bangerskis as local inspector and SS Gruppenführer, though admittedly not its commander.

A good 67.5 per cent of the age groups called up appeared for inspection, of which 5,167 were immediately conscripted into military service. Filled up with new volunteers, the previous legion was formed into the 15th Waffen Grenadier Division of the SS (Latvian No. 1). The unit saw action in the defensive battle near Nevel, followed the retreating Army Group North to Latvia, was reactivated after suffering heavy losses, and, in early 1945, took part in the battles for West Prussia, Pomerania and Mecklenburg. Parts of the division perished in Berlin, the rest went into US captivity near Schwerin at the end of the war.

> Supported by tanks and fighter-bombers, the Bolshevists attacked with powerful forces in the northern sector of the Eastern Front northwest of Nevel, in the Ostrov area, near Pskov and near Narva. Their attempts to break through failed against the stubborn resistance of Army and Waffen SS troops as well as Latvian and Estonian volunteer units. Local breakthroughs were remedied and sealed off with immediate counter-attacks. The enemy lost 101 tanks. (Excerpt from the Wehrmacht report of 11 March 1944)[7]

It was even harder for the 19th Waffen Grenadier Division (Latvian No. 2). The division was formed in early 1944 out of three Latvian police battalions and new recruits, and was promptly deployed with the VI SS Army Corps in heavy defensive fighting on the Volkhov. This division, too, followed the retreating Army Group North, but became caught in the Kurland pocket in October 1944. There the Latvians took part in several defensive battles and were taken prisoner by the Soviets on 8 May 1945.

Many Latvian volunteers who had fled to Sweden were handed over to the USSR.

A total of circa 100,000 Latvian soldiers took part in Hitler's war in the East, including 3,000 in a police regiment and 14,000 in Schutzmannschaft battalions grouped together as 'frontier guard regiments'. Some volunteers were equipped in a makeshift fashion – with Czech helmets, Polish coats and old Latvian gear. On 13 October 1944, in the chaos of collapsing German rule in the Baltics, Riga was occupied by the Red Army. The latter had 20,000 Latvians fighting in its ranks.

A total of 40,000 Latvians perished fighting on the side of the Germans. At the end of the war, another 70,000 were executed or deported by the Soviets. By 1953, an additional 100,000 Latvians had been deported. In their place, 535,000 Byelorussians, Russians and Ukrainians migrated to the country in the postwar period, where they now comprise over 40 per cent of the population. The debate about the past and World War II in Latvia is correspondingly complex.

15

Lithuania

Lithuania, the largest of the Baltic states with 2 million inhabitants, bordered directly on the German Reich. That explains why it became a battlefield for Germans fighting Russians at the beginning and end of both world wars. Occupied and ruled by the German Army as of 1915, it had a limited say only in the social sphere. The forced recruitment of labour battalions gave rise to opposition. In 1917, representatives of all political parties founded a State Council in Vilnius under the leadership of Antanas Smetona and demanded the creation of an independent democratic state. The large Polish minority refused to co-operate, striving instead for the re-establishment of the historical Polish-Lithuanian Union. Byelorussians and Jews – the largest minority with 7.6 per cent – later joined the national movement. In the summer of 1918, there were even negotiations over installing a Lithuanian king of German descent. The armistice in Compiègne ended the political influence of Germany, and Lithuania became a Western-style democracy under Prime Minister Augustinas Voldemaras.

The Red Army, having reached Lithuania in January 1919, was repelled by the newly activated national army using war material left behind by the retreating Germans. Conflict with Poland escalated, however, and the two countries eventually became totally estranged. Given the country's strongly agrarian character and Catholic heritage, the conservatives – unlike in Estonia and Latvia – dominated Lithuanian politics. Agrarian reforms were moderate, mainly affecting large-scale landholdings in Russian and Polish hands. Dependency on an agrarian economy led to the development of an authoritarian form of government as early as 1926, which drew its support mainly from the army. President Smetona was soon exercising dictatorial powers following fascist role models. The 'Iron Wolf' guard movement was modelled on the Italian militia. Attempted putsches and peasant unrest were defining features of 1930s Lithuania.

The country remained isolated in terms of foreign policy, as no international settlement was reached regarding its controversial border with Poland. A latent state of war existed between the two countries. Poland laid claim to Vilnius (Wilno) for ethnographic and cultural reasons, Lithuania for historical and political ones. Its annexation by Poland was not recognized by Lithuania. The so-called Vilnius question was not solved until 1939, when eastern Poland was subjugated by the USSR and Moscow awarded the area to Lithuania, at the cost of a considerable loss of national independence. Relations with Germany were tense as well, despite strong economic ties, the Treaty of Versailles having put the German Memel Territory under French administration before it was occupied by Lithuanian guerrillas in 1923. When the Third Reich occupied Austria and the Sudetenland, Vilnius was put under such pressure that it ceded the Memel Territory to Germany on 22 March 1939. Under different circumstances, Lithuania could have easily been an ally of Hitler in his plans to invade Poland. As it was, he unscrupulously sacrificed his northeastern neighbour for the sake of his pact with Stalin.

Under Soviet pressure, Lithuania was the last Baltic state to sign a pact of mutual assistance with Moscow, on 11 October 1939, and was forced to allow Soviet troops to be stationed on its territory. The end of independence came with the invasion of the Red Army on 16 June 1940, in the wake of rigged elections. A first series of purges affecting 14,000 'anti-Soviet forces' took its toll on 400 Lithuanian officers. The peacetime strength of the Lithuanian Army was about 28,000 men. In June of 1941, 21,000 members of the former elite troops were deported to Siberia. Lithuanian Germans – as small farmers quite different, sociologically speaking, from the Baltic German large-scale landowners – were not 'resettled' to the Reich until March 1941, in accordance with special German-Soviet agreements. At the same time, with Moscow's approval, Lithuanians from the German-ruled Memel and Suwałki territories were shipped off to the Lithuanian heartland.

German military intelligence at this point in time was already preparing its attack on the Soviet Union. It was counting on the support of Colonel Kazys Škirpa, a former Lithuanian ambassador to Berlin who organized the Lithuanian Activist Front (LAF) with more than 36,000 resistance fighters.

Škirpa demanded the restitution of Lithuanian sovereignty, in vain. Together with 200 Lithuanian exiles working in intelligence, the LAF opened their attacks in the hinterland of the Red Army as soon as the war began. The uprising mobilized about 100,000 armed fighters, about 4,000 of whom lost their lives.

Under the pressure of a rapidly advancing Wehrmacht, the Soviets abandoned Lithuania after only five days. Before the eyes of the provisional military administration, anti-Semitic activist groups began organizing pogroms against the Jewish minority, though most soldiers kept their distance from these.[1] Himmler's death squad, the so-called Einsatzgruppe, found willing followers, however. About 6,000 individuals were the victims of these first 'spontaneous' murder campaigns. By the end of the year, Lithuania was 'Jew-free'. The Holocaust took the lives of about 220,000 people in Lithuania. On 25 July 1941, the General District of Lithuania was handed over to a German civil administration under the leadership of Adrian von Renteln which, as in the other two Baltic districts, was largely based on the respective national administration. The latter was headed by General Petras Kubiliūnas, the former Lithuanian chief-of-staff.

Lithuania's part in the Holocaust: Lithuanian nationalists beating Jews to death during the Kaunas pogrom on 27 July 1941.

Every attempt to gain greater autonomy was thwarted by the Germans. A provisional government was boycotted and Škirpa was placed under house arrest in Berlin. His letter to Hitler, in which he offered to be a negotiating partner for a free Lithuania, was left unanswered. Anti-Communist partisan units were for the most part disbanded, only a few of them being engaged by the SS as auxiliary police squads. In an effort to silence the Lithuanians politically, the LAF was outlawed and eventually even the Fascist Iron Wolf movement. The German National Socialists considered Lithuania a valuable land of peasants to be used for future German settlement policies. For this reason alone they tended to view the Lithuanians as the 'most inferior Baltic race', whose co-operation was not highly valued.

Disputes in the civil administration between German authorities and the Wehrmacht about a moderate occupation policy were never settled. The negative course of the war led to some concessions, however. In early 1942, the local auxiliary police were concentrated into 15 Schutzmannschaft battalions. Lithuania was located well behind the Eastern Front, so the units were mainly deployed abroad, in Poland and Byelorussia as well as in the northern Ukraine. These approximately 16,000 men had less to do with partisans than the hunt for Jews. They were particularly zealous in fighting the Polish resistance in the formerly disputed border area.

The German plan of limiting armed collaborators to police duty was increasingly abandoned with the intensification of partisan warfare. Poorly armed Lithuanian volunteers were increasingly used in a military context without fulfilling the hopes of Lithuanian officers that a national army might be established in the process. Instead, about 30,000 Lithuanian Germans left their camps and went back home in 1942. This targeted resettlement only encouraged suspicions and political conflict in the country.

The idea of creating a national legion under the aegis of the SS, proposed in early 1943, was roundly rejected by the Lithuanian General Council, which headed the local administration. Its condition for signing a proclamation of this sort was to combine it with the independence of Lithuania. Only General Kubiliūnas signed a proclamation, under German pressure, in which the Lithuanians were called to join the Germans in a mutual struggle against Bolshevism. As no substantial political concessions were forthcoming, the country's non-Communist passive resistance organized a boycott of recruiting measures. Unlike in Estonia and Latvia, German mobilization was

Members of a Lithuanian
Schutzmannschaft (auxiliary police)
battalion.

a complete failure in Lithuania, with fewer than 20 per cent of those called up actually reporting for inspection.

In retaliation, the Germans arrested leading Lithuanian intellectuals and put them in a concentration camp at Stutthof (Sztutowo) near Danzig. A second appeal by Kubiliūnas also met with little response, so that Commissioner General Renteln abandoned his plans to establish a legion. The new recruits were immediately sent to German armaments factories as forced labourers, and many young men began fleeing to the forests.

In February 1944, the German administration made another attempt to create Lithuanian military units. In private, Renteln made no bones about his opinion of the Lithuanians as a 'completely unwarlike people', marked by 'a lack of discipline, indolence, cowardice and languidness'.[2] With the Soviet Army approaching, the national resistance movement was prepared to support mobilization after all. Under the leadership of Lithuanian officers and the personal responsibility of former General Povilas Plechavičius, there were hopes of forming a last-minute Lithuanian regular army with six divisions for national defence purposes. The Germans were only planning on ten battalions at first, with 15,000 men. Himmler, of course, wanted to put these units at the disposal of the hard-pressed Army Group North to help build defensive fortifications and for use behind the lines, freeing up German soldiers for front-line duty. There were also considerations of deploying them around Vilnius to combat Polish partisans. If the Lithuanians proved battle-worthy, the battalions would perhaps be formed into a division of their own.

To the Germans' surprise, twice as many volunteers signed up as expected. In their negotiations with Lithuanian generals, the distrustful representatives of Himmler demanded that the surplus volunteers be assigned to auxiliary services in the Luftwaffe on Reich territory. If the Germans feared that the Lithuanians might take up arms against them, their absolute demands merely led to the continued failure of their mobilization efforts. The national underground resisted these orders for very clear reasons: the imminent struggle against the Red Army demanded the deployment of all available men, so there could be no thought of shipping off 30,000 of them to Germany. Lithuania had no enemies in the West, and had no interest in entering a war against Britain and the USA.[3]

The Plechavičius battalions mobilized already were sent to Vilnius by the Germans despite their insufficient training and equipment. These men, who had refused to swear an oath to Hitler, showed no particular fighting spirit. Some of them even sold their weapons to the partisans. The general and his staff were ultimately arrested, the battalion was disarmed and some of the men fled into the forests. In mid-May 1944, bitter fighting erupted between Germans and Lithuanians in Mariampole as well as in Kaunas when the Lithuanian military academy was disbanded. One hundred prisoners were shot to death and another 3,500 carted off to Germany where they were given to the Luftwaffe for deployment as auxiliary soldiers. In early 1945, a total of 36,800 Lithuanians were serving primarily in construction units in the Wehrmacht, Reich Labour Service and Organisation Todt.

A comparable number fought against the invading Red Army. The 'Forest Men' put up armed resistance against the Sovietization of their homeland until the late 1940s. In 1944–5 alone, 50,000 Lithuanians were deported or killed by the Stalinist secret police. By 1953, another 260,000 people had been deported. This is how 'peace' was re-established in Lithuania. The country was not to regain its freedom until 1990.

With respect to all three Baltic states, it is evident that the considerable willingness of these nations to collaborate with the Germans after being freed from one year of Soviet rule was not used by the Nazis to their advantage. Caught up in the euphoria of victory in the summer of 1941, ideological and settlement objectives were uppermost in the minds of German planners, along with an interest in ruthlessly exploiting the countries economically. The rather weak Army Group North tried in vain to rekindle the former brotherhood-in-arms of 1918 and utilize the military potential of the Baltic states. The two German armies outside Leningrad and on the Volkhov could presumably have been reinforced by a third army made up of Estonian, Latvian and Lithuanian soldiers. Instead, Hitler pulled out Manstein's 11th Army from the Crimea in the autumn of 1942, while Baltic volunteers were restricted to duty in police battalions and a few infantry units. Racial and political discrimination against them lasted until the bitter end.

16

Poland

The sympathy felt by many Germans for the Polish struggle for national independence in the early nineteenth century had given way by the Bismarck era to a growing sense of antagonism. After three partitions and nearly 120 years of statelessness, Poland became the battleground of foreign powers in World War I and supplied 1.5 million soldiers to both sides of the conflict. With the total occupation of Polish territory, a Kingdom of Poland was declared on 5 November 1916 by the emperors of Germany and Austria. The Central Powers were hoping to deploy a Polish Army with 250,000 soldiers against Tsarist Russia by 1917,[1] but the number of volunteers was limited. The new troops were to wear German uniforms and take an oath of allegiance to the brotherhood-in-arms with the Central Powers. But most of the soldiers refused to do so and were incarcerated along with the commander of a Polish legion which fought on the Eastern Front under Austrian command as of 1914: Józef Klemens Piłsudski. His push for total independence made him even more popular. Not until the defeat of the Central Powers in October 1918 was it possible to found a new state.

The ensuing, violent conflict over the demarcation of the Polish state frontier consolidated a German-Polish antagonism that not even a joint anti-Communist front could overcome. The Polish victory over the Red Army in the Battle of Warsaw in 1920 was achieved with French assistance, making Poland a bulwark of France's anti-German policy of encirclement in the period between the wars. After assuming control of the so-called Eastern Borderlands with the Treaty of Riga in 1921, Poland also played the role of a bulwark against Soviet Russia.

The Reichswehr, for its part, established secret contacts with the Red Army with a strong anti-Polish orientation – a political-military option that Hitler surprisingly reversed after taking power. The non-aggression pact of 1934 introduced a brief phase of relative *détente* between the two states. There was even recurrent talk of a common alliance against the USSR, until the Polish head of state, Marshal Piłsudski, died in 1935. Anti-Polish resentment, to be sure, was still quite rampant in the National Socialist movement as well as in the officer corps of the new Wehrmacht. Nevertheless, there were renewed exploratory talks in late 1938 about a possible German-Polish offensive alliance against the USSR. Poland was to be given the chance of realizing its territorial ambitions in the Ukraine if it came to war between the USSR and Japan in the crisis in the Far East and if Germany followed up on its commitments as Japan's ally.[2] In dividing up Czechoslovakia, Hitler had already made sure that the Poles would receive their share. Thus the country did not have a single border recognized by its respective neighbours. In a country of 35 million inhabitants, the Polish Army with approximately 1 million men and 800,000 reservists was the largest in East-Central Europe, though its equipment was rather outdated. It was in fact the largest 'bulwark' against Bolshevism and for the protection of Europe against possible Soviet expansionism.

Warsaw was rightly concerned, however, that the Germans were merely interested in cutting off Poland's lifeline to the West, forcing the country into satellite status. Hitler needed Poland as a deployment zone against the Soviet Union. If his Polish neighbour acquiesced, its army – as in World War I – would provide welcome auxiliary troops; if not, Poland would have to be conquered and possibly partitioned with Russia once again – the last resort which Hitler turned to in August 1939.[3] Polish leaders insisted on their great-power ambitions, however. And according to the *raison d'état* of Piłsudski, Polish independence meant keeping their distance from both Germany and Russia.

Germany's 'courtship' ended abruptly in March 1939 when Warsaw once again conveyed its clear refusal of Berlin's offer. On 31 March, Prime Minister Chamberlain proclaimed the Anglo-French guarantee to Poland. Only a military alliance with Moscow would have effectively protected Polish independence from possible German aggression, but Anglo-French-Soviet negotiations broke down in the summer of 1939 because of Poland's refusal to grant passage to Russian troops in the event of war. Their fear of Hitler did not make Stalin more palatable to the Poles.

From May 1939 on, the course was set in Berlin to open the struggle for Lebensraum in the East once the invasion of Poland commenced. Hitler was counting on his unexpected alliance with Stalin to prevent the Western Powers from declaring war. Things turned out differently, of course, but the Poles, for a fourth time in their history, would see their country partitioned between the Germans and the Russians. What is more, while the Germans were carrying out a brutal policy of 'Germanization' in the occupied western territories of Poland, the Russians were ruthlessly Stalinizing the eastern part of the country, a policy which ultimately cost more lives than in western Poland under the Nazis up until 1941.[4] The largest massacre was the murder, ordered by Stalin in the spring of 1940, of more than 15,000 Polish officers held in captivity.

Part of the Polish Army had escaped via Romania to France and formed the basis of an army-in-exile which fought on the side of the British until the end of World War II. The Wehrmacht not only profited from the expansion and shift of its basis to the East and the economic exploitation of the country for wartime purposes, but it also won several hundred thousand new recruits from former Polish citizens who were naturalized as ethnic Germans and put into uniforms. Scruples among army leaders about the brutal policy of oppression and anti-Semitic excesses were quickly dispelled, but national conservative elites still held on to the old notion of a certain Polish autonomy.

Following the campaign in France, a number of Polish politicians offered to co-operate with the Germans, a recent discovery which has rekindled discussions in Poland about collaboration.[5] Their main concern was improving the lot of the population. With the Soviet annexation of the Baltics, they probably believed that the Germans might be interested in forming an anti-Communist front. The attempted negotiations fell through, for one thing because the majority of the Polish population supported the government-in-exile in London and the resistance movement, directed from abroad, had a 'disciplinary' effect, for another because German terror, exploitation and racial discrimination continued unabated.

The Polish chapter was settled for Hitler, who passed it on to his henchmen Himmler and Frank. Polish territory, in particular the railway hub of Warsaw, played a key role in the preparations for Operation Barbarossa. The assistance of the Polish population and authorities was essential, but the Germans had absolutely no intention of setting up anything like a Polish legion. Poland was considered a German colony, not a potential ally, and the Poles were certainly not 'comrades' of the Germans. Still, the Wehrmacht enlisted around 20,000 Poles, who were needed as panje

The first talks between German
and Soviet officers to determine the
German-Soviet line of demarcation
take place near Białystok in
September 1939.

wagon (horse-drawn vehicle) drivers to make the unmotorized infantry
divisions mobile. As Wehrmacht auxiliaries and labourers in the German
arms industry, many Poles played their part – more forced than voluntary
– in Germany's Russian campaign.

A good number of Poles were relieved when the war against the Soviet
Union began – most of them probably expecting that German pressure
would then subside, some of them surely with a sense of satisfaction that
their Soviet occupiers were now forced to leave. In eastern Poland, in
particular, which Stalin had occupied in 1939, the Wehrmacht was not
unwelcome. The arrival of the Germans was sometimes combined with
attacks on local Jews, who were suspected of being agents of Stalinism.
The Poles had suffered the most from Stalinist terror. A once self-confident
nation, they were degraded to the status of an inferior people. Many
Byelorussians and Ukrainians, by contrast, had greeted the invading Red
Army in 1939.

The discovery of mass murders perpetrated by the Soviet secret police (NKVD) against Polish prisoners of war at the start of the German invasion fanned the hatred not only of Communists and Russians but also of supposed Jewish collaborators. The Germans knew how to capitalize on these emotions, accelerating their planned extermination of Polish Jews.[6] They did not even try to win the Poles as brothers-in-arms in their 'Crusade against Bolshevism', though there was surely potential at this point in time. The German invasion of eastern Poland actually facilitated the secret advance of the Polish underground army, the Armia Krajowa or 'Home Army', thus fuelling the conflict of nationalities, as Byelorussians and Ukrainians were pursuing their own independence efforts. Armed Ukrainian units attacked Polish villages and engaged in a bitter struggle with the Polish resistance over spheres of power and influence.

July 1944 in the Vilnius area:
members of the Polish Home Army
escort German prisoners of war.

The Germans refused to let go of their anti-Polish stance even after the failure of Barbarossa and the catastrophe of Stalingrad. Even the mass murder at Katyn, disclosed in early summer 1943, was of interest to the Germans merely as a propaganda coup. Polish soldiers would soon be fighting on the side of the British against the Germans in Italy. Despite increasing tensions in the Allied camp caused by Polish fears of a renewed Stalinization of their homeland, Berlin was not prepared to take the step they had already taken with regard to the Russians, as the Poles were still considered unworthy of serving in the Wehrmacht, let alone the Waffen SS, unless they could prove some kind of German ancestry. In 1943–4, however, the hurdles were considerably lowered.

In the meantime, there were Polish legions on the British as well as the Soviet side. Stalin was determined that Poland would be his future war-booty and that he would Sovietize the country. With the approaching German-Soviet Front, especially in the summer of 1944, the Polish Home Army found itself in an unresolvable dilemma. It was preparing an uprising against the German occupiers but at the same time had to assume that the Red Army would not share its control of the country with the Polish government-in-exile. The Poles were caught in a war on multiple fronts: against the German SS and police battalions mostly comprised of Lithuanians, who had their own national claims against a Polish minority, against advancing Soviet partisans who negated the aims of the Armia Krajowa and against Ukrainian nationalists gathered around Stepan Bandera.

During the uprising in Warsaw
against the Wehrmacht in 1944.

It is no wonder that, in 1944, there were even local alliances and agreements between the Wehrmacht, SS and the Home Army.[7] But the arrival of the Red Army spelled disaster for the nationally minded Poles. Their officers had been murdered in eastern Poland, their resistance groups liquidated, and, in October, the Warsaw Uprising failed, with the Red Army watching on the opposite bank of the Vistula as the Germans crushed the Polish attempt at self-liberation. Belated German considerations of mobilizing the Poles' anti-Communism against the Red Army bore no fruit. The tragic struggle of the Armia Krajowa against foreign rule by the Germans and Soviets was not officially recognized until after 1990.[8]

17

Byelorussia

Up until now we have looked at countries with a historically evolved national identity and which were already separated from the Russian Empire after World War I. We will now focus on territories which had been part of Russia and/or the USSR until the invasion of the Wehrmacht and were subject to Stalinism up until that point.

Byelorussia, which did not achieve its independence until after the collapse of the Soviet Union when it was renamed Belarus, had been a recurrent battlefield and marching ground for foreign armies throughout its history. In 1812, soldiers from Germany marched through it in the ranks of Napoleon's Grande Armée towards Moscow; few of these soldiers ever found their way back home. Not until the early twentieth century did a weak Byelorussian national consciousness emerge in a territory that included the regions of Vitebsk, Mogilev, Gomel, Smolensk, Brest-Litovsk and Grodno and had Minsk as its capital, with no clear-cut borders and several nationalities and religious denominations living side by side, as well as isolated German settlements. Alongside Jews, Poles and Russians, the Byelorussians made up the bulk of the rural population.

The Germans made their first appearance as conquerors and occupiers in 1915, when they succeeded in driving back the Tsarist Army and advancing into Byelorussian territory. With the Treaty of Brest-Litovsk in March 1918, they continued their advance all the way to Mogilev. The German military government pursued mainly economic aims, but was open for further-reaching settlement concepts to create a kind of military frontier of German settlers.[1] The Germans had no national ambitions or military expectations of their own for 'Russian Poland', as they called the territory.

With the Treaty of Riga in 1921, the western part of Byelorussia went to Poland, a country exhausted by the war. These Eastern Borderlands (Kresy Wschodnie) remained a poorhouse and a cultural no-man's-land, a stepchild of Polish administration. The cries of nationalist politicians landed on deaf ears. From the viewpoint of the landed Polish gentry, the Byelorussians were the primeval inhabitants of a vast swampland, poor peasants and agricultural workers.

In the Byelorussian Soviet Socialist Republic with its capital Minsk, the national elite, fostered and promoted in the 1920s, was suppressed in the 1930s in the wake of Stalinization. The Polish population was particularly hard hit by the deportation of Soviet citizens. All in all, an estimated half a million people – one-tenth of the area's entire population – were the victims of Stalinist terror.[2] The terror spread to eastern Poland with the invasion of the Red Army on 17 September 1939. The outmatched Polish reservist units hardly put up a fight. In the process of general dissolution there were also spontaneous attacks of Ukrainian and Byelorussian groups against the Soviet Army. Grodno was laid to waste by Soviet artillery. About 800 people died defending the city, among them many volunteers.

On 28 September, after a bogus plebiscite, the eastern Polish and Byelorussian territories were annexed by the USSR, in line with German-Soviet agreements. Byelorussians – about half the population – as well as Ukrainians and Jews automatically became Soviet citizens. Poles could choose their citizenship. About 250,000 of them, half of them soldiers and officers, were held in Soviet captivity. In March and May of 1940, 15,000 Polish officers were secretly shot to death.

The Byelorussian Soviet Socialist Republic thereby doubled its territory, and its population grew to 10.4 million. The redistribution of former Polish estates to impoverished agricultural workers by the Soviet state won the support of many Byelorussians. Sovietization was accompanied above all by an exchange of elites, from which Byelorussian nationalists failed to profit. Stalin's surveillance and police state stoked the fires of existing conflict. And yet the Sovietization of agriculture in the West was not making good progress, a sign of tacit resistance among the rural population. Before the German invasion, every social and national group had been affected by reprisals. Soviet courts convicted 250,000 people and 990,000 inhabitants of the Byelorussian Soviet Socialist Republic were deported to Siberia for being 'unreliable'.

About 220,000 young men were recruited into Soviet industry or for service in the Red Army. A total of 67,000 Germans with Polish passports left the country and headed west, 'home to the Reich'. The potential for resistance in the west of Byelorussia was thereby almost completely destroyed.[3]

Berlin did not waste much thought on the matter in preparing Operation Barbarossa. On the contrary, the concept of economic exploitation and the achievement of racial and settlement objectives found their most radical expression in Byelorussia. From an economic perspective, it was considered essential to plunder the meagre country as fast as possible for the sake of supplying German troops, before the population managed to appropriate the harvest and food supplies for itself. The murder of the relatively large Jewish community was agreed upon well in advance. There was little interest in the Poles, and the Byelorussians were considered 'racially inferior'. The Wehrmacht, at the height of its power, would march through Byelorussia towards Moscow; there was no need to recruit the locals as potential German allies. Armed SS units would take care of security in the hinterland.

The German war machine over-ran the country after its invasion of the USSR on 22 June 1941, the first frontier battles, and especially the battles of encirclement of Białystok and Minsk, leaving a trail of death and destruction in their wake. Endless convoys of prisoners disguised a situation that would eventually get the better of the Germans – namely, that countless Red Army soldiers had managed to escape to the forests and swamps. With the support of NKVD officers, who had gone underground in the cities, a Soviet partisan war was eventually unleashed that the Germans would never succeed in reining in. By mid-August 1941, 231 partisan detachments with more than 12,000 men had already been formed. By the end of the year, another 60 operative groups with almost 2,000 men had been planted behind German lines. They boasted of having killed 669 German soldiers and officers as well as 95 'disloyal ones and traitors'.[4]

Hitler was keen at first to use partisan warfare to his advantage – that is, as a pretext to shoot 'anyone who so much as looks suspicious'.[5] Stalin, his rival, did the same, his partisan commandos ultimately killing more of his countrymen than they did German soldiers. The military usefulness of partisan warfare was, upon closer inspection, probably more negligible than its significance as a means of terrorizing and controlling Soviet citizens.[6] The partisans, after all, had 60 per cent of the territory under their control. Only in 1943–4 with their 'rail war' – the sudden and massive disruption of strategically vital railway connections – did Soviet partisans have any real tactical success. Most of the time they were fighting for their lives in the expansive forests and swampland, attacking occasional German convoys and strongholds, harassing villagers (especially Polish peasants) and fending off major German anti-partisan operations (*Bandenbekämpfung*) mainly by taking flight. In the latter phases of the war, they created large swathes of 'liberated' territory in which the Communist Party held sway.

A Soviet partisan attack against a
German train in Byelorussia, 1943.

The few Wehrmacht security divisions (first three, later six) along with SS and police battalions were able at best to secure the larger towns and important road connections. Under the pressure of the partisan movement, they thought it expedient to win over the anti-Communist-minded population, sometimes arming them. German Gauleiter Wilhelm Kube officially exercised power in the General Commissariat of White Ruthenia. He liked to put on airs and pose as an absolutist ruler in his role as a kind of Byelorussian sovereign or 'father of the people'. In addition to his German guards, he created a personal bodyguard of 50 local youths. The number of administrative experts at his disposal was quite limited. Kube was killed on 23 September 1943 in an assassination organized by the Red Army's secret service.

Representatives of the Byelorussian collaboration hoped that by supporting German rule they could further their cause of national sovereignty. Anti-Communism was the linchpin, tying them to an occupying power that never seriously considered granting the Byelorussians statehood. The multi-ethnic population was mainly interested in improving its social standing, which seemed most achievable by supporting the national movement. Though campaigns and institutions such as the White Ruthenian Self-Aid Association and youth welfare services did draw a certain following, it soon became apparent that the Germans were willing neither to cut back on onerous agricultural quotas nor to minimize the forced recruiting of labourers for the Reich.

Useful from a German perspective were the efforts to form an armed self-defence against partisans, despite the fact that the national movement viewed the founding of the White Ruthenian Home Guard in 1944 as the core element of an independent state. There were protracted discussions in the German security apparatus about the creation of 'fortified villages' (*Wehrdörfer*). Captured weapons would only be supplied to them when their mayors had proved trustworthy. Byelorussians were chiefly recruited as policemen, who were then – just like members of the national movement – used for crimes against the Jewish population and as helpers for deportations to the Reich.

Local police units were officially declared to be 'Ordnungsdienst', 'Hilfspolizei' or 'Schutzmannschaft' units, various names for auxiliary police and security forces. By the end of 1941 they already numbered several thousand, for the most part poorly uniformed and equipped with captured Soviet weapons. They had often been recruited from German POW camps. The SS and police leaders in Byelorussia also had a large number of mixed units for anti-partisan warfare comprising Ukrainian, Latvian and Lithuanian policemen as well. In 1942, two officer-training schools were set up for local policemen. Of great significance were the many small 'police strongpoints' in the villages. These were popular targets for Soviet partisans. A number of German NCOs and active policemen served in this rural police force. In mid-1943, it numbered 6,850 men. Its ethnic composition varied from region to region, though many Poles were among them. In many districts these strongpoints, often under the leadership of older German commanders, remained functional until the summer of 1944.[7]

Above: Byelorussian volunteers
with a captured Red Army machine
gun, autumn 1941.

Below: Byelorussian Self-Defence
in the Minsk region, winter
1941–2.

In the 4.5-hour fight, 200 members of the Self-Defence were killed, moreover 4 heavy machine guns, 13 light machine guns, 4 mortars, 10 submachine guns, 93 rifles, over 20,000 rifle cartridges, numerous mines and hand grenades were destroyed, burned or captured. The power station, saw mill, barracks, lookouts, administration and a German estate were burned down, and up to 100 cows and 70 horses carried off. I extend my thanks to the leaders of the Stalin Brigade, the 'Dzerzhinksy', 'Bolshevik' and 'Suvorov' detachments, and all of the partisans male and female who took part in the engagement, for their exemplary fulfilment of the combat mission to destroy the Naliboki garrison as well as for the boldness and bravery they demonstrated. ... Our detachments counted six dead and six wounded as a result of the battle. Glory to our courageous patriots! (Excerpt from the order of the authorized representative of the Central Staff of the Partisan Movement at the Supreme Command Headquarters and of the Central Committee of the CP(B) of Byelorussia of 10 May 1943 concerning the attack on the village of Naliboki)[8]

These policemen were not particularly reliable. Many of them switched sides, sometimes several times. And yet the SS dared, in 1944, to include them in their ranks after retreating from Byelorussia. The nationalists were more trustworthy, having burned their bridges behind them on account of their hatred for Stalinism as well as their participation in German war crimes. The Schutzmannschaft battalions of the German Ordnungspolizei in Byelorussia were organized into the 30th (White Ruthenian) Waffen Grenadier Division of the SS. Following the collapse of Army Group Centre they were temporarily consolidated into a brigade with four regiments that included Ukrainian and Russian volunteers. The brigade was assembled in the Warsaw area and transferred to the French city of Belfort. But the Byelorussians did not want to fight against the Western Powers.

While being reorganized and trained as the 30th Waffen Grenadier Division of the SS, a mutiny and conspiracy broke out among the soldiers. The German officers in two battalions were killed on 27 August 1944 and the troops defected to the French Resistance. Another 2,300 men were deemed useless and unreliable. They were transferred to the Karlsruhe Transport Command where they were used as entrenchment construction regiments ('Schanzregiment' 1 and 2). Only one battalion remained that was considered operational. Filled up with Russian volunteers from the Vlasov movement, a brigade was created at first, then, in March 1945, after the Russians were pulled out, the unit was renamed the 30th Waffen Grenadier Division of the SS (White Ruthenian No. 1). This division consisted of only a single regiment, which survived the end of the war at the Bavarian training grounds of Grafenwöhr. Hectic reorganization on the part of SS leaders reveals that they were at a loss about what to do with these few thousand Byelorussians – a confusing conclusion to the Byelorussians' role as armed combatants in Hitler's war against the Soviet Union.

In the western part of Byelorussia, the situation had become more complicated by the spring of 1944 thanks to the growing activities of the Polish underground army. In areas settled predominantly by Poles, the Armia Krajowa mobilized the population in the fight against the Germans as well as against the Soviets. Temporary alliances between Germans and Poles likewise emerged, especially in the Vilnius area. The city was ultimately liberated through the joint efforts of Polish and Soviet units. The Armia Krajowa was then disbanded by the Soviets and Byelorussia re-Sovietized. The armed 'pacification campaign' of the NKVD and the Red Army in the spring of 1945 mainly targeted the Polish underground and was perfidious in its use of Nazi methods. In the course of 'ethnic cleansing', some 274,000 people were resettled to Poland. Apathy spread among the remaining Byelorussian populace. An atomized war society buckled down to the task of survival under Soviet rule.

18

Ukraine

It was clear as early as World War I that, of all the nations in Eastern Europe, the Germans could find the most support in the Ukraine, if only they were willing to capitalize on it. As in Byelorussia, a national movement had formed which strove for independence from the Russian Empire. The movement, to be sure, was divided, and met with varying responses in different parts of the country. Just like in Byelorussia, the diverging interests and peculiarities of different regions and nationalities were a big problem. The largely agricultural western Ukraine had belonged to the Austrian dual monarchy for more than a century. Galicia was oriented more towards Vienna than Kiev, the religious divide between the Catholic and Orthodox churches coming into play here. The eastern Ukraine, on the other hand, was largely Russified and had a powerful industrial core in the city of Kharkov, which was strongly influenced by the Bolshevist Party.

It was precisely in the Ukraine, however, that the Germans had made a considerable effort to create a national government centred in Kiev, which would join the German Reich in an anti-Russian alliance. The war with Russia was officially over with the Treaty of Brest-Litovsk in 1918. As an agent of the German military administration, though, the Ukrainian government had a hard time getting its way in the country, since the Germans were mainly interested in exploiting it economically. The Ukrainian 'breadbasket' promised to offer major relief to the starving empire's war machine.

The creation of a Ukrainian army was stalling partly because of internal Ukrainian conflicts, but also because the German military administration had no need at first for military allies, being interested at best in policemen who could help bring in the harvest.[1] But alongside rebellious peasants they also had to deal with advancing Red partisans. The anti-Communist linchpin with the national Ukrainian movement was of limited use, however, because the German Reich had officially made peace with the Bolshevist government in Moscow.

The overall strategic situation was the deciding factor in the end, though, as German troops withdrew from the Ukraine after signing an armistice with the Entente. It now became apparent that Germany's Ukraine policy in 1917–18 had failed to create a viable state. The civil war escalated, ultimately ending with the victory of the Moscow Red Army. In the interwar period, Soviet Ukraine with its 30 million inhabitants was debilitated by forced collectivization, famines and mass repression. Historians now assume that Stalin's fight against the 'kulaks' with its artificially induced famine resulted in the deaths of up to 6 million people between 1930 and 1933. Western Ukraine was divided between Poland (Galicia with 6 million inhabitants), Czechoslovakia (Carpathian Ruthenia with about 500,000 people) and Romania (Bukovina with 800,000 inhabitants). The political environs there were relatively free. A group of *émigré* Ukrainian officers had organized a revolt movement as early as 1920, targeted mainly against Poland and Soviet Russia.[2]

In 1938, the organization, which secretly collaborated with German intelligence, split into two bitterly feuding factions under Andriy Melnik (OUN-M) and Stepan Bandera (OUN-B). When Hitler occupied the remainder of the Czech state in March 1939 and put Slovakia under the 'protection' of the Reich, Carpatho-Ukraine declared its independence as well, albeit to no avail, for the Germans had already promised the territory to the Hungarians. A Ukrainian defence organization of 15,000 men offered futile resistance and continued to play the German card.

For its Polish campaign, the military secret service assembled a Ukrainian legion in battalion strength that was supposed to create unrest in Galicia. But with the Hitler-Stalin Pact, the territory was ceded to the USSR. The Ukrainians in exile were deceived once again. The Stalinization of Galicia, a region with historically evolved social and economic structures, was a veritable nightmare. About 400,000 people were allegedly exiled to Siberia and Kazakhstan. The forced collectivization of agriculture, the nationalization of factories and political purges gave rise to a situation in which the majority of the population eventually welcomed 'liberation' by the Wehrmacht in 1941.

Both exile groups of the OUN (Organization of Ukrainian Nationalists) vied for the Germans' good graces. There was much linking them to National Socialism. Anti-Communism and anti-Semitism were among the things they had in common. With regard to the aim of independence, however, the Ukrainian nationalists harboured false hopes. Hitler and his chief ideologue Alfred Rosenberg had learned from World War I that making Germany blockade-proof and securing its world-power status were unthinkable without the Ukrainian breadbasket, and that this region therefore had to be ruled with a heavy hand.

Rosenberg, though, as the future Reich minister for the occupied eastern territories and with his concept of 'decomposing' the Russian Empire, was prepared to give the Ukrainians preferential treatment and a certain degree of autonomy, though naturally nothing approaching full sovereignty. Hitler, on the other hand, was primarily interested in the wholesale economic exploitation of the country and thus appointed East Prussian Gauleiter Erich Koch to the position of Reich commissioner of the Ukraine. Koch ruled 'his' country with an iron fist and was not particularly interested in the political ambitions of his minister, so that Germany's Ukraine policy zigzagged, blocking its own scope of action on account of internal conflicts.

There were varied opinions in the Wehrmacht as well. The military's economic organization was naturally concerned about supplying its own troops and meeting delivery obligations to the Reich. They saw no need to worry about 'useless eaters' – a strategy of plunder and extermination aimed mainly against the eastern Ukrainian industrial region. Among army generals there was also the view that it might be expedient to win over the Ukrainians for the German cause and use them in the fight against the Red Army. In the eyes of the SS, the Ukraine was first and foremost a potential German settlement area that had to be 'purged' of supposed 'racial inferiors' and 'subhumans'. Added to this were the murder of Communist elites and the repression of undesirable political movements and resistance among the population.

In preparing Operation Barbarossa, Admiral Wilhelm Canaris, head of military intelligence, turned to exiled Ukrainians for help. He was expecting to recruit upwards of 30,000 combat-willing sympathizers of the OUN-B in western Ukraine. Followers of Bandera were formed into the Nachtigall and Roland battalions, which, acting as vanguards of the Wehrmacht, carried out acts of sabotage and destabilized the hinterland of the Red Army. The Ukrainians, for their part, were hoping that these units would be the core of a future national army, bolstered by Ukrainian deserters and prisoners of the Red Army. The legionnaires wore uniforms reminiscent of the first national army of 1918. Unlike the other legions of the Wehrmacht, they did not swear an oath to Hitler, but vowed: 'With this gun I fight for the freedom of the Ukraine or I shall die.'[3]

Advising German officers, among them Lieutenant and Professor Dr Theodor Oberländer, who later served as federal minister for displaced persons, refugees and victims of war in Bonn, did not always intervene when Ukrainian members of the Wehrmacht took part in popular riots against Jewish citizens. In beating a hasty retreat, the Soviet NKVD murdered up to 30,000 Polish and Ukrainian prisoners being held in numerous prisons. In their wrath many Ukrainians blamed the Jews, who they thought had profited inordinately from Soviet rule.[4]

The worst massacres took place in the Galician metropolis of Lemberg (Lviv). Ukrainian insurgents penetrated the city and proclaimed the Ukraine's independence, but did not initially succeed in capturing it. The murder of about 3,500 prisoners by the NKVD continued until the Wehrmacht's invasion on 29 July 1941. Ukrainian militiamen added fuel to the fire. Following spontaneous pogroms, the SS Einsatzkommando continued murdering the Jewish population in a more systematic way. There were also many instances, however, of Ukrainians attacking the Polish minority.

Ukraine's part in the Holocaust: Ukrainian auxiliary police guard a group of Jewish women and children from Mizocz (in the Volhynia region) on 14 October 1942 before they are shot by an SS unit in a nearby pit.

Parade of Ukrainian nationalists in Galicia.

The OUN was the perfect partner for the Wehrmacht on its march through Galicia, as the nationalists had many years of experience in their underground war against the Soviet system. But this brotherhood-in-arms only went so far. In a memorandum to Hitler, Bandera pleaded for the re-establishment of the Ukrainian state. Just like the Melnik wing of the OUN, Pavlo Skoropadskyi, the former Hetman or head of state in Kiev (1918), made an offer to Berlin to set up an army of 2 million men for the fight against Stalinism.[5] A staff of experienced officers was to lead these troops.

The Germans soon put a damper on the political ambitions of the Ukrainians. One of the techniques of rule of the newly installed German administration was to replace the Ukrainian mayors appointed by the OUN with Polish ones. On 30 June 1941, a national assembly met in Lemberg and proclaimed the restoration of the Ukrainian state without consulting Berlin beforehand. The Ukrainian National Revolutionary Army would 'fight with its ally the German Army against Muscovite occupation for a United Ukrainian State and a new order throughout the world', the proclamation read.[6] A provisional government decided, moreover, to create its own Ukrainian militia. Though Skoropadskyi had little influence, the new set of Ukrainian politicians was confident of persuading their countrymen to fight alongside the Germans against Russian Bolshevism.

German security police quickly intervened, however, because Hitler was furious when he heard about the Ukrainian's declaration of independence. Bandera was placed in 'honourable detention' and a new Ukrainian self-government was installed in Lemberg. Eastern Galicia was incorporated – against the protest of Ukrainian nationalists – into the General Government of Poland, whereas the rest of the Ukraine was placed under a Reich Commissariat. Bandera, whose followers at times controlled 50 per cent of German-conquered territory, and many other Ukrainian nationalists had once again misjudged the Germans. The Ukraine-friendly attitude of certain Wehrmacht officers and official 'liberation' propaganda obscured the fact that Berlin was solely interested in the economic exploitation and subjugation of the country.

The two Ukrainian Wehrmacht battalions were pulled out of the front in August 1941 and their members retrained as policemen. As of March 1942, they were sent to Byelorussia to combat partisans as Schutzmannschaft Battalion 201. When their tour of duty expired in September, most of the

Ukrainians refused to stay on. The Germans thereupon disbanded the unit and imprisoned its officers in Lemberg.

OUN march groups were formed in July of 1941 to accompany the German advance in the Ukraine, establishing regional strongholds to the rear of the Wehrmacht. From now on they avoided confrontation with the Germans and offered to secure the hinterland with their militia. For want of its own police forces, the Wehrmacht and Einsatzkommandos of the Security Service were happy to fall back on these armed groups in order, for instance, to comb the forests for hidden Red Army soldiers. Anti-Communism and anti-Semitism were their common political foundation. The militias were instrumental in carrying out countless mass murders of Jews. Renouncing for the time being its claims to founding an independent state modelled after the one of 1918, the OUN-M sought to consolidate its power basis 'from below' under German protection. Unlike the OUN-B, it was hoping for a gradual road to independence, and advised its followers to offer their services to the Germans as interpreters and in local administration.

Unlike during World War I, police and SS units as well as the German civil administration intervened between the German military and the Ukrainian national movement. Propaganda Minister Joseph Goebbels complained about the consequences one year later:

> The Ukrainian population was initially more than willing to view the Führer as the saviour of Europe and to warmly welcome the German Wehrmacht. This attitude has totally changed over the months. Our policies have continually snubbed the Russians and especially the Ukrainians. Being cudgelled over the head is apparently not always a convincing argument to the Ukrainains and Russians. We are slowly beginning to change these tendencies, however, if only still to a small degree. ... Our troops are all for it, as it would surely make their job easier.[7]

Himmler had been counting in particular on the support of ethnic Germans in the Ukraine, but his settlement and police specialists were extremely disappointed by the impression made in German villages. The human material was hardly convincing from a 'racial' standpoint, the men being suited for a 'self-defence' unit at best.

It took a military setback outside Moscow and the failure of their blitzkrieg strategy to cause the Germans to rethink their stance. But apart from using Ukrainian auxiliary police and Schutzmannschaft battalions, they were still not interested in harnessing the country's full military potential in the struggle against the USSR. There were two Schutzmannschaft battalions in western Ukraine, nos. 201 and 212. Yet Hitler – in contrast to his generals in the Eastern Army – was not willing to make the political and economic concessions required to build up a Ukrainian national army.

The Ukrainian paramilitary formations set up at local German headquarters relieved the Wehrmacht in its fight against the Red Army to no small degree. Though the Ukrainians' political aims had to be scaled back drastically and their real intentions hidden from view upon surrendering the militias to German security and rural police, the OUN-B – once again active underground – nevertheless called on its followers to sign up for police duty, join the railway defence, or seek employment with the postal service and other administrative agencies. The Polish underground in Galicia acted in a similar way, inevitably giving rise to a covert civil war, given the Ukrainian-Polish conflict.

Unlike in western Ukraine, in the eastern part of the country there was a clearly delineated common front of Ukrainian 'willing helpers' and Germans who resisted infiltration by Soviet partisans. Ukrainians and Cossacks were assembled into 70 Schutzmannschaft battalions with 35,000 men. Added to this were 15,665 uniformed police and 55,094 men in rural police forces posted at various stations.[8]

Support of the Wehrmacht among the local population in areas close to the front decreased in inverse proportion to their perception of German rule as oppressive and enslaving thanks to the closing of factories, the introduction of forced labour and a general disregard for the people's welfare and nutrition. The Germans' hesitation over dissolving the hated kolkhoz farms cost them the sympathy of the majority of the rural population. But it was the hundreds of thousands of people in the Ukraine being dragged off to Germany, even hunted down as slaves, for 'employment in the Reich' (*Reichseinsatz*) starting in the spring of 1942 that produced a drastic change in mood. There were hardly any recruitable young men left in the villages, as many of them preferred to run off to join the partisans, especially since the German defeat at Stalingrad made plain that the Red Army would be likely to return to the Ukraine.

Eastern Ukraine was, of course, affected much earlier. In Galicia and western Ukraine the situation was more stable at first, at least from a German perspective, especially in those parts heavily under the influence of the former Austro-Hungarian monarchy. Erich Koch, Reich commissioner of the Ukraine, played a key role in the constant struggle of the military administration of the OKH and reasonably-minded generals against the hardliners of the SS and the economic administration. Contrary to his minister's intentions, he viewed the Ukraine as German colonial territory and the Ukrainians as German 'niggers', so to speak, whose role it was to work and obey, just as Hitler envisioned it. He therefore gave his officials the following guidelines: 'We have liberated them; in return they shall know no other aim than to work for us. There can be no human camaraderie. ... Strictly speaking, we are dealing with niggers here. ... The population is quite simply filthy and lazy. ... In my jurisdiction anyone who shows the least bit of intelligence is shot.'[9]

Thus in spring 1942, the OUN was faced with the question of whether it should form a partisan detachment to protect its own population from the Germans. The Ukrainian nationalists' enemy number one was still the USSR, but they could not ingore the suffering of their people in the German hinterland. Launching military operations against the Germans before the outcome of the war between the two empires was evident could turn out to be a mistake. Unlike the Polish Armia Krajowa, the Ukrainian underground could not hope for the backing of a Western power that would champion Ukrainian independence against the claims of the USSR. The OUN's situation was rather hopeless in this respect.

Following the spontaneous emergence of self-defence groups against the Germans and – in western Ukraine – against the Polish underground, the OUN declared open warfare against the German occupying power in early 1943 (in the shadow of the Stalingrad catastrophe).

We ... fight so that every nation lives a free life in its own independent state. The end of national oppression and exploitation of one nation by another nation, a system of free peoples in their own independent state – this is the only order that offers a just solution to the national and social question throughout the world. We fight against imperialists and empires because in them a ruling people oppresses other peoples culturally, politically and economically; that is why we are against the

USSR, and against the German 'New Europe'. (From the resolution of the Third Great Assembly of the OUN in February 1943)[10]

The newly formed Ukrainian Insurgent Army (UPA) found a rapidly growing following, many of its armed and equipped fighters having previously served in the German auxiliary police. Within a matter of weeks, German forces were driven from large parts of the countryside into western Ukraine. The Germans managed to hold their ground only in the larger cities, barely securing important railway connections. The UPA, moreover, sent units into central and eastern Ukraine to recruit forces for the common struggle and win the support of former Soviet Ukrainian citizens for the national independence movement. They naturally became embroiled in fighting with Soviet partisans. The latter were given the task of liquidating the UPA to the rear of retreating Germans during the Red Army's advance through the Ukraine in the spring of 1944.[11]

Hungarian occupying troops in the Ukraine played an important role in securing the hinterland. The UPA reached a secret agreement with them as early as 1943 to organize an armistice while exchanging information and food for weapons and equipment. Rival armed factions of the national movement were sometimes disbanded by force and integrated into the UPA. Thus by 1944, about 30,000 fighters were ready for battle in strictly organized military units. The Red partisans, by contrast, had about 24,000 men in western Ukraine.

The UPA was a well-organized infantry army with a hotchpotch of captured weapons, supported by cavalry and artillery as well as a few tanks. Save for its officers, the army's young men and women had no prior military training. They were conducting a war on multiple fronts. Against the backdrop of shifting fronts, they attacked the Germans and even succeeded in repelling an enemy division on 9 July 1944 at Lopata Hill. At the same time, the UPA was engaged in out-and-out warfare with the Polish Armia Krajowa, which had set up a division in Galicia and Volhynia to promote the return of these regions to a future Polish state. Both sides perpetrated brutal 'ethnic cleansing' in villages – a repeat of the conflict at the end of World War I. An estimated 100,000 Poles and 20,000 Ukrainians were killed in the course of this curious war within a war.[12]

The UPA also conducted raids into central Ukraine from its strongholds in the west. They ambushed and killed the supreme commander of the 1st

Ukrainian Front, General Nikolai Vatutin. The NKVD assembled 30,000 men – in vain – to prevent the advance of the UPA into the Soviet hinterland. Thus, the underground state remained intact even after the withdrawal of the Germans, and fought against the Soviet regime until the early 1950s. Upwards of 30,000 communist functionaries, Chekists and Red Army members were killed in the process. In return, about 500,000 western Ukrainians were deported to Siberia between 1946 and 1949.[13]

Ukrainians from the Lemberg (Lviv) district volunteering for the Waffen SS, May 1943.

After the catastrophe of Stalingrad, the Germans finally made their own effort to set up Ukrainian military units to compete with the UPA. Ideological scruples against the deployment of Slavic soldiers (they preferred to call them 'non-German' volunteers) had now been dropped, even within the SS. With the Ordnungspolizei having set up armed units on its own initiative in the spring of 1943, Heinrich Himmler now approved the suggestion of the governor of Galicia, SS Brigadeführer Dr Otto Wächter, to recruit volunteers for the Waffen SS in this still relatively peaceful region.

The three regiments were preferably to be made up of men whose fathers had served in the Austro-Hungarian Army. The OUN thought it sensible to support these recruiting efforts so as to gain access to weapons and trained soldiers. A good 84,000 men had signed up by June of 1943, of which only a quarter were selected by the SS. The latter were careful to keep away the 'germ' of Ukrainian nationalism. After several renamings, the newly formed 14th Waffen Grenadier Division of the SS, Halytschyna (Galician No. 1) comprised 15,299 soldiers by the end of the year. The additional label 'Ukrainian' was prohibited by Himmler. An unusual concession on the part of the SS was the inclusion of nine army chaplains. Most of the troops were ethnic Germans and Ukrainians from the Lemberg region. The remaining volunteers were used by the police to form five additional SS volunteer regiments (nos. 4 to 8).

Their training was completed in the summer of 1944, resulting in the creation of a powerful fighting unit within the ranks of the Waffen SS. A combat group had meanwhile been deployed to fight partisans. In June, the division was attached to the 1st Panzer Army in response to a major Soviet offensive and found itself in the Brody pocket on 19–20 July. Despite courageous resistance, only 3,000 of the division's men managed to escape behind German lines. About 1,000 of them fought their way to the UPA.

Disbanded Galician police regiments were used in reactivating the division. Higher-ranking Ukrainian officers, on the other hand, were not included. German commanders were unsympathetic towards their foreign troops. But tensions were kept at bay by transferring the division to Slovakia as an occupying army. They were now given the additional label of 'Ukrainian No. 1'. Occasional clashes with Slovakian insurgents and Tito partisans were not a big problem. Hence, the rate of desertion (3 per cent) was modest until spring 1945.

The Ukrainian Schutzmannschaft battalions of the Ordnungspolizei were sometimes redeployed in police regiments of the SS after withdrawing from the Ukraine. As with the Byelorussians, they proved unreliable in battle situations on the western front. A Ukrainian regiment was deployed on the Upper Rhine in the XVIII SS Army Corps in February 1945 but had to be pulled out after numerous complaints by the German population. The Nazi regime could not put up with German civilians being molested by Ukrainians in German uniforms.

In late September 1944, Berlin let go of all its inhibitions. Bandera was released from prison and the Jagdverband Ost of notorious SS Hauptsturmführer Otto Skorzeny was to establish contact with the UPA in occupied Ukraine with the aim of intensifying partisan warfare against the

Red Army – an illusionary undertaking. The SS Head Office in Berlin decided – much too late – to revolutionize Nazi policy in the East and endorsed the formation of a Ukrainian National Committee under the leadership of Pavlo Shandruk. The latter had fought against the Red Army as a Ukrainian colonel from 1918 to 1920, then joined the Polish Army in 1936, hoping to save the country's 'substance' – by which he meant rescuing from the Red Army as many Ukrainian 'Eastern workers' (Ostarbeiter), prisoners of war and volunteers as possible.[14]

The idea of Ukrainian independence was so important to him that he rejected an assignment in General Vlasov's Russian National Committee, put in place by Himmler. In March 1945, Shandruk was officially recognized by the government of the German Reich, which at this point was ruling from its bunker in Berlin. The superficiality of this change of heart became evident, however, when Hitler, having learned about the Ukrainian SS division, recommended it be disarmed. Instead, it was placed under the command of Shandruk and, in April 1945, renamed the 1st Division of the Ukrainian National Army – little more than a symbolic gesture in the waning days of the war, with the Red Army already at the gates of Berlin. In late April, in far-away Austria, its German cadre personnel had to take an oath to the foreign flag as well: 'I will always and everywhere with weapon in hand fight for my Ukrainian homeland under the Ukrainian national flag.' If the Germans thought they could avoid captivity by doing so, they learned in just a matter of days how mistaken they were.

Except for the 2nd Ukrainian Division – in the midst of reorganization after being wiped out by the Red Army in Bohemia – the units of the 1st Division in Austria (as well as the 281st Reserve Regiment in Denmark and two guard units in Holland) were lucky to be called 'Galician', because the Western Powers declared them a 'Polish outfit' and did not turn them over to Stalin but interned them in Rimini – surely not the worst place to be as Ukrainians at this bleak hour. Upon their release, many of them emigrated to Canada or the United States, where large Ukrainian communities emerged which upheld the idea of an independent homeland. Some of these immigrants were paid a visit by public prosecutors as late as the 1980s and 1990s for lying about their military service with the Germans or for being suspected of war crimes. Bandera was assassinated by Soviet secret agents in Munich in 1959. A large Ukrainian exile community was living there as well.

The total number of Ukrainians bearing arms for the German war effort is estimated at 250,000.[15] If Hitler had allowed the formation of a national army and a certain degree of national autonomy in 1941, as suggested by many experts and officers, and to a certain extent even by Eastern Minister Rosenberg himself, the army of 2 million men envisioned by Skoropadskyi may very well have become reality. Yet unlike in other areas of Eastern Europe, Hitler was not so much guided by racial ideology here as he was by radical economic motives. Learning from the experiences of 1918, his ruthless 'squeezing dry' of the Ukraine was to enable the Germans to continue their war effort. And so the Ukraine was conquered once again by the Germans, but its brutal policy of exploitation failed. The Ukrainians who were willing to fight against Stalinism could not help falling into resignation or eventually switched sides and joined the Soviets.

19

Russia

Positive German-Russian military relations from the era of the Napoleonic Wars had been replaced by increasing tension between the two countries by the end of the nineteenth century. Power-political rivalries and ideological differences led to a mutual sense of being threatened, making military confrontation seem ever more likely. By the early twentieth century, the German General Staff considered Russia a sure enemy in future armed conflict. With the outbreak of war in August 1914, both sides struggled bitterly to defeat the other. Neither Berlin nor Moscow even thought about forming legions with citizens from their respective rival. This did not apply, however, to national minorities in the enemy camp. Their mobilization and arming could – so both sides calculated – shake the imperial foundations and undermine the cohesion of the enemy.

The German Empire was the most successful with this policy, especially in promoting the creation of nation-states in the territory of the ultimately vanquished Russian Empire. Even during World War I, German war aims sought to dismantle Russia into its various national components through a 'policy of decomposition', thus reducing a defeated Russia to its 'Old Russian' core and eliminating the competition of a great power to the East. The Germans even co-operated with the hated Russian Bolshevists in order to weaken and then defeat their opponent. Though they hardly sympathized with the Communists in the ensuing Russian Civil War, they considered the White Guard army their enemy, supported as it was by the Entente.

This cynical game of power politics was continued even after German defeat. The Reichswehr even secretly intensified its co-operation with the Bolshevik regime in military and armament matters. Some individuals – for instance, Count Brockdorff-Rantzau, the German ambassador to Moscow

– imagined making common cause with the 'Red Cossacks' in a 'war of liberation' on the Rhine against France. The chief of German Army Command, General Hans von Seeckt, was cool and calculating in his contacts with Red Army leaders. If Communism failed in Soviet Russia, as most people in the West expected it to, the Germans would maintain their influence in Russia by virtue of their alliance with former Tsarist officers in the Red Army, thereby preventing Russia from drifting to the Western camp.

Hundreds of thousands of Russian *émigrés* in Germany were able to become politically active, but former Tsarist Army officers hoped in vain to return to their homeland sometime soon. The notion, defended by the last German commander-in-chief in the East, General Max Hoffmann, of waging a future war against the Soviet regime with the help of the local population met with no response from Reichswehr leaders with their power-political calculations. On the contrary, numerous German officers were sent to the USSR for training prior to 1933, just as key Red Army cadre received their general staff training in Germany.

Though a potential alliance with the Soviet regime remained controversial among national conservative elites, here, too, the basic idea of Bismarck's Russian policy lived on. Ideas of a German-Russian alliance of various shades even existed among the radical right. The Führer, in any case, had an uncompromising vision when the National Socialists took power in 1933: Lebensraum for Germany could be found only in the East, and this at the expense of Russia. Any co-operation with the Russian population was therefore out of the question. Hitler had concocted a lethal mixture of racial ideology, anti-Semitism and anti-Communism, inspired by the Baltic-German emigrant Alfred Rosenberg. Rosenberg advocated a strict 'programme of decomposition' for Russia in which non-Russian nationalities would be considered as potential German allies, depending on their racial value, but not the population of the Russian heartland, the 'Muscovites'.

To be sure, Germany's Russian policy remained divided after 1933. With Joachim von Ribbentrop as head of the Foreign Office, the 'continental bloc' concept of a German-Russian alliance gained in importance once again. In 1939, it became even more important when Stalin was forced to admit the failure of his system of collective security, which he had tried to use to keep the ambitions of his rival great power Germany in check. Even today there are speculations that a Berlin intrigue led Stalin to purge the higher officer corps of his Red Army. Whatever the case, the murder or deportation of thousands of veteran commanders severely crippled the Soviet Army well into World War II and was one cause of the catastrophic defeat they suffered in the summer of 1941.

Stalin's enticements in the summer of 1939 gave Hitler the chance to invade Poland without immediately risking a world war. Thus, in September, a kind of brotherhood-in-arms emerged reminiscent of the Brest-Litovsk era of 1918, this time, however, 'at eye level', and at the cost of re-establishing the old frontiers of the Russian Empire. German-Soviet co-operation flourished for both sides in almost every respect during the first year of the war and – as some national conservatives in Germany saw it – could have rekindled German-Russian relations of the Bismarck-era type. But Hitler, we now know, was merely waiting for the right moment to launch the real war he had in mind – the conquest of Russia.

German leaders had varied expectations. Diplomats to Russia were keen to expand relations with the USSR, as were some parts of German industry. Initial military considerations of a possible armed encounter with the Red Army assumed they were facing an unequal opponent and expected a rapid victory, especially considering that for the time being – in June of 1940, after the defeat of France – they were merely thinking about a 'small' solution; that is, the conquest or 'liberation' of the western fringes of the Soviet Union, the areas just recently occupied by Stalin: the Baltics, eastern Poland and Ukraine. It was clear that the territorial expansion of the USSR had not increased its military potential in any dependable way. The Germans could count on the willingness of non-Russian nationalities to co-operate with them, as in World War I.

Even as Hitler was mapping out an overall solution to defeat the USSR in July 1940, Wehrmacht leaders were still only planning a brief conflict, rendering superfluous the inclusion of the local population. Though the army's quartermaster general, Eduard Wagner, expected to take large numbers of prisoners, these would be used as labourers or otherwise quickly released. But Hitler's intervention and the appointment of Rosenberg to the position of Reich minister for the occupied eastern territories in March–April 1941 led to a radical change in plans. Hitler's notorious address of 30 March 1941, delivered to the commanders of the future Eastern Army, made this change of policy clear.[1] The Russians would not be the Germans' 'comrades', but by killing off their commissars would become a leaderless mass, at best slave labourers without any rights, who could starve by the millions if need be. The future Reich Commissariat Muscovy under the leadership of SA Obergruppenführer Siegfried Kasche was to be 'held down' under Rosenberg's plan.[2] In contrast to the Baltics, the Ukraine and the Caucasus, the Russian heartland was predestined in Hitler's view to be plundered and, in the long term, robbed of its people. Russian 'subhumans' had no place in the German Eastern Empire.

This is the reason why Hitler was so adamant about refusing to arm the Russians and putting them in the service of Germany. Minor exceptions would be made in the case of non-Russian peoples. Although German leaders assumed at the start of Operation Barbarossa that Stalinist rule was tolerated rather than supported by the majority of the Russian population, they were convinced in their initial euphoria that the Russians would not be needed to win a victory. Hence building a Russian 'liberation army' was not in the picture at all.

The arrogance of Nazi leaders was particularly tenacious and was only gradually undermined by military constraints and pressures. Front troops, on the other hand, were forming the first units out of deserters and prisoners as early as summer 1941, starting in the 'liberated' borderlands of the USSR, where armed militias had to be handed over to the higher SS and police leaders of Heinrich Himmler. Russian prisoners of war and volunteers were then increasingly used for auxiliary services in the Wehrmacht. They were already being put to use as interpreters, guards and labourers by military commands and sub-units. But Hitler strictly refused to accept the offers, for example, of Russian exiles or local mayors to form a common anti-Communist Front or even independent Russian troops.

There was only one exception to this racial-ideological policy towards the Russians: an almost clichéd benevolence towards the Cossacks. When the Soviet 436th Infantry Regiment under the command of Major Ivan N. Konosov defected almost wholesale to the Wehrmacht on 22 August 1941, Army Group Centre renamed it the 600th Cossack Detachment and used it for security tasks as well as to combat partisans. The number of 'genuine' Cossacks in its ranks was small, but the 'packaging' at least was convincing. Rosenberg originally wanted to expand the Cossack Don and Volga area into an independent buffer state between the Ukraine and Muscovy, but later abandoned the idea when he failed to see any kind of distinct national consciousness among the Cossacks.[3] Their supposedly warlike spirit and historic track record of anti-Communism made them an exception to the category of 'subhumans'. Long-standing contacts between the Cossack leadership in exile, especially Ataman Pyotr Krasnov, and the Wehrmacht were probably paying off here as well. In late 1941, the OKW at any rate approved the creation of Cossack units to fight on the side of the Germans. This at least gave them equal status with the non-Russian peoples, if not more.

Indeed, during preparations for the summer offensive of 1942, which would pass through the historic settlement areas of the Cossacks, Hitler approved their deployment not only in combating partisans but also for front-line duty. The military situation after the setback outside Moscow had forced the Führer to press his allies for greater help as well as to open up and accommodate a more 'moderate' policy of occupation in the East.[4] The Eastern Ministry seemed convinced that the populations of the Caucasus and southern Russia could be induced to collaborate through political and cultural concessions. Again it was military officers who took the initiative here. After occupying the Kuban region, the military administration proclaimed on its own authority the creation of a 'test area' with a Cossack self-government. An ataman government was promised, as well as the dissolution of collective farms.

A Cossack in Germany's service.

Suddenly the trumpeter sounded his horn above them, piercing their ears: the alluring signal for 'parade at a walk'! The colourful mass of horsemen ordered itself at the edge of the field, the first regiment crossed the line in five blocks. At the fore rode a heavyset colonel on a white horse that fumed and overbridled, behind him a grim yesaul, and finally a saucy lieutenant on a bay horse. Then the first squadron followed, the Ataman's guard, all of them in black cherkesskas. They sat on large bay horses, his Guard Cossacks on the brigade's best horses. Their pride shone in their savage faces, which incidentally looked as shiny as if they had just been scrubbed with scouring powder. They kept a relatively straight line, glanced like lined-up marionettes over at their Ataman, above whose head the new flag was flapping lazily: the old white-blue-red cloth, a Madonna embroidered in its middle, entirely of precious gold thread, extending her hands in a blessing. ... They were riding there again, the Tsar's black Cossacks. ... To Russia's rebirth, to Russia's old greatness. ... The next to come was the brown squadron, their horses were smaller but adorned twice as beautifully in exchange, some of them with gay little patterns on their croups. The Cossacks were wearing German uniforms which did not quite want to fit them properly but nevertheless gave an army-like impression. These men seemed even more marionette-like than the first ones; is that because they were making an extra effort in their uniforms? Were they trying to honour this uniform, is that why they sat there as stiff as ramrods, did they think in their childish simplicity that they owed it to the German general? (from a description of a parade of Kuban Cossacks)[5]

The quartermaster general of the army, General Eduard Wagner, broke a lance in favour of the Cossacks, even against the protests of the SS. A Cossack army commander was even supposed to be appointed in order to turn a provisional police force into a front-line unit with the help of an additional 25,000 volunteers. Germany's defeat at Stalingrad and its withdrawal from the Caucasus shattered these plans in early 1943. Thousands of local refugees nonetheless joined the Germans, among them numerous smaller Cossack units which the Germans themselves had created.

As with other foreign volunteer units, Hitler did not really want any formations larger than battalion strength. Thus, about 20 Cossack battalions were scattered along the Eastern Front. This restriction was weakened in 1943, for the Cossacks as well. Three full-scale regiments were already deployed by springtime. And as of May, a complete cavalry division was to be created out of volunteers, though nearly half of the troops were to come from POW camps. The existing 600th Detachment, meanwhile renamed 5th Don Cossack Regiment, formed the core of the division, which was placed under the command of the German General Helmuth von Pannwitz, an adventurer and former Freikorps fighter. It was an explosive mixture of old emigrants and civil-war veterans, of defectors and Red Army prisoners of war. Turning these motley troops – touchy to the point of mutual assassination attempts – into a powerful fighting unit was a difficult task indeed. The influence of Orthodox priests as well as the introduction of an old form of Cossack grass-roots democracy, which the older members were familiar with from Tsarist times, were helpful.[6]

By September 1943, the division was considered complete. It comprised one regiment each of Siberian and Terek Cossacks, and two regiments each of Don and Kuban Cossacks. Several squadrons of young Cossacks – orphans between the ages of 14 and 18 – also served in a training and replacement regiment. At a strength of 2,000 men, each regiment was provided with 160 Germans as cadre personal. The division was ready for action, but disappointment soon followed. Hitler had meanwhile changed his mind and ordered the withdrawal of Russian auxiliary units from the Eastern Front. The 1st Cossack Cavalry Division was transferred to Yugoslavia, where they were used to secure the German hinterland against Tito partisans. The fight against Communists was ruthlessly pursued by the Cossacks, or by those claiming to be Cossacks.[7] They had little sympathy with Croatian Ustaša units and their murderous campaign of extermination against Orthodox Serbs.

> 30 November [1943]. In the morning a ride with the general. As an escort we had ten Old Cossacks who sang marvellously on our ride through the villages. The locals stared at us aghast. Fear of the Cossacks spread. Villages went up in flames again and inhabitants were shot to death. It is very hard for the troops to wage a war here, because it is awfully difficult, if not impossible, to differentiate between partisans and non-partisans. Artillery fire could be heard all the time. There is no unified front to speak of. The enemy is everywhere. ...

26 December. Mounted our horses at 9 a.m. Dressed in Cossack-style. Rode with Schultz, the trumpet corps and a platoon from the guard squadron, all of them wearing their cherkesskas, to the quarters of Colonel v. Bosse to sing him a song in honour of his 25 years of service. Afterwards a procession through the town with a lot of hoopla. Went for black coffee to Logornik Faget, who invited us all to go dancing in the synagogue [!] that evening. Went for half an hour with dread. Fortunately people came, cold as hell and, as luck would have it, miserable drinks. (From the war diary of Major Erwein Karl Graf zu Eltz from the staff of the 1st Cossack Division about their deployment in Yugoslavia)[8]

Discipline in the division could only be maintained with draconian punishments. The 'organization' of food and, especially, alcohol was part of daily business. Other Cossack battalions were sent by the Germans to the Atlantic Wall, where they fought as infantry against British and Americans invasions. Ideological pragmatism, promoted even by Himmler in the face of impending defeat, led to the further build-up of Cossack formations in late 1944. Cossack nationalists knew how to impress the Reichsführer SS with anti-Semitic and anti-Western arguments. The claim to have 'strong blood ties with their original German homeland' was to bolster their demand for a 'Greater Cossackia'.[9] They were at least successful in having the Cossack cavalry expanded to a corps with two divisions in northern Yugoslavia, which had meanwhile become a hinterland of the Eastern Front. The XV Cossack Cavalry Corps, formed at the end of the year, had a fighting strength of no fewer than 25,000 men. General Krasnov swore to the Führer 'loyalty unto death', which the Cossacks – most of whom had taken their families along with them to Southeastern Europe – subsequently underscored with a low desertion rate.

About 35,000 Cossacks were evacuated from the East in the summer of 1944, being resettled to northern Italy in 50 railway transports. Their headquarters were in Dolmezzo, with 2,800 officers and 20,000 soldiers deployed exclusively to combat partisans. On 25 March 1945, the participants at a congress of Cossack front-line soldiers in Virovitica elected Helmuth von Pannwitz as their supreme commander or 'Field Ataman'. At the end of the war, men, women, children and the German general were all handed over to the Red Army by their British captors.[10] Pannwitz and an unknown number of his men were convicted and executed in the USSR.

But the tanks were faster because the tanks had engines. Monstrous things began. Shell after shell wailed into the mass of cavalrymen, tore the horses into bloody shreds, often knocked down entire lines like practice targets. The Cossacks pressed themselves flat on the necks of their horses, their eyes bulged, popping out of their heads, but the slope of the hollow robbed the horses of their last ounce of strength. The tanks rattled ever closer, the cracking and bursting were becoming clearer, they could already smell the fumes of burning oil, could feel the hot flashes of machine guns. One platoon after the other was mowed down, dying horses thrashed about, mangled humans screamed with ghastly voices. The bolting horses jumped with their hooves right into the ones that lay there on the battlefield in bloody gelatinous masses, hacked to pieces as if by a butcher's knife. Some of the fallen Cossacks raised their hands beseechingly in the hope of being taken along, but their yellow faces usually betrayed their imminent deaths. Others tried to crawl forward on all fours, often dragging one leg behind them, like a block of wood dangling from them. The only thought was how to escape this steaming hell of death, this bloody slaughterhouse in which even the air condensed into blood! The battle turned ever more frantically into a horrifying hare-hunt, horses began to fall from faintness and exhaustion, throwing their riders out of their saddles in their fear of death. (Report on the events following the last successful attack of the Kuban Cossacks on a Soviet infantry division in Yugoslavia in 1945)[11]

Similarly tragic was the fate of the overwhelming majority of Russians who were willing to fight on the side of the Germans. They were by far the greatest potential resource that Hitler – under other circumstances – could have mobilized in his war against Stalinism. Instead, until 1942, they were classified as 'subhumans', the last vestiges of discrimination not being lifted until the spring of 1945, with the Red Army already outside Berlin.

German reservations about the idea of a Russian 'liberation army' were so great that, up until 1944, the deployment of Russian volunteers was generally only possible in the unarmed auxiliary troops scattered without any sense of solidarity along the Eastern Front. There was only one exception where – unlike in the case of the Cossacks – no ideological contortions were possible. In late 1941, in the Bryansk region, the 2nd Panzer Army conducted an experiment on its own initiative, installing a largely autonomous Russian administration with its own police force in the remote area of Lokot, the latter being threatened by partisans. It was led by Bronislav V. Kaminski, a half-Polish, half-German engineer who had recently been released from a Soviet concentration camp.

Under German supervision, he consolidated this area of 1.7 million inhabitants – comparable to one of the Baltic states – into his personal sphere of influence. Schools and cultural facilities flourished, and a cleverly contrived tax system rewarded anti-Communist activities. Kaminski gained particular popularity by abolishing the hated kolkhoz system. He doled out land to merited anti-partisans who then farmed these lands as 'soldier-peasants' (*Wehrbauer*), so to speak, generating surpluses – in stark contrast to German economic and occupation policy in the rest of occupied Russia. His National Socialist Russian Workers' Party remained a phantom, in any case, with no political impact.

Kaminski had to use his own soldiers to defend his independence against attacks by Soviet partisans. By spring 1943, his Russian National Liberation Army (RONA), which included Russian Jews in its ranks, had grown to 10,000 men, half of them deserters from the partisan camp or former prisoners of war – dimensions likewise reminiscent of the Baltic states. His home-defence troops, as it were, were mainly equipped with captured Soviet weapons, and their uniforms were a veritable hotchpotch. The 15 battalions were supported by an artillery detachment as well as T-34 tanks. According to German assessments, they relieved the Wehrmacht with a strength equivalent to one division.

The situation changed when the Germans began to withdraw. Kaminski was evacuated to Byelorussia in August 1943 with 6,000 soldiers and 25,000 civilians. There the troops had to hold their own in an arduous struggle against a hostile civilian population and powerful partisan groups. The 'Kaminski Brigade' was now operating as an occupying army. One battalion defected to the partisans during a revolt. In the summer of 1944, Himmler decided to convert the demoralized troops into a regular division of the Waffen SS. They were called the 29th Waffen Grenadier Division of the SS (Russian No. 1) and were led by Kaminski in the rank of SS Brigadeführer. Though still being activated and trained, parts of the unit were used to suppress the Warsaw Uprising in August 1944. Looting and rape by Kaminski's men assumed such proportions that Himmler eventually disbanded this marauding band of mercenaries. Kaminski was apparently the victim of a murder conspiracy engineered by his masters. His men were put in the Vlasov Army shortly before the end of the war.

Bronislav Kaminski in Lokot, 1943.

The greatest number of Russian volunteers on the Eastern Front are linked to the name Vlasov. The origins of his army go back to 1942, when the OKH was faced with the problem of no longer being able to fill the gaps in the Eastern Army with German forces. Men like Stauffenberg and Wagner, who had been pleading for a change of course with regard to Germany's Russian policy, saw that the opportunity had come to officially integrate a large number of Russian 'willing helpers' into Germany's armed forces – that is to say, to put them into official positions provided for in the staff plan. Numerous German units already contained about 250,000 Russian prisoners of war who had escaped the gruelling life in the camps by offering indispensable services as panje-wagon drivers and unskilled labourers in German baggage trains, or as lightly armed guard and security personnel. As such they took the place of German soldiers who were then freed up for deployment at the front.

By the summer of 1942, Stauffenberg had seen to it that up to 10 per cent of the permanent posts in German divisions could be filled with so-called 'willing helpers'. If these margins of manoeuvre had been used to maximum capacity, a fighting strength of about 25 divisions, basically an entire army, could have been mobilized. If the eastern legions and the numerous formations made up of former Soviet citizens are included in the equation, about 1 million men were potentially available. These numbers correspond to the expectations of the army commanders who were hoping that military circumstances and practical constraints would force a change of course in occupation policy. The number actually reached was about 250,000, which nevertheless made up about 10 per cent of the Eastern Army's actual strength.[12] But the OKH had still not established full recognition and equality for the various voluntary units active on the Eastern Front, its Basic Order No. 800 falling short of this. For the time being, only Caucasians and Cossacks were considered 'combatants with equal rights'. Great Russians were excluded from armed service, though various formations of auxiliary guard (*Hilfswachmannschaften*) and municipal combat units (*Einwohnerkampfverbände*) had long since been created in the different army groups.

Russian 'voluntary helpers'.

The Wehrmacht had taken many prisoners in its 1942 summer offensive, at least in the south. This made the recruitment of 'willing helpers' easier, especially considering that more than half of the prisoners taken the year before had died. Thus the German 6th Army had more than 10 per cent Russians in its ranks, at least 19,000 men, in the battle for Stalingrad. The Italian 8th Army on the Don had even assembled an armed security battalion from Russian deserters.

In late 1942, it looked as though numerous memoranda and political talks in German leadership circles would perhaps soften up the harsh ideological stance towards the 'Russian question'. Though Rosenberg held staunchly to his rejection of the 'Muscovites', some of his leading officials had already broken the spell in collaboration with the OKH.[13] For the sake of 'saving German blood' – for this was apparently the most practical argument to convince the ideological hardliners – Russian volunteers were to be recruited into armed Eastern legions alongside unarmed 'willing helpers' and non-Russian military units; these legions would be under the care of the newly created 'general of the Eastern troops' in the OKH, as would existing units.[14] General of the Cavalry Ernst Köstring, who served as military attaché in Moscow until 1941, was chosen for this position. Major in the General Staff Claus Graf Count von Stauffenberg, in his function as group leader in Organization Department II, proved to be the actual driving force behind these plans. General Reinhard Gehlen, responsible for military intelligence as chief of the Foreign Armies East Department, noted in a memorandum that these Russian soldiers could not be treated like mercenaries (Landsknechte) who have to fight for a piece of bread.[15]

Italian Colonel General Gariboldi reviews the march-past of a Russian security battalion on the Don.

Andrey A. Vlasov.

The political basis for the recruitment of Russians – though still insufficient – was established in the course of 1943 despite the stubborn resistance of Hitler. It was only the strategic necessity of pulling out troops from the Eastern Front on account of an impending Allied invasion in the west and/ or the south that caused Hitler – as he put it – to tolerate temporary helpers of this sort. He still used every opportunity, however, to block any further move towards a Russian Liberation Army of the kind certain protagonists in the OKH hoped for.

In Soviet Lieutenant General Andrey A. Vlasov, the Germans had found a man who seemed to have the calibre required to lead such an army. Vlasov had been instrumental in the defence of Moscow and was captured by the Wehrmacht in July 1942 on the Volkhov Front south of Leningrad. His 2nd Assault Army had been surrounded and left in the lurch. Disillusioned by Stalinism, he showed himself to be open to leading an anti-Communist movement. His aim was a free and democratic Russia which had nothing in common with the many German variants of Russian policy he would encounter over the next three years.[16]

The national conservative representatives of a possible German-Russian alliance, such as officers Stauffenberg, Rudolf Christoph von Gersdorff and Henning von Tresckow, were part of the clandestine military opposition and ultimately had to keep their cover, just like the earlier Russian diplomats in the Foreign Office, but their support of the Vlasov movement was linked to the hope of a fundamental reorientation of German policies. This co-operation may have strengthened the illusions on both sides about such a change of course, but they were determined to leave no stone unturned in their piecemeal gathering of information and in trying to persuade others of their cause. Opinions wavered among Nazi leaders, but were cemented in place among the key individuals. Hitler, in particular, strengthened by his secretary Martin Bormann, persisted in his conviction of the racial inferiority and political unreliability of Russian 'subhumans'. If Vlasov proved to be a 'useful idiot' for propaganda purposes and could shake the morale of the Red Army, all the better; but under no circumstances was Hitler willing to allow the actual creation of a Russian Liberation Army.

Vlasov's illusions were strengthened in late 1942 when the OKH began a large-scale propaganda campaign using the phantom of a political liberation movement against Stalinism to recruit followers for the German cause. The public appearance of the former Soviet general in occupied Smolensk on 26 February 1943 was not without effect, as he promised a free Russia within the European community of states. He rejected National Socialism for the future of Russia, but affirmed his respect for the Germans as allies against Stalin, however many mistakes and misunderstandings there had been on the part of the Germans towards the Russian population.[17]

On his tour of the Army Group Centre zone he visited several Russian volunteer units and encountered a noticeable enthusiasm there as well as among the populace. The number of armed Russians in German security forces in rearward areas of the army group was already nearly 100,000, and they formed an indispensable element in the Germans' war against partisans. There were several other battalions apart from the Kaminski Brigade which Vlasov tried to inspire with courage and whose support he tried to enlist for the idea of fighting together in a future army against the Bolshevist regime. Though the OKW once again refused to allow the concentration of armed Russian units beyond the battalion level, there was still hope that the Germans might alter their stance, especially since Vlasov had received considerable support on his visits with German officers. Even Propaganda Minister Joseph Goebbels appeared impressed, and regretted East Minister Rosenberg's categorical refusal of a Great Russian movement.

The propaganda campaign was the only concession Hitler was willing to make at this point. In Dabendorf, to the south of Berlin, Stauffenberg assembled 1,200 Russians into the East Propaganda Department for Special Purposes (Ostpropagandaabteilung z. b. V.). The future propagandists were recruited in POW and labour camps as well as from volunteer units, and began their training on 1 March 1943. They were allowed to wear German uniforms with the insignia ROA (Russkaya Osvoboditel'naya Armiya, or Russian Liberation Army).[18] In the ensuing months, Dabendorf developed into a political centre where various Russian movements were brought together under the cloak of propaganda. An unresolved issue was the strained relations with other non-Russian national movements that had their own legions on the Eastern Front and were not willing to go along with the restoration of an anti-Communist Russian empire. The dilemma, caused not least of all by Rosenberg's 'policy of decomposition', remained until the very end and diminished Vlasov's room for manoeuvre as did the recalcitrance of Hitler, who ordered Vlasov to be taken captive again after another spectacular appearance of the Russian general on the Eastern Front. From now on he merely used the name, not the person, for propaganda purposes.[19]

The Army General Staff, however, was pushing more and more for a change of course. In the meantime, Stalin had founded his National Committee for a Free Germany among German prisoners of war, but likewise only used it for propaganda purposes. On 8 June 1943, Hitler decided in a heated military conference that he would not abandon his war aims and that he would rather bring the Russians to Germany as labourers: 'I can only say, we will never build up a Russian army, that's a phantom of the first order.'[20] Of course, Vlasov was never told about this decision. According to a statistical survey conducted in the Eastern Army in June 1943, there were still more than 600,000 'willing helpers' and about 200,000 men in volunteer units.[21]

When another 560,000 men were detailed to the front through rigorous economizing in the rearward organization of the army after heavy losses in the autumn of 1943, 260,000 Russian 'willing helpers' alone were used to replace German personnel,[22] But desertion rates were also increasing, especially among the Eastern troops, with the start of the German withdrawal. The perceptible turning point of the war in the East and troop transfers were reason and opportunity enough for some volunteers to desert. The Germans decided to integrate their scattered Eastern troops into security divisions at a ratio of one to two, while also exchanging personnel with security units in the

West. In this manner a large number of Russian units ended up in Western Europe, where the Germans felt they could control them better. Given the general lack of German cadre personnel, the Eastern battalions quickly became a burden to German formations. Thus, the OKH ordered this cadre personnel to be taken from the respective divisions and the ensuing gaps to be filled with 'willing helpers', which unintentionally resulted in a strong intermixing in immobile German fortress divisions, weakening their already debilitated fighting strength.[23] The political impulse of Russian volunteers – that is, anti-Bolshevism – had no value on the Western Front.

Loyalty among unarmed 'willing helpers' was somewhat stronger, at least from the German perspective. Their permanent attachment to German troop formations created a lasting emotional bond that was not so easy to sever. But the transfer or exchange of divisions from the Eastern to the Western Front meant that they, too, were soon scattered throughout all of Europe. The majority of them, however, remained in the baggage trains and rearward units on the Eastern Front. As late as April 1945, 15,000 Soviet 'willing helpers' were assembled in Norway for deployment in the Vlasov Army. As it was too difficult to transport them to southern Germany, they were integrated into German units as armed volunteers.

The position 'general of the Eastern troops' was renamed 'general of the volunteer units' in May 1944, signalling the intent of some army leaders at the start of the last year of the war to lend greater support to the Vlasov movement. ROA propaganda courses were now organized in areas close to the front as well. In June 1944, Hitler was still assuming that after successfully warding off the invasion in the west more than 30 divisions could be transferred to the Eastern Front and go on the offensive there once again. From this perspective there was no need for a Russian Liberation Army.

The war took a different course, however, leading to the catastrophic collapse of Army Group Centre with the start of the Soviet summer offensive on 22 June 1944. In no time the Wehrmacht was virtually thrown back to its starting position, losing all the ground it had gained since launching Operation Barbarossa in 1941. There were two events that gave the Vlasov movement a sudden boost. First, with the Wehrmacht being beaten back, a large number of Russian units and auxiliary troops had reached the border of the Reich, raising the question of their further use. Second, with the failed assassination attempt on 20 July, Heinrich Himmler became commander-in-chief of the reserve army and thus became a key figure in the organization of the army.

The result was that the Reichsführer SS was willing to receive General Vlasov – whom a year earlier he had called a 'swine' – for talks in Prague. Ideological reservations about deploying armed 'non-Germanic' volunteers had long since been abandoned in the thinning ranks of the Waffen SS and police. If the SS was meanwhile recruiting anyone it could get its hands on, the ambitions of the army could no longer be ignored. Vlasov presented extensive plans to build up ten infantry divisions, a tank regiment, several reserve brigades, an independent air force and an officer-training school within a year. This probably sounded utopian to Himmler, especially considering that he had to use his own remaining weapon reserves to raise the new Volksgrenadier divisions.

Given the enemy's superior strength of up to 500 divisions, a Vlasov Army of these proportions could not have changed the course of the war. Apparently the general was not concerned about saving Hitler's Eastern Front. It is likely he was aiming to create a military basis to survive the inevitable downfall of the Third Reich. The whole world was banking on the fragile anti-Hitler coalition collapsing, and why should an anti-Communist Vlasov Army not be a potential partner of the Western Powers, just as the latter had come to the aid of the Whites on Russian soil in the civil war at the end of World War I?

Time was of the essence, however. If he wanted to build up combat-ready units fast, he had to concentrate the already existing, albeit heterogeneous Russian troops under his command. This quickly proved to be a virtually impossible task. Vlasov's talks with Major-General Boris A. Smyslovsky did not result in any agreement. The Russian *émigré* leader and former captain in the Imperial Guards had been promoted by the OKH as an alternative to Vlasov. In 1941, he set up a Russian battalion on the northern front and, in April 1944, he was given the task of combining 12 Eastern battalions into a division.

By early 1945, Smyslovsky had about 6,000 men under his command and called himself commander of the 1st Russian National Army, troops made up of former Tsarist officers in exile and very young recruits. In April–May 1945, they fled to Liechtenstein, the officers heading to Australia from there and the homesick youths back home.

Émigré Russians in 1944 could not relate to Vlasov's political slogans. The former Soviet general was too much of a Bolshevist for them. It was therefore unclear to which formation the Russian Defence Corps – a unit stationed in Serbia and likewise made up mainly of emigrants – was assigned. The same applied to the Cossack cavalry in northern Yugoslavia. General Krasnov, the legendary civil war hero, refused to co-ordinate his troops with Vlasov's ROA in early 1945. Not only was there a clash of generations but also of worldviews.[25] General Pannwitz had to exert a good deal of pressure to create an organizational network in March 1945. The non-Russian national units categorically refused to co-operate.

Perhaps Vlasov's claim to be able to recruit a large number of volunteers from the millions of Soviet prisoners of war and forced labourers was nothing more than an illusion.[26] There were indeed some new recruits after his propagandists appeared in German camps, since many prisoners feared the wrath of Stalin or simply wanted to escape the mass deaths in German captivity which increased as the end of the war approached. But Vlasov and his staff were especially lacking the officers needed to set up the first three divisions, which Himmler, for his part, considered realistic. Only if they proved their worth would the Reichsführer SS and the commanders of the reserve army contemplate creating further divisions.

Interned Russian soldiers with auxiliary police and firemen in Liechtenstein, 1945.

Vlasov, at any rate, was allowed to reappear in person at public rallies in Prague and Berlin, conjuring up for the international press the phantom Russian army which was to take up arms with the Germans in the fight against Bolshevism. In the Prague Manifesto of 14 November 1944, he proclaimed the creation of a Committee for the Liberation of the Peoples of Russia along with a 14-Point Programme with 'progressive, social-democratic' ideas – without the requisite anti-Semitic passages Himmler wanted, and without even mentioning Hitler. Goebbels expected to profit from the campaign, having long since pleaded for more political warfare and relying to this end on anti-Communism as the most effective bait to win the support of the Western Powers.

On 28 January 1945, two weeks after the start of the Soviet Vistula-Oder Offensive and at a time when the Red Army was about to pounce on Berlin, Hitler appointed Vlasov 'supreme commander of Russian armed forces'. The ROA was now at least nominally an ally of the German Reich.[27] Off the record, though, Hitler was true to his principles: 'Vlasov is nothing'.[28] Former Soviet officers dominated its staff positions. Among the few *émigrés* were members of the Cossack movement. On paper and in official decrees, a flourishing organization and competence centre had developed in which ideas were born, plans were forged, hectic activities unfolded and dreams of equality and camaraderie were dreamt. The reality was much more sober. Thus, for example, at Nuremberg Central Station, a Russian captain from Vlasov's bodyguard was shot on the spot by a sergeant from the station patrol during an altercation with German Luftwaffe officers who refused to give him a proper seat. The perpetrator went unpunished.[29]

The Army General Staff ordered the creation of the first Russian division as soon as late November 1944. The 600th Infantry Division (Russian), under the command of Colonel Bunyachenko, was assembled at the Münsingen troop training grounds in Württemberg. The remnants of the Kaminski Brigade – which even the SS refused after the atrocities it committed in Warsaw – were used as a foundation for the division. Himmler thus abandoned his experiment of a 29th and 30th Waffen Grenadier Division of the SS (Russian No. 1 and No. 2). A few battalions of the Eastern Army were also attached to it. Turning this motley assortment of troops into a combat-ready unit was not an easy task for Vlasov's officers, especially with the Germans insisting on their rapid deployment at the imperilled Oder line. The division was fully activated by 10 February 1945, despite extremely difficult circumstances. The planned second division of the ROA, the 650th Infantry Division (Russian), was merely an assemblage of former Soviet prisoners of war armed with nothing but handguns. The third division did not make it past the formation of a training staff, whereas the establishment of an officer-training school and an air force was still virtually on the drawing board.

Thus, even in the Wehrmacht's final days Vlasov had access to only a small minority of the Russian volunteers fighting on the German side. Apart from the 20,000 men of the 1st Division (ROA), another 30,000 men in various formations were under his command. Several so-called Panzerjagd or 'tank-hunter' units of the ROA assigned to German units were partly disarmed by their German 'comrades' in April. As early as 9 February, a small, select group of volunteers was pulled out to support the German attack on the Soviet bridgehead near Wriezen an der Oder. The combat group's fighting vigour even earned the praise of Himmler. Grenadier Regiment 1604 (Russian), previously used as occupying troops in Denmark, was withdrawn and held its ground in a northern sector of the Oder Front.

The march-off of the 1st Division (ROA) from Württemberg to the Oder Front in March 1945 was not without inner resistance. Some Russian officers preferred to march towards Switzerland instead of – predictably – serving as 'cannon fodder' for the Germans. On 27 March, the division was supposed to support an attack north of Frankfurt an der Oder. But the venture ended in failure, without the Russians' participation. The Germans needed a visible Russian success they could use for propaganda purposes. They also believed that the division, deployed on its own, could not be expected to fight to the end. The entire ROA as a unified formation would have to be at its disposal, because if the 1st Division suffered a disaster, the overall project of building up the army would be doomed to failure.

Thus a new assault plan with more favourable conditions was sought and ultimately found: taking out a small Soviet bridgehead south of Fürstenberg. Russian staff officers, of course, deemed the combat mission 'madness'. Given the imminent German collapse, they had long since been thinking about gathering the various parts of the ROA and the Cossack cavalry corps in Austria and Bohemia, where they were most likely to make contact with the US Army. Being taken prisoner by Soviet troops was something Russian volunteers must have feared more than the Germans. But Vlasov recognized that he had to make a symbolic gesture towards the Germans, at least for the time being. Withdrawing from the Eastern Front without a fight was unthinkable under the circumstances, however low the fighting spirit of his Russian soldiers may have been. For them it was important to show their morale and escape with the fewest casualties possible. The 7th Army provided the 1st Division with unusually heavy fire support. On 13 April 1945, Operation April Weather was

At the 1st Division in Münsingen: Sakharov, Bunyachenko, Vlasov.

to begin. After some initial successes, the Russian regiments became stuck in the Soviet defence system. Despite German threats, Divisional Commander Bunyachenko used his cunning and deceit to disengage his unit from the front and get them into Bohemia.

They did actually succeed in gathering together the various parts of the ROA. The Germans could do nothing but observe their movements. The Vlasov units were only willing to fight if attacked. Contacts were made with the Czech resistance, which was planning an uprising against the Germans to liberate the capital, Prague, before the Red Army moved in. The poorly organized and insufficiently armed civilian uprising was hoping to receive support from the ROA, whereas the latter hoped to be taken into the Allied camp this way. On 6 May, the Russians had their first engagements with their hitherto German allies and succeeded in taking Prague the following day despite stubborn German resistance. The very same day, Czech communists, who had originally approved the alliance between the ROA and the military command of the National Council, declared the Vlasov men to be criminals and traitors.

With the backing-off of the National Council and the realization that the Americans, who had already advanced to Pilsen (Plzeň), would not come to their aid, Bunyachenko had to stop fighting and find a safe haven in the face of rapidly approaching Soviet forces. Parley delegates made their way to American lines, which were preparing to take the 'White Russian Corps' captive. Only some sections of the ROA managed to fight their way to the Americans. As late as 12 May, four days after the armistice, countless units were still roaming around in no man's land, hoping to find asylum with the Americans. But the latter did not want to burden themselves politically, and played Vlasov and his staff into Soviet hands. Numerous officers and soldiers were shot to death while being taken prisoner by the Red Army.

About 20,000 Russians were in American captivity after the end of the war. Their leaders were hoping to be politically active again and declared their willingness to take up arms immediately against the Bolshevist menace.[30] In Carinthia, the British handed over the Cossacks with extreme brutality.[31] By 1946, in line with the agreements reached at Yalta, they had surrendered to the USSR more than 32,000 Russian prisoners of war who had fought in German uniforms. The Americans were more hesitant with regard to forced deportations, but gradually followed suit, though not without generously overlooking numerous escapes, sometimes even aiding them.

The ultimate fate of Vlasov soldiers, Eastern legionnaires and 'willing helpers' was unknown for decades. Vlasov himself and his officers were put before Soviet tribunals as traitors and executed. It was known that the majority of the rank and file had landed in the 'Gulag Archipelago', the prison camps of Siberia. They were part of the millions of Soviet prisoners of war and 'Eastern workers' who were put through 'filter camps' upon returning to their homeland. Even the overwhelming majority of Russian POWs who had refused to collaborate with the Germans were considered suspicious by Stalin. Most of them, however, got off with mild sentences and short 'probation' periods,[32] whereas the Vlasovites were generally punished more severely, the survivors being stigmatized for the rest of their lives.

The political objective of free national self-determination, for the sake of which many Russians were willing to fight on the side of the Germans against Stalinism, was only possible after 1990. Most of them did not swear an oath to Hitler, and had no need to either, since the Führer wanted nothing to do with them. And yet they still formed the largest group of non-German auxiliaries on the Eastern Front. Their military usefulness for the Germans was not restricted to the brief deployment of the ill-starred Vlasov Army in the final days of the war. Without the help of Russian volunteers in varied formations, the Wehrmacht would have reached its limit and could not have continued the war in the East after the disaster of Stalingrad.

20

The Caucasus

In the early nineteenth century, the Caucasus was not much more than a geographical term to most Germans, one that more educated citizens associated with Antiquity. When the conquest of these mountains and their foothills by the Tsarist Army turned into a protracted, decades-long struggle, an interest in the region was gradually awakened, along with a sense of astonishment at its cultural, religious and social diversity. The image of a wild and romantic Caucasus emerged, inhabited by warlike mountain peoples who resisted Russian subjugation. Sympathies varied, though they tended to be with the Christian Cossacks, the Georgians and other pro-Russian ethnic groups. With rapprochement between the German Reich and the Ottoman Empire in the late nineteenth century, there was increasing interest in the Muslim areas of the Caucasus as well.

Strategic considerations played an ever greater role here. According to geostrategic notions of the time, the Caucasus was a bridge to the 'heartland' – to Central Asia, the centre of world-controlling forces. On the eve of World War I, a 'big game' was emerging between the major powers for influence in this region. The Germans came up with adventurous ideas of a possible diversionary operation via Turkey, Persia and Afghanistan to strike their future opponent Russia in its 'soft underbelly' and Great Britain in its 'crown jewel', India. The German thrust with the help of local forces was to push back Russian influence in the region as well as British positions in the Near East, not least of all the new oil fields of its two great-power adversaries in Caucasian Baku and Persia. 'Inciting' Islam seemed a useful means to achieving this end. Bavarian officer Oskar Niedermayer had been scouting the terrain before World War I and became the operation's mastermind during the conflict.[1]

With the collapse of the Tsarist Empire in 1917 and the dictated peace of Brest-Litovsk, it seemed possible, in 1918, for Germany to open up the Caucasus from the Russian side as well. A Mohammedan Legion had already been formed from the more than 100,000 Muslim prisoners of war in Germany and a Georgian Legion had been formed in Turkey from Russian prisoners of war. German troops finally reached Georgia and entered a race to Baku with British units. Niedermeyer, who had settled down in Kabul, suggested mobilizing the small Russian-German minority in the Caucasus to have a base for advancing to Persia. There was not enough time, however, to put these audacious plans into practice or to exert any lasting influence on the Caucasian peoples. The rapid collapse of the Central Powers in the autumn of 1918 meant the end, for the time being, of Germany's intense interest in the military potential of the Caucasus and Near East.

In the years of civil war, the anti-Communist regime and tribal rule in the Caucasus could not prevail against the Moscow central government's Red Army. And yet the conflict of nationalities remained a constant source of unrest in the region, which not even Stalinism was able to eliminate. The Caucasus became a laboratory for human experiments of re-education and 'ethnic cleansing' under totalitarianism; a culture of excessive violence emerged.[2] At the same time, the Germans changed their course. Niedermayer spent the 1920s in Moscow as the representative of General Hans von Seeckt, chief of German Army Command, and directed the Reichwehr's secret rearmament measures in Russia. His vision, which found some supporters in national conservative circles, was of a German-Soviet Russian co-operation which, relying on the Caucasus, would mainly still act as a counterweight to the British world empire. Thus, the voices of prominent Caucasian and Turkic-Tatar political *émigrés* from the Soviet Union met with no response in Germany. Hundreds of Georgian officers, for example, served in the Polish Army instead in the period between the wars.[3]

In the heterogeneous world of ideas of National Socialism, the image of warlike, fanatical anti-Communist mountain peoples was interwoven with modern Pan-Turanism, which gave rise to ideas of reviving the German-Turkish axis but inevitably collided with the interests of Christian peoples in the region, such as the Armenians and the Georgians. With Hitler's rise to power in 1933, at any rate, the old national conservative ideas of a German-Soviet power bloc receded into the background. The vociferous anti-Communist thrust of German foreign policy up until 1939 did, however, promote an interest in finding potential allies in the Caucasus. The Reich Security Main Office of Himmler had been gathering information since 1936 at a so-called Caucasian Liaison Office (Kaukasische Vertrauensstelle) led by the Georgian Lado Akhmeteli with his staff of experts. There were also a number of Georgians and Tatars in the Foreign Policy Office of the NSDAP under party ideologue and later Reich Minister for the Occupied Eastern Territories Alfred Rosenberg, as well as in the training centres of military intelligence, where as of 1938 they were prepared for deployment as partisans against the USSR.

The divided and mutually hostile organizations of the Caucasian Turkic-Tatar emigration had already begun to approach the fascist movement of Europe. With the Hitler-Stalin Pact, however, they were given orders not to disturb the official foreign policy of the Reich. Their activities were prohibited in occupied Poland as well, and a year later in France. Emigrants from the Caucasus were barely taken into consideration in planning Operation Barbarossa. Here, too, German policy-makers were playing it by ear and acting inconsistently. The Caucasus, of course, played a prominent role in military and economic planning with a view to its strategically vital oil reserves. But with the USSR expected to collapse quite rapidly, there were no plans for engaging the military assistance of Caucasian and Oriental peoples.

The construction of a Reich Commissariat Caucasia was part of the longer-term plans adopted in April 1941 by the later Reich Ministry for the Occupied Eastern Territories. In line with Rosenberg's concept of a 'decomposition' of the Russian empire, the demand for a certain autonomy for the diverse ethnic groups in the region gained in significance. He imagined instrumentalizing the Russian Cossacks at the foothills of the Caucasus as well as the Christian and Muslim peoples, despite their all being viewed as 'alien to the race' (*rassefremd*) and therefore not equal-ranking partners.

Old clichés were not unimportant in this political fermentation process. The general warning given to German troops to beware of 'Asian' Soviet soldiers – because they are 'obscure, unpredictable, underhanded and unfeeling'[4] – was interpreted by the SS at first as authorization to shoot the very captured Red Army soldiers who might have been the most likely to sign up for the fight against Stalinism.[5] Hitler's indifferent notion of the Caucasus, Rosenberg's policy of 'decomposition', the Wehrmacht's falling back on the experiences of World War I, and not least of all the presence of various political *émigré* groups in the apparatus of the Third Reich created more favourable conditions on the whole for the Caucasian and Turkic-Tatar peoples than for the Russians. But the racial delusions and stereotypes such as 'Asian subhumanism' were always there, and were a frequent cause of irritation in propaganda as well as in the constant internal debates about the 'right' course to take in Nazi Eastern policy.

Even in implementing the murderous anti-Semitic policy of extermination, there were contradictions and sometimes absurd problems of definition in the case of the Caucasus. Thus, for example, in the initial phase of the war in the East, thousands of Muslim Caucasians, Turkestans and Tatars were shot as purported Jews simply because they were circumcised. Experts had to be called in to instruct SS troops about local customs and religious practices in order to stop the mass murder of Soviet Muslims. Military intelligence and the Eastern Ministry had to take considerable pains to prevent such 'special treatment' of Caucasians for racial-ideological reasons. Some conflicting objectives, however, were unresolvable for Nazi ideology. The existence of smaller tribes in the Crimea and in the Caucasus which had converted to Judaism centuries before reduced the idea of racism to absurdity. The respective Einsatzgruppe of the Security Service did not know if it was allowed to kill the Turkic-Tatar population or not, because it could not clearly identify their origin. It was finally decided to murder entire villages in the Caucasus in 1942 and to order the so-called Mountain Jews to wear the yellow star as the preliminary stage to their being exterminated. Only in December, when the Wehrmacht began its withdrawal from the Caucasus, did the Eastern Ministry and military intelligence succeed in putting an end to discrimination against the Mountain Jews.[6]

The Georgians, on the other hand, were presumed to be descendants of the Germanic Goths because of their 'Nordic appearance', whereas the Armenians were generally subject to the same prejudices as the Jews and were even suspected of having considerable Jewish 'racial admixtures'. That the SS was not willing to set aside its racism toward these peoples until 1944 for the sake of winning recruits for the 'final struggle' shows how strongly anchored this ideological madness was. An important counterweight to this was Otto Bräutigam, a career diplomat who lived in Tbilisi and Baku and was the last German consul general in Batumi in 1940–1. By 1942, he had succeeded in his efforts to institute a more constructive policy towards the Caucasian peoples in his function as head of the Policy Department (Grundsatzabteilung) in the Eastern Ministry and an expert on the Caucasus.[7]

As with the recruitment of Russians, the Germans were comparatively late in harnessing the military potential of the Caucasus and Far East. Here, too, when the Germans began their invasion of the USSR, there were initially thousands of emigrants residing in all parts of Europe who volunteered to join the fight against Stalinism in the hope of securing future independence for their nations.[8] These volunteers were registered in July 1941, but not accepted in the German armed forces. The Nazis refused for political reasons to fall back on former White Guardsmen and Russian elites. Their only interest for the time being was in forming auxiliary troops from Soviet prisoners of war and defectors.

Thus two special formations were created under the auspices of military intelligence. In October 1941, 700 Caucasians were selected from among the POWs in Poltava. This so-called Bergmann Special Unit was deployed in 1942 for reconnaissance and diversionary purposes as part of the German advance into the region, and attained a maximum strength of 2,900 men. Its commander was Lieutenant of the Reserve Professor Theodor Oberländer, who had already gained experience with the Ukrainians and was one of the most active minds in the internal discussion about the focus of Nazi occupation policy. He was discharged from the Wehrmacht in 1943. Parallel to this was the so-called 450th Turk Battalion, created by the Wehrmacht from Turkic-Tatar soldiers and under the command of China expert Major Andreas Mayer-Mader. Both battalions retained their special status within the Wehrmacht throughout the course of the war.[9] Mayer-Mader, the 'Chinese major', was criticized internally for his maverick leadership style, soon lost his post, and tried in 1943 to set up a 1st East Muslim Regiment within the Waffen SS. This enigmatic figure fell out once again with his superiors and disappeared under mysterious circumstances in 1944.

As of August 1941, commissions were charged with the task of setting up regular national 'legions' and were to make sure, in the interests of the Eastern Ministry, that the various nationalities in the POW camps were kept apart from each other. Prominent Turkish generals made a case on their visit to Berlin in October 1941 for the fair treatment of Turkic-Tatar prisoners, which prompted Rosenberg in December to ask Hitler for permission to set up 'Turkish' legions.[10]

A Georgian soldier of the
Bergmann Special Unit.

When German operational objectives were not achieved in the East and it became clear that the thrust into the Caucasian oil fields, of such paramount importance to the war effort, could only be undertaken the following summer, the Führer, on 22 December 1941, approved the creation of a Turkestani, a Georgian and a Caucasian Mohammedan legion, the latter being later divided into an Azerbaijani and a North Caucasian legion. A special legion was likewise created for the Volga Tatars in autumn 1942. The 444th Security Division in the southern Ukraine had already created hundred-man units of Caucasian and Turkic-Tatar origin in November 1941 on its own initiative to combat the growing threat of partisans. Their consolidation into a regiment – called the 444th Turkic Battalion – reinforced the Security Service at the mouth of the Dnieper.

The military training of the legions began in January 1942 in occupied Poland. After being inspected, the recruits were officially discharged from captivity, clothed and treated like German soldiers. The units were placed under a German 'commander of the Eastern legions' and assumed training duties as a stationary organization in the General Government. Their job was to form combat-ready field battalions for deployment at the front. The legions were constantly redivided and renamed, and strict attention was paid to even the most subtle differences between nationalities. Hence, the 450th Turkestani Infantry Battlaion, in addition to its staff, was comprised, for example, of the 1st Company (Kyrgyz), the 2nd Company (Uzbeks and a platoon of Tajiks), the 3rd Company (Kazakhs), the 4th Company (Turkmens and a platoon of Eastern Tatars) and an MG company with one platoon each of Kyrgyz, Uzbeks and Kazakhs. The anti-tank, sapper and mortar platoons were each mixed. The German system made sure that no nationality felt disadvantaged.[11]

The Supreme Commander began with the Führer's order that the Wehrmacht was to win the friendship of the people of Caucasia. This is why the Caucasian people need to be treated in a special way. The population of Caucasia includes the Russians living there. The preconditions are there for a positive political development in occupied Caucasian territory. Army Group A is the most forward-deployed of all German army groups. We stand at the gates of the Islamic world. What

Legionnaires in a Turkestani infantry regiment with camels.

we do here and how we act here will radiate all the way to Iran, to India, even to the frontiers of China. We have to be aware of the long-range effects of all our actions. The best inward and outward propaganda is a satisfied and hopeful populace which knows that a better future awaits it than under the rule of the Tsar and Stalin. The population must know that we are doing our best for them even if we cannot give them all that they wish. This is impossible given the conditions of war. The population must realize that we have the good will to help them, and that we are helping in little ways too, within our means …. We cannot, on principle, differentiate between mountain tribes, Cossacks and Russians. We need them all. The Russians are no exception, because in their case we are dealing with especially valuable human beings, who once came to the occupied areas as an elite, as colonists. Back then they were pioneers, today they are locals, and no longer stand in contrast to the native population. As far as the Communists are concerned who have stayed behind in the occupied Caucasian territory, it is necessary to keep an eye on them. But we have to beware of seeing ghosts, and keep in mind that the population spied and informed on each other in the long years of Bolshevist rule. We must try to educate these remaining Communists and influence them through hard facts and better living conditions. (From the report on an address by Colonel-General Ewald von Kleist, Supreme Commander of Army Group A)[12]

According to army regulations, the members of the legions were considered 'volunteer fighters for the liberation of their homeland from Bolshevism and for the freedom of their faith'. 'They are not foreign legions. Only by awakening idealism, a sense of responsibility and of honour can the legions be made into useful units.'[13] They were therefore not to be confused with the French Foreign Legion. Nevertheless, the command posts were exclusively filled by Germans, who had orders to treat the legionnaires as brothers-in-arms and to respect their national peculiarities. We can assume that the Caucasian and Turkic-Tatar minorities in particular were motivated by the understandable need to move in a familiar national context while in German captivity or under German occupation more than they were by the anti-Bolshevism that linked them to the Germans.[14] The Wehrmacht, for its part, though trying to bolster the mood of the legionnaires for deployment at the front with the use of anti-Communist slogans, was relatively restrained in its political propaganda measures otherwise, especially considering that many of the so-called 'Turkos' were illiterate and could only communicate in their native language. Moreover, the sympathy and understanding of German cadre personnel for other mentalities and traditions was not always sufficient to prevent discord, a lack of discipline and desertion.

> The manner of training and commanding Turkos is significantly different from that of German soldiers; e.g. if a Turko is yelled at he becomes confused, because he generally doesn't understand the language, becomes stubborn and counters with Asian passive resistance, which can and must be broken with patience – the man has to repeat something 10 times till he's got it down, and once he has it down properly he needs to be praised for it. ... But one thing is for sure: never will the Turkos rebel against their German leaders, however imperfect these may be, and defect to the Russians, because they know all too well what the Russians have in store for them as traitors to their fatherland, and no amount of agitation will persuade them of the contrary. They cling to their German superiors because they are convinced that German leaders are their only salvation. Besides, they trust in the Germans' promises wholly. ... The Turkos are in many respects still rather primitive people: thus, e.g., when they hear good news they clap their hands for joy, regardless of the fact that they are standing at attention. Punishing them for this would be wrong, because they would not understand it. 16.) They have the greatest interest for everything German, and the greatest wish of every Turko soldier is to go to Germany some day. Many, especially craftsmen, have often asked if they can work in Germany after the war. (From a progress report on the training of Turkic volunteers)[15]

Having their own national insignia on Wehrmacht uniforms – whose rank insignia, too, were different from their German counterparts – was the only concession the Germans were willing to make. The battalions were sent to the front separately, and for this reason alone could not be considered the basis for future Georgian, Armenian or other such armies. By late autumn, the OKH had deployed a first wave of 15 reinforced field battalions, Army Group South being badly in need of troop reinforcements for its thrust into the Caucasus.

After sometimes extremely brief training and with inadequate equipment and supplies, these troops did not always live up to expectations, but did generally fight better than their respective national units in the Red Army. Not without good reason were they afraid of being shot if captured by Red Army soldiers. Red Army loudspeaker propaganda urged them to desert, and pointed out that in failing to do so revenge would be taken on their women and children. And yet the number of desertions was low. There was no lack of tension, however, between the various nationalities on the German side. There were even some downright clashes between Caucasians and Russian Cossacks.[16]

The Caucasians fought better when side by side with the Germans than when they were put into mixed-ethnic battalions and were left to their own devices. At an attack to mop up the Popova Ridge on 30 October 1942, for instance, the 125th Infantry Division deployed German alarm units and an anti-tank company in close co-operation with four Slovak companies of the Mobile Brigade and a subordinate company of the 800th North Caucasian Infantry Battalion, and this with such success that the enemy was driven away and the front was cleared.[17]

At the command post, I ran into Major Rank (Rank Group), battalion commander of the 805th and captain in the Medical Corps. One hundred and forty men, who took Tukhu Mountain – close to Verkhniy-Zhemgala – a few days ago in three attempts, sat on top of the wooded mountain. ... Around 11 o'clock, reports began coming in that the Russians had surrounded the mountain. The forest terrain is completely broken there. ... Three people brought in three Russian prisoners, dropped them off, were excited, and went straight back to the mountain. You know already that the battalion suffered heavy losses up till that day. ... The mood was not at all gloomy among the Azerbaijani, although their footwear was quite poor, some of their shoes had no soles, some of them had no socks, and they occasionally had to go a day without rations. ... My overall impression from my last trip to the front is that these people are indeed quite useful. But they need the support of Germans. Every platoon and every group needs a German NCO or corporal. The Russians have probably learned from experience that the machine guns and heavy artillery in Caucasian units should be operated by Russians. With more German personnel, the combat strength of these units will be quite different. If we do things like before, we will waste too quickly the valuable support of this human material. (Report on the deployment of the 805th Azerbaijani Infantry Battalion on 3 December 1942 at Tukhu Hill)[18]

The 804th Azerbaijani Infantry Battalion.

The Wehrmacht extended training in the General Government for the second wave of divisions so that 21 of the more battle-tested battalions went to the Ukraine in the spring of 1943. By the end of the year, a third wave with 17 field battalions followed.

All in all, the staff of the Eastern legions in occupied Poland alone provided the Wehrmacht with 53 field battalions of about 53,000 men. Added to this was a substantial number of smaller construction and supply units comprised of legionnaires not entirely fit for duty. The total number of volunteers deployed on the side of the Germans is estimated at least at 110,000 Caucasians, 35,000 Volga Tatars and 110,000 Turkestans.[19] There were special units made up of Crimean Tatars (20,000) and Kalmyks (5,000), the latter in a cavalry corps used to secure the weak flank of the 6th Army facing the steppe, towards Astrakhan.

Crimean Tatar units were not raised in Poland but close to home in the Crimea. Almost all of the able-bodied men of this minority offered their services to the Germans in 1942 (about 20,000 men, twice as many as were conscripted into the Red Army). The 11th German Army found them to be a valuable reinforcement for securing the hinterland and combating partisans. Smaller groups of Tatars were directly assigned to most German units and were usually better off than their Romanian allies. Larger combat formations, however, were only used by the Security Service in rearward areas. Alongside these Schutzmannschaft battalions, the bulk of the Crimean Tatars formed a local self-defence in their villages. The attempt to create a Waffen Mountain Brigade of the SS (Tatar No. 1) from these auxiliary police battalions following the evacuation of the Crimea in 1944 failed, as the units fell apart being so far away from home.

More impressive was the deployment of Kalmyks.[20] With the capture of Elista on 26 August 1942, the 16th Motorized Infantry Division attempted to control the huge steppe area in its security zone with the help of local forces. After building a local Kalmyk self-defence, which defended itself against the requisition of its livestock by the Red Army, the Germans called upon the people to join them in a common struggle against Bolshevism, creating volunteer cavalry squadrons for reconnaissance and smaller combat missions. A larger formation under German command with upwards of 5,000 men was then formed which eventually followed the Wehrmacht upon its withdrawal from the region.

More Kalmyks served in the Wehrmacht's Kalmyk cavalry corps than in comparable units of the Red Army. The Kalmyks, led by the charismatic former intelligence officer Dr Rudolf Otto Doll, provided valuable support in 1943 in protecting the coast of the Sea of Azov, in combating partisans in the Dniepropetrovsk area, then in Poland in 1944. 'Of some use as a fighting unit at the front due to their courage and hatred for Bolshevism and as enemies of the exterminators of the Kalmyk people', was the German assessment.[21]

The Kalmyks took their families and livestock with them, so the Germans tried to find a new settlement area for them. Overrun by the Red Army near Lublin in July 1944, the remainder of the unit received the protection of the

SS, replenished itself from the POW camps, and was again overrun by the Red Army in January 1945, which this time destroyed them. Their family members were evacuated to Bavaria, a newly activated cavalry regiment was attached to the Cossack cavalry corps of Pannwitz stationed in Croatia and shared their fate, being handed over to the Red Army at the end of the war.

Whereas the Wehrmacht was able to recruit Crimean Tatars and Kalmyks in the occupied territories of these nations, they could not do so when entering the Caucasus, having no direct contact with most of the ethnic groups there. They became stuck in the outlying areas. But they found enough volunteers from among the three major ethnic groups there – the Armenians, Georgians and Azerbeijani – who, as prisoners of war, were willing to co-operate with the Germans. And they probably could have found many more volunteers had the Wehrmacht succeeded in advancing into these countries. An anti-Soviet uprising throughout the entire region was hindered by numerous NKVD units. In Azerbeijan alone about 32,000 'unreliable' persons were supposedly 'exterminated' in 1942.[22]

The Caucasian Turkic-Tatar volunteers were not permanent reinforcements of the Wehrmacht, because when the Germans withdrew from the region some of the formations disappeared,[23] and the combat efficiency, too, of the field battalions led by German cadre personnel diminished with every kilometre westwards. Thus quite a few units that had fought valiantly up until then had to be disbanded, their volunteers being allotted in smaller groups to German regiments. The Armenians were particularly unreliable, with an increasing number of mutinies and desertions among them in 1942–3. The Georgians, too, tended to defect to the partisans for the slightest reason, whereas the Muslim regiments were more dependable. Hence, in 1943–4, most of the legions were withdrawn from the Eastern Front and spread throughout occupied Europe. There they frequently established contact with local resistance movements.

The Caucasians and Oriental peoples had little military value for the Germans on the Western Front, their first enemy contact often rendering them useless. The last mutiny was by the 822nd Georgian Infantry Battalion, which was supposed to be transferred from the Dutch island of Texel to the front in April 1945. The uprising – long in the making – of 750 legionnaires began with the Georgians killing 200 German cadre personnel and unpopular superiors. The 2,000 SS soldiers who landed on the island eventually suppressed it with extreme brutality, but nevertheless failed to break it before the Canadian landing.

General Köstring (right) talking with a Turkestani NCO.

The formation of military units from the southern fringes of the USSR was the army's preserve between 1942 and 1944. Count Stauffenberg, in the Organization Department of the OKH, played a leading role.[24] He saw to it that a series of key positions was filled by officers who, as Russian experts in the army, did not approve of the official anti-Russian course and saw the creation of so-called Eastern troops and 'Eastern ethnic' (*ostvölkisch*) volunteer units as a chance to achieve a political and military watershed on the Eastern Front. The most important appointment was that of Cavalry General Köstring, the former German military attaché in Moscow, first to the position of 'commissioner-general for Caucasian affairs' (1942), then of 'general of the Eastern troops' (1943) and 'general of the volunteer units with the chief of the General Staff of the Army' (1944).

Stauffenberg was instrumental in the Turkic-Tatars, Caucasians and Cossacks being allowed as early as 1942 to fight in the Wehrmacht as 'co-combatants with equal rights', even on the front lines – the only nations of the USSR granted this privilege. Russians, Byelorussians, Ukrainians and Balts, by contrast, were consigned to duty in rearward areas. Stauffenberg was able to attain this special status in August 1942, arguing that the field battalions of the Eastern troops at this point in time were the only operative reserve of the High Command in the Eastern theatre of war and that their build-up therefore had to be accelerated.[25] Stauffenberg was also involved behind the scenes in the decision to reactivate Oskar Ritter von Niedermayer, thus consciously re-establishing a direct link with a prominent figure from World War I and the Reichswehr era, a period not yet contaminated by the murderous racial ideology of the ruling National Socialists. Niedermayer left his chair at the university in Berlin in 1942 and, as a general, was given the task of taking the staff of the disbanded 162nd Infantry Division and creating the framework for deploying Turkic-Tatar and Caucasian units in a major formation. Niedermayer's plans were to deploy these troops east of the Caucasus, where he had operated successfully in World War I. The fusing together of heterogeneous units and the creation of a major formation proved to be a difficult task. Hence, the 162nd (Turk) Infantry Division, comprising about 35,000 men in late 1942 and stationed in the eastern Ukraine, did not see action in the area it was intended for, but following the disaster of Stalingrad was deployed in Yugoslavia in the fight against partisans. The division went under in Northern Italy in 1945.

The efforts of the SS to become involved in Oriental policy were not successful until 1944. A Volunteer Control Office East was formed in the summer of 1944, with separate Caucasian and 'East Turkish' offices. There were experts who complained about the relatively unpolitical course of the Wehrmacht and who saw an opportunity to weaken the enemy by revolutionizing the Turkic peoples, even if this meant abandoning their racial-ideological misgivings.[26] A Caucasian and an 'East Turkish armed unit' were thus formed to gather the remains of the legions commanded by the Wehrmacht up until then. Personnel was sought at first, however, among the members of SS auxiliary troops, as well as in POW camps and among the 'Eastern workers'. The two units were to comprise four regiments each, but were only partly assembled by the end of the war. All in all only 5,000 men were mobilized. Their military value was less than the positive political echo which the SS obtained in the national assemblies of the Caucasians and Turkic-Tatars. The units used to quell the Slovakian national uprising in late 1944 had a high rate of desertion. And yet the SS continued pushing its recruiting and deployment measures. The last volunteers were four Caucasians who signed up in April 1945 to help defend Berlin.[27]

Major in the General Staff Claus Count Schenk von Stauffenberg (left) and Major-General Oskar Ritter von Niedermayer (centre) with the staff of the 162nd (Turk) Division in the Ukraine, 27 September 1942.

The total number of Caucasians and Turkestans who fell fighting on the side of the Germans is estimated to be at least 100,000.[28] Presumably even more perished, when Stalin, in an act of vengeance, deported entire ethnic groups after reconquering these borderland areas of his empire. Immediately after 'liberation' of the northern Caucasus, all able-bodied men were forcefully recruited by the Red Army and – some with no uniforms or training – forced to take on well-fortified German machine-gun positions on the Taman Peninsula.[29] Then the NKVD troops arrived to cleanse the towns and villages of 'hostile elements'. Hundreds of thousands are said to have perished.[30] In Elista a proper bloodbath ensued. In 1943–4, in line with a resolution of the

Politburo, the Kalmyks, Karachays, Chechens, Ingush, Balkars and some of the Kabardins were deported from their ancestral homelands to Siberia or Central Asia.[31] Their autonomous republics were dissolved. Only in the 1950s were the survivors permitted to return to their homeland.

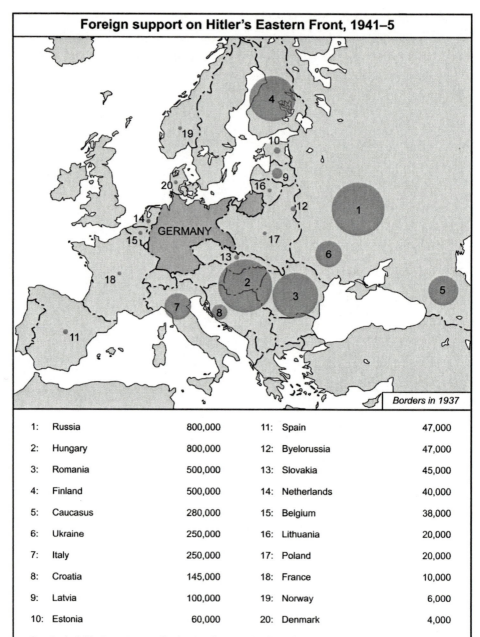

Foreign support on Hitler's Eastern Front, 1941–5

Borders in 1937

1:	Russia	800,000		11:	Spain	47,000
2:	Hungary	800,000		12:	Byelorussia	47,000
3:	Romania	500,000		13:	Slovakia	45,000
4:	Finland	500,000		14:	Netherlands	40,000
5:	Caucasus	280,000		15:	Belgium	38,000
6:	Ukraine	250,000		16:	Lithuania	20,000
7:	Italy	250,000		17:	Poland	20,000
8:	Croatia	145,000		18:	France	10,000
9:	Latvia	100,000		19:	Norway	6,000
10:	Estonia	60,000		20:	Denmark	4,000

See the individual country-specific chapters for more detailed information about these figures. The numbers refer to all the forces mobilized for German-allied troops, Wehrmacht, SS, police and local paramilitary units which fought on the side of the Germans against the Red Army during the entire period. Not taken into account are ethnic German conscripts, e.g. from Poland and Alsace-Lorraine, whose numbers on the Eastern Front cannot be determined. Most of the figures found in the sources and in the respective literature vary to some extent, particularly with regard to the Russians.

Concluding Remarks

What do the figures about the number of Hitler's foreign helpers on the Eastern Front tell us, figures which cannot be considered entirely accurate but are largely based on estimates? The sheer magnitude is impressive, at any rate. Even in the initial phase of the German-Soviet conflict, Wehrmacht allies and volunteers from throughout Europe amounted to nearly a million men (476,000 Finns, 325,685 Romanians, 45,000 Hungarians, 41,000 Slovaks and 43,000 foreign volunteers) as opposed to the 3 million Wehrmacht soldiers stationed on the Eastern Front. Whereas the average strength of the Wehrmacht sank to about 2.5 million in the ensuing years, the number of foreigners deployed increased by another million men. Most of the latter were former Soviet citizens who were prepared to fight on the side of the Germans against Bolshevism or to support the German struggle through auxiliary services.

These numbers force us to re-evaluate the military dimensions of this collaboration. To put it pointedly:

1. Without the inclusion of allied armies, which Hitler pursued rather unenthusiastically and without expecting very much, the Wehrmacht would never have made it to the gates of Moscow in 1941. The deployment of Finnish, Hungarian and Romanian conscripts enabled the Eastern Front to be expanded considerably to the north and south and be well covered. Out of a 2,000-kilometre-long front line, 600 kilometres were held by the Finns and another 600 kilometres by the Hungarians and Romanians. This allowed the Wehrmacht to concentrate the bulk of its Eastern Army in the central thrust towards Moscow. By tying up the main Soviet army in the Ukraine, mostly

thanks to Germany's allies, the Germans were able, near Kiev, to win the greatest battle of encirclement in history.

2. Without mobilizing additional allied forces, Hitler could not have carried out his new summer offensive towards the Volga and Caucasus in 1942. These allies secured the broad flank on the Volga and Don, enabling the risky advance towards the oil fields of the Caucasus. Hundreds of thousands of local volunteers supported the advancing Wehrmacht divisions as 'willing helpers' or in armed formations.

3. At the latest after the catastrophe of Stalingard, it was only with the aid of foreign helpers that the Wehrmacht could keep the Eastern Front from collapsing. Their most important role was in securing the hinterland and combating partisans. Thus in the Baltics alone 107 Schutzmannschaft battalions with 60,000 men were fighting partisans in 1943.[1] At the same time, they were still helping stabilize the Eastern Front in Finland and the Ukraine, sometimes in front-line units. The loss of Germany's biggest allies, Finland, Italy and Romania, was not as critical as it might have been, as German withdrawals in 1943–4 had effectively shortened the front. It was thanks to Hungary, his last ally, that Hitler could launch his final offensive on the Eastern Front at all, in the spring of 1945. Even during the last year of the war, the mobility of the Wehrmacht was not only dependent on fuel, but on nearly a million volunteers from the nations of Eastern Europe.

Also not to be overlooked is the fact that, as of 1942, it was the millions of foreign forced labourers and prisoners of war in Germany, as well as production in the hinterland of the Eastern Front, that provided the Wehrmacht with the necessary material resources in the first place to carry on a war of attrition against a superior foe for another three years. In 1944, in the final phase of the war, when the Nazis threw all of their ideological and racial prejudices to the wind and were merely recruiting cannon fodder, 763,000 men alone came from annexed and 'Germanized' territories (Alsace, Lorraine, Eupen-Malmedy and Polish Germans of category IV on the 'Volksliste'), in other words, 8 per cent of the Wehrmacht's actual strength.[2] If foreign soldiers and 'willing helpers' are included in the equation, the total number of non-German soldiers within the ranks of the Wehrmacht, Waffen SS, etc. was probably almost 20 per cent – most of them deployed on the Eastern Front, where their share was considerably higher.

Compulsory or Voluntary?

This political and moral dimension is difficult to define given the varied forms of foreign involvement and the changes that occurred throughout the course of the war. Whether the conscripted soldiers in Germany's allied armies marched to the East enthusiastically or not, very few of them fought there of their own free will. This presumably applies to most of the German soldiers as well. A politically motivated spirit of voluntarism was most likely to be found among the foreign legionnaires from Southern, Western and Northern Europe. But only a part of these belonged to the so-called Germanic volunteers to whom the SS gave priority in recruiting. The extent of other motives is hard to discern and probably quite individual in nature. Adventurism and right-wing-radical convictions are not to be excluded.

In the case of the peoples of Eastern Europe, the yearning for independence from the Russian empire and the experiences of Stalinism played a role. As hinterland or front-line areas they were immediately affected by the war in the East, were harassed by partisans and had to fear the wrath of Stalin. In parts of East-Central Europe, civil-war-like situations emerged along with disintegrating war societies where only the fight for survival counted. But even after the Germans retreated, and well into the postwar era, some larger military formations survived which continued to battle the Soviet system.

The Nazi policy of decomposition succeeded in giving nationalism in Eastern Europe an anti-Soviet strain and allowed the Nazis to harness this force for their own purposes. By the same token, however, it stirred up nationalist conflicts to the point of tearing each other to pieces, which ultimately limited its usefulness for the Nazi 'Crusade against Bolshevism'. It was true that anti-Bolshevism was the Nazis' strongest argument, but their racial ideology and ruthless policy of exploitation damaged their reputation and thus their chances of winning over the peoples of Eastern Europe to their cause.

On the 'battlefield of dictators', neither side was sparing in terms of harshness and brutality. Despite elaborate propaganda warfare, neither Stalin nor Hitler was interested in the hearts and minds of the people. Soviet ideology, at least, contained a promise for the future, which ultimately made the victorious Red Army somewhat more attractive, even though the 'liberators from Fascism' were hard on the heels of the 'liberators from Bolshevism' and failed to bring the people freedom. Stalin, unlike Hitler, set up only a small number of foreign volunteer units throughout the course of World War II. German prisoners of war, even if they joined the National Committee for a Free Germany, were never armed. The largest foreign unit was made up of Polish prisoners of war – a total of about 200,000 men. Added to this were a Czechoslovakian army corps with about 16,000 men and a Romanian volunteer division – all in all no more than 300,000 troops.[3]

It is evident that the common notion of 'collaboration' is unsuited to capturing the phenomenon of foreign 'helpers' in Hitler's Wehrmacht in all their varieties and complexity. Unpolitical in its literal meaning ('to work together'), during the war the term came to be used by the anti-Hitler coalition as a label for the enemy – the purported traitors in their own ranks or from the occupied territories. At the end of the war, collaboration became a stigma for anyone considered undesirable. It was applied to the guilty and innocent, offenders big and small who not only fought on the side of the enemy but took part in Nazi war crimes as well.

Anti-Communism and anti-Semitism did indeed incite many volunteers and collaborators to commit acts of terror and murder against their own countrymen. The front-line soldiers among them could not expiate themselves from this responsibility, just as the German legend of a 'clean' or 'innocent' Wehrmacht could not hold up in the long run. It took more than a generation for a more differentiated picture of Hitler's war in the East to emerge in Germany, though even today his foreign helpers are generally disregarded. In many of the volunteers' homelands, this historical debate has yet to take place.

Notes

Preface

1   Gnauck, Gerhard, 'Zwischen allen Fronten. Kollaborateure oder Freiheitskämpfer? Die Ukraine ringt um die richtige Deutung ihrer Partisanen zwischen Roter Armee und Wehrmacht', *Die Welt* (19 July 2007), with reference to Kiev historian Volodymyr Sergiychuk.

Introduction: Operation Barbarossa and Its Consequences

1   For a more detailed account of the following overview see the serialized work in ten volumes *Das Deutsche Reich und der Zweite Weltkrieg* published between 1979 and 2007, also available in a one-volume edition under the title *Der letzte deutsche Krieg*; for an overview of the scholarly work done on this topic see Müller and Ueberschär, *Hitlers Krieg im Osten*. Some of the ideas presented here appeared previously in *Der 2. Weltkrieg*, pp. 114–25.

2   *Deutsch-polnische Beziehungen 1939–1945–1949*. German occupation policy became considerably harsher with the start of the German-Soviet war, resulting in millions of deaths in the country, particularly through the Holocaust.

3   File memo of Martin Bormann from a meeting on 17 July 1941, reprinted in *'Unternehmen Barbarossa'*, pp. 330 f.

4   File memo from an undersecretary meeting on 2 May 1941, reprinted in ibid., p. 377.

5   File memo of Bormann, reprinted in ibid., p. 331.

6   Besymenski, *Die letzten Notizen von Martin Bormann*; Domarus, *Hitler*.

PART I: THE ALLIES

Finland

1   For a detailed discussion see Kesselring, *Des Kaisers 'Finnische Legion'*.

2   Kirke (1877–1949) directed the British military mission in Finland in 1924–5.

Halder was aware of the former's attempt to solicit the Finns' support on 19 June 1939; see Bundesarchiv-Militärarchiv (BA-MA) Freiburg, N 220/19.

3   *Das Deutsche Reich und der Zweite Weltkrieg*, vol. 4, p. 367; for a more detailed assessment see Ueberschär: *Hitler und Finnland*.

4   Quoted in *Das Deutsche Reich und der Zweite Weltkrieg*, vol. 4, p. 375; see also Besymenski: *Molotows Berlin-Besuch*.

5   *Heeresadjutant bei Hitler*, p. 93.

6   Finnish memorandum from 2 June 1941, reprinted in Ueberschär: *Hitler und Finnland*, p. 335.

7   Stein / Krosby: *Freiwilligen-Bataillon*.

8   File memo of Bormann from 16 June 1941, reprinted in '*Unternehmen Barbarossa*', p. 331.

9   Erfurth: *Der Finnische Krieg*.

10   Quoted in Gosztony, *Deutschlands Waffengefährten*, p. 28.

11   Schreiber, *Nordlicht*, p. 127.

12   Neulen, *Am Himmel*, p. 214.

13   *Das Deutsche Reich und der Zweite Weltkrieg*, vol. 4, p. 841.

14   Ibid., p. 843.

15   On the situation in Scandinavia in 1943–4 see ibid., vol. 8.

16   Quoted in Mannerheim: *Erinnerungen*, pp. 526 f.

Hungary

1   *Das Deutsche Reich und der Zweite Weltkrieg*, vol. 4, p. 350.

2   *Allianz Hitler-Horthy-Mussolini*, doc. 93.

3   Quoted in *Das Deutsche Reich und der Zweite Weltkrieg*, vol. 4, p. 359.

4   Quoted in Gosztony, *Deutschlands Waffengefährten*, p. 137.

5   Quoted in ibid., p. 142.

6   Quoted in *Andere Helme*, p. 87.

7   Quoted in Gosztony, *Deutschlands Waffengefährten*, pp. 160 f.

8   Order of the day of 24 January 1943, quoted in ibid., p. 161.

9   For a general overview see Aly and Gerlach: *Das letzte Kapitel*.

10   Hillgruber, *Staatsmänner*, vol. 2, pp. 245 f.

11   For more detail see Ungváry, *Die ungarische Besatzungstruppe*.

12   See Ránki, *Margarethe*.

13   Quoted in *Das Deutsche Reich und der Zweite Weltkrieg*, vol. 8, p. 858.

14   Ungváry, *Robbing the Dead*, pp. 212–29.

15   Army General Staff on the situation in Hungary, 16 April 1944, quoted in *Das Deutsche Reich und der Zweite Weltkrieg*, vol. 8, p. 861.

16   For a comprehensive approach see Kissel, *Panzerschlachten*.

17   For a more detailed treatment see Ungváry, *Schlacht*.

Romania

1   Eichholtz, *Deutsche Politik*.

2   See Hanfland, *Die internationale Lage*.

3   Quoted in Hürter, *Hitlers Heerführer*, p. 8.

4   Quoted in *Das Deutsche Reich und der Zweite Weltkrieg*, vol. 4, p. 344.

5   On the history of the Romanian Army see Axworthy, *Third Axis*.

6   For more detail see Ancel, *Antonescu*; Deletant, *Hitler's Forgotten Ally*.

7   *Akten zur deutschen auswärtigen Politik (ADAP)*, D, vol. XIII, 1, doc. 159.

8   Hitler, *Monologe*, p. 75.

9   *Romania in World War II*, pp. 76–9.

10 *Das Deutsche Reich und der Zweite Weltkrieg*, vol. 4, p. 887.

11 Ibid., p. 885.

12 Ibid.

13 Letter from 17 August 1941, *ADAP*, D, vol. XIII, 1, doc. 210.

14 *Romania in World War II*, pp. 67–9.

15 This corresponds to the self-critical appraisal of Antonescu of 14 December 1941, who saw faulty training as a product of the prewar period; reprinted in ibid., p. 89. A detailed analysis can be found in Axworthy, *The Romanian Soldier*.

16 Quoted in Hillgruber, *Hitler*, p. 144 (12 December 1941).

17 Ancel, *Stalingrad und Rumänien*, pp. 196 f.

18 Statement of the chief of the German army mission in Romania, 11 January 1942, quoted in *Das Deutsche Reich und der Zweite Weltkrieg*, vol. 4, pp. 887 f.

19 Talks on 26 August 1941, *ADAP*, D, vol. XIII, 2, doc. 505.

20 Talks with Göring on 13 February 1942, ADAP, E, I, doc. 241.

21 Gosztony, *Hitlers fremde Heere*, p. 267.

22 Förster, *Stalingrad*, p. 138.

23 Notes for Führer speech, September 1942, reprinted in Zeidler, *Experiment*, p. 497.

24 Degrelle, *Die verlorene Legion*, p. 90.

25 Quoted in Ancel, *Stalingrad und Rumänien*, p. 199.

26 Gosztony, *Deutschlands Waffengefährten*, p. 104.

27 Letter from Antonescu to Manstein of 9 December 1942, reprinted in Kehrig: *Stalingrad*, pp. 588–94.

28 Memorandum from 11 January 1943, quoted in Ancel, *Stalingrad und Rumänien*, p. 207.

29 Reprinted in Förster, *Stalingrad*, p. 138.

30 Quoted in Ancel, *Stalingrad und Rumänien*, p. 210.

31 Talk between the head of the Mineral Oil Department in the Reich Ministry of Economics, Ernst Rudolf Fischer, and Speer on 29 November 1943, quoted in *Das Deutsche Reich und der Zweite Weltkrieg*, vol. 5, no. 2, p. 533.

32 Hillgruber, *Hitler*, p. 205.

33 Hillgruber, *Staatsmänner*, vol. 2, p. 498.

34 See the report on their in-depth talk in the memoirs of Friessner, *Verratene Schlachten*, p. 80.

35 *Romania in World War II*, p. 219.

36   Ibid., pp. 166, 299. The extremely high number of soldiers missing in action on the Eastern Front is probably attributable to deaths, whereas on the Western Front many of these are likely to have been deserters, for which no figures are available.

Italy

1   *Das Deutsche Reich und der Zweite Weltkrieg*, vol. 3, p. 13.
2   Ibid. vol. 4, p. 897.
3   Halder, *Kriegstagebuch*, vol. 3, p. 10 (24 June 1941).
4   Schreiber, *Italiens Teilnahme*, pp. 250–8.
5   *Die Italiener*, p. 11.
6   From a letter from the front, 2 September 1941, quoted in ibid., pp. 15 f.
7   See Neulen, *Am Himmel*, pp. 64–8.
8   Degrelle, *Die verlorene Legion*, pp. 25 f.
9   Ibid., pp. 28 f.
10   For a self-portrayal see the memoirs of Messe, *Hitlers Krieg im Osten*.
11   Letter from Hitler to Mussolini, 29 December 1941, *ADAP*, E, vol. 1, pp. 104 –13.
12   Schreiber, *Italiens Teilnahme*, pp. 268 f.
13   Telex from the head of the German liaison staff at the Italian 8th Army Headquarters to Army Group Ruoff, I a, 17 July 1942, quoted in *Die Italiener*, p. 31.
14   There is much work to be done in this field of historical research.
15   Quoted in *Die Italiener*, p. 40.
16   Quoted in ibid., p. 42.
17   Ibid., p. 37.
18   Quoted in ibid., p. 54.
19   Ibid., p. 57.
20   Memorandum on the situation of the 8th Army, reprinted in ibid., here p. 188.
21   Quoted in Beevor, *Stalingrad*, p. 217.
22   Quoted in *Die Italiener*, p. 71.
23   Report of the 221st Security Division from 31 March 1943, reprinted in ibid., doc. 15, here p. 156.
24   Schreiber, *Die italienischen Militärinternierten*, p. 208.
25   Battle report of the German liaison command at the Ravenna Division, 20 March 1943, reprinted in *Die Italiener*, doc. 9, here p. 126.
26   Schreiber, *Die italienischen Militärinternierten*, pp. 209–12.

Slovakia

1   Venohr: *Aufstand*, p. 22.
2   Quoted in ibid., p. 30.
3   *Das Deutsche Reich und der Zweite Weltkrieg*, vol. 4, p. 362.
4   See also the overview of Axworthy, *Axis Slovakia*.
5   Gosztony, *Deutschlands Waffengefährten*, p. 218; see also Schönherr, *Die Slowakei*.

6   Major v. Lengerke, report from 2 August 1941, quoted in *Das Deutsche Reich und der Zweite Weltkrieg*, vol. 4, p. 896.
7   Schreiber, *Die Niederschlagung*.
8   Venohr, *Aufstand*, p. 274.

Croatia

1   For a comprehensive treatment see Schmider, *Partisanenkrieg*.
2   Divisional order from 12 October 1941, reprinted in Neidhardt, *Mit Tanne und Eichenlaub*, pp. 425 f.
3   Quoted in ibid., p. 170.
4   This was at least the opinion of Lieutenant General Arthur Schmidt, chief-of-staff at 6th Army Headquarters, quoted in Gosztony, *Deutschlands Waffengefährten*, p. 240.
5   A detailed account can be found in *Das Deutsche Reich und der Zweite Weltkrieg*, vol. 5, no. 2, p. 990.
6   Ibid., vol. 8, pp. 1061–70.

PART II: THE VOLUNTEERS FROM
NEUTRAL AND OCCUPIED TERRITORIES

Spain

1   For a comprehensive account see Ruhl, *Spanien im Zweiten Weltkrieg*.
2   Kleinfeld and Tambs, *Hitler's Spanish Legion*.
3   *Das Deutsche Reich und der Zweite Weltkrieg*, vol. 4, p. 914.
4   Hitler, *Monologe*, p. 178 (4–5 January 1942).
5   Neulen, *An deutscher Seite*, pp. 116–25.
6   Muñoz Grandes became Spain's defence minister in 1951 and was deputy prime minister from 1962 to 1967.
7   OKH / GenStdH / Org.Abt.(III a), Nr. 1023 / 43 gKdos., betr. Waffen-Zuweisung für die 250. Spanische Division, 12 March 1943, BA-MA Freiburg, RH 2 / 934 b.
8   Esteban Infantes, *Die Blaue Division*, p. 99.
9   Neulen, *Am Himmel*, p. 287.
10   *Das Deutsche Reich und der Zweite Weltkrieg*, vol. 4, p. 915.

France

1   Quoted in Gosztony, *Deutschlands Waffengefährten*, p. 254.
2   Bormann protocol of 16 July 1941, reprinted in '*Unternehmen Barbarossa*', p. 330.
3   Neulen, *Am Himmel*, p. 268.
4   For more detail see Michel: *Deutsche in der Fremdenlegion*.
5   Gosztony, *Deutschlands Waffengefährten*, p. 254.

6   Quoted in Neulen, *Europas verratene Söhne*, p. 137.
7   Quoted in Selder, *Der Krieg der Infanterie*, p. 309.
8   Ibid., p. 312.
9   Facsimile of the battle report in Gosztony, *Deutschlands Waffengefährten*, p. 256. See also the novelistic account of former NCO in the legion and later writer Marc Augier de Saint-Loup, *Legion*, pp. 33 f. and Philippe Carrard, *The French Who Fought for Hitler. Memories from the Outcasts.*
10   Ibid., p. 61.
11   Gosztony, *Deutschlands Waffengefährten*, p. 257.
12   Saint-Loup, *Legion*, p. 92.
13   Neulen, *Europas verratene Söhne*, p. 138.
14   A French NCO with the task of tranferring 30 Turkestanis from Warsaw to the front had an SS recruiter arrested who tried to kidnap the men. The occurence is documented in BA-MA Freiburg, RH 53–23 / 52.
15   Saint-Loup, *Legion*, p. 177.
16   Gosztony, *Deutschlands Waffengefährten*, p. 262.
17   See Mabire, *Berlin im Todeskampf.*
18   One such fate can be found in the first-hand account of writer Guy Sajer (*Denn dieser Tage Qual war gross*), who reported to the elite division 'Grossdeutschland' as a 17-year-old and lived through the war on the Eastern Front. Other assessments put the number of Frenchmen forcefully recruited into the Wehrmacht and SS at upwards of 130,000; see Allainmat and Truck, *La Nuit.*

Belgium

1   Quoted in Neulen, *Europas verratene Söhne*, p. 132.
2   For more biographical information see Kurowski, *Grenadiere*, pp. 257–69.
3   Degrelle, *Die verlorene Legion*, pp. 11 ff.
4   Ibid., p. 25.
5   *Das Deutsche Reich und der Zweite Weltkrieg*, vol. 4, p. 923.
6   Neidhardt, *Mit Tanne und Eichenlaub*, pp. 164 f.
7   See Ott, *Jäger*, pp. 215 f. and Degrelle, *Die verlorene Legion*, pp. 101 ff.
8   Wagner, *Belgien*, p. 26.
9   Neulen, *Europas verratene Söhne*, p. 201.

Netherlands

1   For an overview see *Das Deutsche Reich und der Zweite Weltkrieg*, vol. 5, no. 2, pp. 19–21.
2   On occupation policy see, in general, Hirschfeld, *Fremdherrschaft.*
3   *Das Deutsche Reich und der Zweite Weltkrieg*, vol. 4, p. 911.
4   *Die deutsche Wirtschaftspolitik*, pp. 139 f.
5   Kwiet, *Reichskommissariat*, p. 150.

Denmark

1   *Das Deutsche Reich und der Zweite Weltkrieg*, vol. 5, no. 1, p. 50; see, in general, Ueberschär, *Besatzungspolitik*.

2   *Das Deutsche Reich und der Zweite Weltkrieg*, vol. 4, pp. 932 f.; a scholarly overview is now available in the work of Werther *(Dänische Freiwillige in der Waffen-SS)*.

3   Werther, *Dänische Freiwillige*, pp. 65 f.

4   Tieke, *Geschichte des 'Freikorps Danmark'*. This older, uncritical work is now considered outdated.

5   Neulen, *Am Himmel*, pp. 264–7. Ove Terp was one of them. Seriously wounded, he survived the war and adopted German citizenship, eventually serving as a lieutenant colonel in the new Luftwaffe of the Federal Republic.

6   Werther, *Dänische Freiwillige*, pp. 55 f.

7   Quoted in ibid., p. 81.

8   Ibid., p. 83.

9   *Das Deutsche Reich und der Zweite Weltkrieg*, vol. 9, no. 2, p. 756.

10 Proposal of Divisional Commander Major-General Wagner, quoted in Neulen, *An deutscher Seite*, p. 144.

Norway

1   On occupation policy see Bohn, *Reichskommissariat*.

2   *Das Deutsche Reich und der Zweite Weltkrieg*, vol. 4, p. 934. On the unusual instance of a Norwegian who managed to be taken on as a pilot in Göring's Luftwaffe see Neulen, *Am Himmel*, pp. 257–62.

3   Quoted in Neulen, *An deutscher Seite*, p. 155.

4   *Das Deutsche Reich und der Zweite Weltkrieg*, vol. 9, no. 2, pp. 757.

5   Lang, *'Mitleid'*.

PART III: THE EASTERN EUROPEAN NATIONS IN THE STRUGGLE AGAINST STALINISM

Estonia

1   Volkmann, *Ökonomie und Machtpolitik*.

2   Schlussurteil Estland, BA-MA Freiburg, N 220/19.

3   Neulen, *An deutscher Seite*, p. 281.

4   For a detailed account see Birn, *Sicherheitspolizei*.

5   Kaasik, *Estonian Military Units*; Adamson: *Eesti idapataljonid*.

6   Isberg, *Zu den Bedingungen des Befreiers*.

7   Quoted in Neulen, *An deutscher Seite*, p. 283.

8   Quoted in Jahnke, Kessel, pp. 103 f.

9   Myllyniemi, *Neuordnung*, p. 206.

10   Ibid., p. 233.

11   For more detail see Uustalu, *For Freedom Only.*

12   Mood report of 21 June 1943, quoted in *Das Deutsche Reich und der Zweite Weltkrieg,* vol. 5, no. 2, p. 53.

13   Myllyniemi, *Neuordnung,* p. 253.

14   Garleff, *Die baltischen Länder,* p. 170.

15   Ibid., p. 171.

Latvia

1   Garleff, *Die baltischen Länder,* p. 96.

2   Angrick and Klein, *Die Endlösung,* p. 65.

3   Myllyniemi, *Neuordnung,* S. 227 f.

4   Ibid., p. 231.

5   Ibid., p. 238.

6   Quoted in ibid., p. 254.

7   'Das Oberkommando der Wehrmacht gibt bekannt ...', p. 54.

Lithuania

1   Stang, *Hilfspolizisten,* p. 863.

2   Quoted in Myllyniemi, *Neuordnung,* p. 235.

3   Ibid., p. 279.

Poland

1   Król, *Besatzungsherrschaft,* p. 580.

2   Müller, *Das Tor zur Weltmacht,* p. 310.

3   On this development see Schmidt, *Aussenpolitik,* pp. 316 ff.

4   The Institute of National Remembrance in Warsaw has been commissioned by the Polish government to investigate the overall number of Polish deaths. About 2.5 million Poles are estimated to have suffered from reprisals in eastern Poland; the number of actual deaths is the subject of debate but is currently estimated at 570,000, 200,000 of which have been documented. The figures are not definitive for the period of German occupation either, but most historians assume that around 250,000 Poles were victims of German mass executions, 150,000 of these after the Warsaw Uprising of 1944. Added to this, of course, are the victims of concentration and extermination camps, most of whom were not murdered until after the German invasion of the USSR. The aforegoing assessment, based on more recent literature, therefore merely serves as a guideline.

5   For a more detailed account see Wiaderny, *Untergrundstaat.*

6   For an in-depth analysis see Musial, *'Konterrevolutionäre Elemente'.*

7　Chiari, *Kriegslist.*
8　*Die polnische Heimatarmee.*

Byelorussia

1　See the brief history of Byelorussia with a comparative approach to both world wars in Chiari, *Geschichte als Gewalttat.*
2　*The Soviet Takeover.*
3　Chiari: *Alltag.*
4　Pavlov: *Belorusskie partizany.*
5　Notes of Martin Bormann from a meeting on 16 July 1941, reprinted in '*Unternehmen Barbarossa*', p. 331.
6　See the documentation *Sowjetische Partisanen in Weissrussland.*
7　Chiari, *Alltag*, p. 312.
8　According to Polish accounts, Naliboki was a stronghold of the Polish Self-Defence, armed with 26 rifles and two light machine guns. Soviet attackers killed 128 innocent civilians, ransacked the village and burned it down; see *Sowjetische Partisanen*, pp. 116 f.

Ukraine

1　An interesting comparison between the invasion of German troops in World War I and World War II is offered by Grelka, *Die ukrainische Nationalbewegung.*
2　See the overview of Pavlenko, *Die Ukrainische Aufständischenarmee.*
3　Quoted in Neulen, *An deutscher Seite*, p. 308.
4　On the following see Musial, '*Konterrevolutionäre Elemente*'.
5　Bräutigam, *So hat es sich zugetragen*, pp. 460, 504.
6　Quoted in Grelka, *Die ukrainische Nationalbewegung*, p. 257.
7　*Die Tagebücher von Joseph Goebbels*, entry from 25 April 1942.
8　Neulen, *An deutscher Seite*, p. 310.
9　Quoted in Grelka, *Die ukrainische Nationalbewegung*, p. 391.
10　Quoted in Pavlenko, *Die ukrainische Nationalbewegung*, p. 75.
11　Ibid., p. 78.
12　Motyka, *Der polnisch-ukrainische Gegensatz*, p. 544.
13　Pavlenko, *Die Ukrainische Aufständischenarmee*, p. 86.
14　Neulen, *An deutscher Seite*, p. 313.
15　Ibid., p. 314.

Russia

1　The more recent in-depth account and analysis of Hürter is impressive: *Hitlers Heerführer*, pp. 1–13.

2   Memorandum of Rosenberg, 7 April 1941, quoted in Dallin, *Deutsche Herrschaft*, p. 307.

3   Ibid, p. 310.

4   On this phase of occupation policy see Mulligan, *Politics*.

5   Dwinger, *Sie suchten die Freiheit*, pp. 72 f. The writer was a war reporter on the Eastern Front and was placed under house arrest in 1943 for his open support of Vlasov.

6   Neulen, *An deutscher Seite*, p. 317.

7   See the eye-witness account from a German perspective of Eltz, *Mit den Kosaken*.

8   Ibid., p. 69.

9   Dallin, *Deutsche Herrschaft*, p. 312.

10 For more detail see Tolstoy, *Victims*, and more recently Stadler, Kofler and Berger, *Flucht*.

11 Dwinger, *Sie suchten die Freiheit*, pp. 344 f.

12 *Das Deutsche Reich und der Zweite Weltkrieg*, vol. 5, no. 2, p. 989.

13 For a detailed account see the memoirs of Bräutigam, *So hat es sich zugetragen*.

14 *Das Deutsche Reich und der Zweite Weltkrieg*, vol. 5, no. 2, p. 986.

15 Memorandum of 25 November 1942, reprinted in Hoffmann, *Kaukasien*, p. 43.

16 See the biography of Steenberg, *Wlassow*.

17 Ibid., pp. 76 f.

18 See the memoirs of the former director of Dabendorf, Strik-Striktfeld, *Gegen Stalin*.

19 Steenberg, *Wlassow*, p. 99.

20 *Lagebesprechungen*, p. 109.

21 Steenberg, *Wlassow*, p. 111. Kurt Zeitzler, chief of the General Staff of the Army, cited the figure of 220,000 'willing helpers' in his military conference with Hitler, which did not tally with the statistics of the Foreign Armies East Department.

22 See the chart in *Das Deutsche Reich und der Zweite Weltkrieg*, vol. 5, no. 2, p. 973.

23 Ibid., pp. 988 f.

24 Vogelsang, *Nach Liechtenstein*.

25 Hoffmann, *Geschichte*, p. 83.

26 Ibid., pp. 21 f.

27 Ibid., p. 32.

28 Quoted in Neulen, *An deutscher Seite*, p. 348.

29 Hoffmann, *Geschichte*, p. 54. The Russian was, however, buried with military honours in the presence of the German commandant of the city, something normally denied to Soviet prisoners of war till then.

30 Ibid., p. 288.

31 See the very polemic account of Tolstoy, *Die Verratenen*.

32 For more detail see Polian, *Deportiert*.

The Caucasus

1   For an account of his adventurous life see Seidt, *Berlin, Kabul, Moskau*.

2   For the case of Azerbaijan see Baberowski, *Feind*.

3   Mühlen, *Zwischen Hakenkreuz und Sowjetstern*, p. 24.

4   Guidelines for the behaviour of troops in Russia, May 1941, reprinted in '*Unternehmen Barbarossa*', p. 312.

5   Mühlen, *Zwischen Hakenkreuz und Sowjetstern*, pp. 47 f.

6   Ibid., p. 50.

7   See, in general, his autobiography, Bräutigam, *So hat es sich zugetragen*.

8   Mühlen, *Zwischen Hakenkreuz und Sowjetstern*, p. 57.

9   See, in general, Hoffmann, *Ostlegionen*, as well as his expanded and systematic study *Kaukasien 1942 / 43*.

10 Mühlen, *Zwischen Hakenkreuz und Sowjetstern*, p. 58.

11 Hoffmann, *Ostlegionen*, p. 32.

12 Closing remarks of Kleist, 15 December 1942, quoted in Hoffmann, *Kaukasien*, pp. 464–66.

13 Activation order of the OKH for the legions in Poland, 24 April 1942, quoted in Hoffmann, *Kaukasien*, p. 89.

14 This corresponds to Mühlen, *Zwischen Hakenkreuz und Sowjetstern*, pp. 63 f.

15 Lieutenant Colonel Wendt, instructor at the training course for 3rd higher ordnance staff, 12 February 1943, BA-MA Freiburg, RH 19V/5.

16 Hoffmann, *Kaukasien*, p. 242.

17 Ibid., pp. 206 f.

18 Major Bake to Army Group A, 13 December 1942, BA-MA Freiburg, RH 19V/5.

19 Mühlen, *Zwischen Hakenkreuz und Sowjetstern*, p. 60.

20 See Hoffmann, *Deutsche und Kalmyken*.

21 Notes of Dr. Doll, July 1944, reprinted in ibid., p. 194.

22 Ibid., p. 393.

23 Steiner, *Die Freiwilligen*, p. 183.

24 Key documents on this are reprinted in Hoffmann, *Kaukasien*, appendix.

25 Hoffmann, *Ostlegionen*, p. 64.

26 Mühlen, *Zwischen Hakenkreuz und Sowjetstern*, pp. 144 f.

27 Ibid., p. 157.

28 Ibid., p. 68.

29 Hoffmann, *Kaukasien*, p. 395.

30 Tolstoy, *Victims*, p. 400; Hoffmann, *Kaukasien*, p. 457.

31 Conquest, *Deportation*.

Concluding Remarks

1   Figures according to Neulen, *An deutscher Seite*, p. 278.

2   *Das Deutsche Reich und der Zweite Weltkrieg*, vol. 5, no. 2, p. 983.

3   For more detail see Gosztony, *Stalins fremde Heere*.

Bibliography

Ádám, Magda (ed.), *Allianz Hitler-Horthy-Mussolini. Dokumente zur ungarischen Außenpolitik (1933–1944)* (u.a. Budapest, 1966).

Adamson, Andres (ed.), *Eesti idapataljonid idarindel 1941–1944* (Tallinn, 2004).

Akten zur deutschen auswärtigen Politik 1918–1945. Serie B (Göttingen, 1966–78).

Allainmat, Henry, and Truck, Betty, *La Nuit des Parias. La tragique histoire des 130 000 Français incorporés de force dans la Wehrmacht et la Waffen-SS* (Paris, 1974).

Aly, Götz, and Gerlach, Christian, *Das letzte Kapitel. Realpolitik, Ideologie und der Mord an den ungarischen Juden 1944 / 45* (Stuttgart and Munich, 2002).

Ancel, Jean, 'Antonescu and the Jews', in *Yad Vashem Studies on the European Jewish Catastrophe and Resistance*, vol. 23 (1993), pp. 213–80.

———, 'Stalingrad und Rumänien', in Jürgen Förster (ed.), *Stalingrad. Ereignis. Wirkung. Symbol* (Munich and Zurich, 1992), pp. 189–214.

Anders, Wladyslaw, *Russian Volunteers in Hitler's Army, 1941–1945* (New York, 1997).

Andreyev, Catherine, *Vlasov and the Russian Liberation Movement. Soviet Reality and Émigré Theories* (Cambridge, 1987).

Angrick, Andrej, and Klein, Peter, 'Die "Endlösung"', in Riga, *Ausbeutung und Vernichtung 1941–1944* (Darmstadt, 2006).

Axworthy, Mark, 'The Romanian Soldier at the Siege of Odessa', in Paul Addison and Angus Caldor (eds), *Time to Kill* (London, 1997), pp. 228–32.

———, *Axis Slovakia: Hitler's Slavic Wedge 1938–1945* (New York, 2002).

———, *Third Axis Forth Ally. Romanian Armed Forces in the European War, 1941–1945* (London, 1995).

Baberowski, Jörg, *Der Feind ist überall. Stalinismus im Kaukasus* (Stuttgart, 2003).

Bartusevičius, Vincas, Tauber, Joachim, and Wette, Wolfram (eds), *Holocaust in Litauen. Krieg, Judenmorde und Kollaboration im Jahre 1941* (Cologne and Weimar, 2003).

Beevor, Antony, *Stalingrad* (Munich, 1999).

Besymenski, Lew, *Die letzten Notizen von Martin Bormann* (Stuttgart, 1974).

———, 'Wjatscheslaw Molotows Berlin-Besuch vom November 1940 im Licht neuer Dokumente', in Bianka Pietrow-Ennker (ed.), *Präventivkrieg?* (Frankfurt am Main, 2000), pp. 113–27.

Bethell, Nicholas, *The Last Secret. The Delivery to Stalin of Over Two Million Russians by Britain and the United States* (New York, 1974).

Birn, Ruth Bettina, *Die Sicherheitspolizei in Estland 1941–1944. Eine Studie zur Kollaborationim Zweiten Weltkrieg* (Paderborn, 2006).

Bohn, Robert, *Reichskommissariat Norwegen. 'Nationalsozialistische Neuordnung' und Kriegswirtschaft* (Munich, 2000).

Borodziej, Wlodzimierz, and Ziemer, Klaus, *Deutsch-polnische Beziehungen 1939–1945 –1949. Eine Einführung* (Osnabrück, 2000).

Bräutigam, *Otto, So hat es sich zugetragen. Ein Leben als Soldat und Diplomat* (Würzburg, 1968).

Brüggemann, Karsten, 'Der Widerstand gegen die deutsche Besatzung in Estland 1941–1944', in Gerd R. Ueberschär (ed.), *Handbuch zum Widerstand gegen National-sozialismus und Faschismus in Europa 1933 / 39–1945* (Munich, 2008).

Burgdorff, Stephan, and Wiegrefe, Klaus (eds), *Der 2. Weltkrieg. Wendepunkt der deutschen Geschichte* (Munich, 2005).

Carnier, Pier Arrigo, *L'Armata Cosaca in Italia 1944–1945* (Mailand, 1990).

Chiari, Bernhard, 'Kriegslist oder Bündnis mit dem Feind? Deutsch-polnische Kontakte 1943 / 44', in *Die polnische Heimatarmee*, pp. 497–530.

——, *Alltag hinter der Front. Besatzung, Kollaboration und Widerstand in Weißrussland 1941–1944* (Düsseldorf, 1998).

——, 'Geschichte als Gewalttat. Weißrussland als Kind zweiter Weltkriege', in *Erster Weltkrieg – Zweiter Weltkrieg*, pp. 615–31.

—— (ed.), *Die polnische Heimatarmee. Geschichte und Mythos der Armia Krajowa seit dem Zweiten Weltkrieg* (Munich, 2003).

Conquest, Robert, *The Soviet Deportation of Nationalities* (London, 1960).

Constantiniu, Florin, *1941. Hitler, Stalin si România. România si geneza operatiunii 'Barbarossa'* (Bucharest, 2002).

Corti, Eugenio, *Few Returned. Twenty-eight Days on the Russian Front, Winter 1942–1943* (London, 1997).

Dallin, Alexander, *Deutsche Herrschaft in Russland 1941–1945. Eine Studie über Besatzungspolitik* (Düsseldorf, 1958).

Das Deutsche Reich und der Zweite Weltkrieg, ed. by the Militärgeschichtlichen Forschungsamt, 10 vols (Stuttgart, 1979–2008).

Degrelle, Léon, *Die verlorene Legion* (Preußisch Oldendorf, 1972).

Deletant, Dennis, *Hitler's Forgotten Ally: Ion Antonescu and His Regime, Romania 1940 –1944* (New York, 2006).

Dieckmann, Christoph, and Quinkert, Babette (eds), *Kooperation und Verbrechen: Formen der »Kollaboration« im östlichen Europa 1939–1945* (Göttingen, 2003).

DiNardo, Richard L., *Germany and the Axis Powers. From Coalition to Collapse* (Lawrence, KS, 2005).

——, 'The Dysfunctional Coalition: The Axis Powers and the Eastern Front in World War II', *The Journal of Military History*, vol. 60, no. 4 (1996), pp. 711–30.

Domarus, Max, *Hitler. Reden und Proklamationen 1932 –1945*, vol. II / 2 (Wiesbaden, 1973).

Dwinger, Erich Edwin, *Sie suchten die Freiheit … Schicksalsweg eines Reitervolkes* (Munich and Salzburg, 1952).

Eichholtz, Dietrich, *Deutsche Politik und rumänisches Öl (1938 –1941). Eine Studie über Erdölimperialismus* (Leipzig, 2005).

Eltz, Erwein Karl Graf zu, *Mit den Kosaken. Kriegstagebuch 1943–1945* (Donaueschingen, 1970).

Erfurth, Waldemar, *Der Finnische Krieg 1941–1944*, 2nd edn (Wiesbaden, 1977).

Ertel, Heinz, and Schulze-Kossens, Richard, *Europäische Freiwillige im Bild* (Osnabrück, 1986).

Esteban Infantes, Emilio, *Die Blaue Division. Spaniens Freiwillige an der Ostfront* (Leoni am Starnberger See, 1958).

Estonia 1940–1945. Reports of the Estonian International Commission for the Investigation of Crimes Against Humanity, collected by Toomas Hiio (Tallinn, 2006).

Förster, Jürgen (ed.), *Stalingrad Ereignis. Wirkung. Symbol* (Munich and Zurich, 1992).

Friessner, Hans, *Verratene Schlachten* (Hamburg, 1956).

Fröhlich, Elke (ed.), *Die Tagebücher von Joseph Goebbels*, pt 2, vol. 4 (Munich, 1995).

Garleff, Michael, *Die baltischen Länder. Estland, Lettland, Litauen vom Mittelalter bis zur Gegenwart* (Regensburg, 2001).

Gosztony, Peter, *Deutschlands Waffengefährten an der Ostfront 1941–1945* (Stuttgart, 1981).

——, *Stalins fremde Heere. Das Schicksal der nichtsowjetischen Truppen im Rahmen der Roten Armee 1941–1945* (Bonn, 1991).

——, *Hitlers fremde Heere. Das Schicksal der nichtsowjetischen Truppen im Rahmen der Roten Armee 1941–1945* (Stuttgart, 1991).

Grelka, Frank, *Die ukrainische Nationalbewegung unter deutscher Besatzungsherrschaft 1918 und 1941/ 42* (Wiesbaden, 2005).

Halder, Franz, *Generaloberst Halder. Kriegstagebuch. Tägliche Aufzeichnungen des Chefs des Generalstabes des Heeres 1939–1942*, ed. Hans-Adolf Jacobsen, 3 vols (Stuttgart, 1962–4).

Hanfland, Jens, *Die internationale Lage Rumäniens im Vorfeld des 'Unternehmens Barbarossa' Vom deutsch-sowjetischen Nichtangriffsvertrag bis zum Überfall auf die UdSSR* (Münster, 2004).

Hausser, Paul, *Soldaten wie andere auch* (Osnabrück, 1982).

Heeresadjutant bei Hitler 1938–1943. Aufzeichnungen des Majors Engel, ed. and with a commentary by Hildegard von Kotze (Stuttgart, 1974).

Heiber, Helmut (ed.), *Lagebesprechungen im Führerhauptquartier* (Stuttgart, 1963).

Hillgruber, Andreas, 'Der Einbau der verbündeten Armeen in die deutsche Ostfront 1941–1944', in *Wehrwissenschaftliche Rundschau* (1960), pp. 659– 82.

——, *Hitler, König Carol und Marschall Antonescu. Die deutsch-rumänischen Beziehungen 1938–1944* (Wiesbaden, 1965).

—— (ed.), *Staatsmänner und Diplomaten bei Hitler. Vertrauliche Aufzeichnungen über Unterredungen mit Vertretern des Auslandes 1939–1944*, 2 vols (Frankfurt am Main, 1967).

Hirschfeld, Gerhard, *Fremdherrschaft und Kollaboration. Die Niederlande unter deutscher Besatzung 1940–1945* (Stuttgart, 1984).

Hitler, Adolf, *Monologe im Führerhauptquartier 1941–1944*, ed. Werner Jochmann (Hamburg, 1980).

Hoffmann, Joachim, *Deutsche und Kalmyken 1942 bis 1945* (Freiburg, 1974).

———, *Die Ostlegionen 1941–1943. Turkotataren, Kaukasier und Wolgafinnen im deutschen Heer* (Freiburg, 1976).

———, *Die Geschichte der Wlassow-Armee* (Freiburg, 1986).

———, *Kaukasien 1942 / 43. Das deutsche Heer und die Orientvölker der Sowjetunion* (Freiburg, 1991).

Hürter, Johannes, *Hitlers Heerführer. Die deutschen Oberbefehlshaber im Krieg gegen die Sowjetunion 1941 / 42* (Munich, 2006).

Isberg, Alvin, *Zu den Bedingungen des Befreiers. Kollaboration und Freiheitsstreben in dem von Deutschland besetzten Estland 1941–1944* (Stockholm, 1992).

Jahnke, Günter, *Der Kessel von Tscherkassy 1944. Analyse und Dokumentation* (Donauwörth, 1996).

Jurado, Carlos Caballero, *Breaking the Chains. 14. Waffen Grenadier Division der SS and Other Ukrainian Volunteer Formations, Eastern Front 1942–1945* (London, 1998).

Kaasik, Peeter, 'Estonian Military Units in German Armed Forces and Police during the Second World War', in *Yearbook of the Museum of Occupation of Latvia* (Riga, 2004).

Karashuk, A. (ed.), *Russkiya Osvobodetelnya Armia 1939–1945* (Moscow, 1999).

Kehrig, Manfred, *Stalingrad. Analyse und Dokumentation einer Schlacht* (Stuttgart, 1975).

Keßelring, Agilof, *Des Kaisers 'Finnische Legion'. Die finnische Jägerbewegung im Ersten Weltkrieg im Kontext der deutschen Finnlandpolitik* (Berlin, 2005).

Kissel, Heinz, *Die Panzerschlachten in der Puszta im Oktober 1944* (Neckargmünd, 1960).

Kleinfeld, Gerald R., and Tambs, Lewis A., *Hitler's Spanish Legion. The Blue Division in Russia* (St Petersburg, 2005).

Król, Eugeniusz Cezary, 'Besatzungsherrschaft in Polen im Ersten und Zweiten Weltkrieg: Charakteristik und Wahrnehmung', in *Erster Weltkrieg – Zweiter Weltkrieg*, pp. 577–91.

Kurowski, Franz, *Grenadiere – Generale – Kameraden* (Rastatt, 1968).

Kwiet, Konrad, *Reichskommissariat Niederlande* (Stuttgart, 1968).

Lang, Armin, '"Mitleid mit der Bevölkerung ist nicht am Platze". Die Zerstörung Nordnorwegens durch deutsche Truppen 1944', *Militärgeschichte*, vol. 4 (2004), pp. 14–17.

Littlejohn, David, *The Patriotic Traitors: The History of Collaboration in German Occupied Europe, 1940–45* (Garden City, NY, 1972).

Logusz, Michael, *The Waffen-SS 14th Grenadier Division, 1943–1945* (Atglen, PA, 1997).

Mabire, Jean, *Berlin im Todeskampf 1945. Französische Freiwillige der Waffen-SS als letzte Verteidiger der Reichskanzlei* (Preußisch Oldendorf, 1977).

Malaparte, Curzio, *The Volga Rises in Europe* (Edinburgh, 2000).

Mannerheim, Carl Gustav, *Erinnerungen* (Zurich and Freiburg i. Br., 1952).

Messe, Giovanni, *Der Krieg im Osten* (Zurich, 1948).

Michaelis, Rolf, *Russen in der Waffen-SS* (Berlin, 2000).

Michel, Eckard, *Deutsche in der Fremdenlegion 1870–1965. Mythen u. Realitäten* (Paderborn, 1999).

Motyka, Grzegorz, *Der polnisch-ukrainische Gegensatz in Wolhynien und Ostgalizien*, in *Die polnische Heimatarmee*, pp. 531–47.

Mühlen, Patrik von zur, *Zwischen Hakenkreuz und Sowjetstern. Der Nationalismus dern sowjetischen Orientvölker im 2 Weltkrieg* (Düsseldorf, 1971).

Müller, Rolf-Dieter, *Das Tor zur Weltmacht. Die Bedeutung der Sowjetunion für die deutsche Wirtschafts- und Rüstungspolitik zwischen den Weltkriegen* (Boppard, 1984).

—— (ed.), *Die deutsche Wirtschaftspolitik in den besetzten sowjetischen Gebieten 1941–1943* (Boppard, 1991).

Müller, Rolf-Dieter, and Ueberschär, Gerd R., *Hitlers Krieg im Osten 1941–1945. Ein Forschungsbericht* (Darmstadt, 2000).

Müller, Rolf-Dieter, *Der letzte deutsche Krieg 1939–1945* (Stuttgart, 2005).

Mulligan, Timothy P., *The Politics of Illusion and Empire. German Occupation Policy in the Soviet Union, 1942–1943* (New York, 1988).

Muñoz, Antonio J., *The Kaminski Brigade: A History, 1941–1945* (Bayside, WI, 1996).

——, *Hitler's Eastern Legions. Vol. I: The Baltic Schutzmannschaft 1941–1945* (Bayside, WI, 1996).

——, *Hitler's Eastern Legions. Vol. II: The Osttruppen* (New York, 1997).

—— (ed.), *The East Came West: Muslim, Hindu, and Buddhist Volunteers in the German Armed Forces, 1941–1945* (Bayside, WI, 2002).

Muñoz, Antonio J., and Romanko, Oleg V., *Hitler's White Russians: Collaboration, Extermination and Anti-Partisan Warfare in Byelorussia, 1941–1944* (Folkestone, 2003).

Musial, Bogdan, *'Konterrevolutionäre Elemente sind zu erschießen'. Die Brutalisierung des deutsch-sowjetischen Krieges im Sommer 1941* (Berlin and Munich, 2000).

—— (ed.), *Sowjetische Partisanen in Weißrussland. Innenansichten aus dem Gebiet Baranoviči 1941–1944. Eine Dokumentation* (Munich, 2004).

Myllyniemi, Seppo, *Die Neuordnung der baltischen Länder 1941–1944. Zum nationalsozialistischen Inhalt der deutschen Besatzungspolitik* (Helsinki, 1973).

Neidhardt, Hanns, *Mit Tanne und Eichenlaub. Kriegschronik der 100. Jäger-Division vormals 100. leichte Infanterie-Division* (Graz and Stuttgart, 1981).

Neitzel, Sönke, 'Hitlers Europaarmee und der "Kreuzzug" gegen die Sowjetunion', in Michael Salewski und Heiner Timmermann (eds), *Armeen in Europa – Europäische Armeen* (Münster, 2004), pp. 137–50.

Neulen, Hans Werner, *Europas verratene Söhne* (Munich, 1980).

——, *An deutscher Seite. Internationale Freiwillige von Wehrmacht und Waffen-SS* (Munich, 1985).

——, *Am Himmel Europas. Luftstreitkräfte an deutscher Seite 1939–1945* (Munich, 1998).

Newland, Samuel J., *Cossacks in the German Army, 1941–1945* (London, 1991).

Niehorster, Leo W.G., *The Royal Hungarian Army, 1920–1945* (Bayside, WI, 1998).

Ott, Ernst, *Jäger am Feind. Geschichte und Opfergang der 97. Jäger-Division 1940–1945* (Munich, 1966).

Out, Petre (ed.), *Romania in World War II 1941–1945*. Institute for Operative-Strategic Studies and Military History (Bucharest, 1997).

Pavlenko, Irina, 'Die Ukrainische Aufständischenarmee (UPA). Ein Abriß der Geschichte ihres Widerstandes', *Militärgeschichtliche Zeitschrift*, vol. 61 (2002), pp. 73–90.

Pavlov, V. Ja., 'Belorusskie partizany uni čtožali vraga bez poščady', *Voenno-istoričeskij žurnal*, vol. 5 (2001), pp. 28–34.

Polian, Pavel, *Deportiert nach Hause. Sowjetische Kriegsgefangene im 'Dritten Reich' und ihre Repatriierung* (Munich and Vienna, 2001).

Ránki, György, *Unternehmen Margarethe. Die deutsche Besetzung Ungarns* (Wien, 1971).

Ready, J. Lee, *The Forgotten Axis: Germany's Partners and Foreign Volunteers in World War II* (Jefferson, FL, 1987).

Robinson, Paul F., *The White Russian Army in Exile 1920–1941* (Oxford, 2003).

Ruhl, Klaus-Jörg, *Spanien im Zweiten Weltkrieg. Franco, die Falange und das 'Dritte Reich'* (Hamburg, 1975).

Saint-Loup, *Marc Augier de, Legion der Aufrechten. Frankreichs Freiwillige an der Ostfront* (Leoni am Starnberger See, 1977).

Sajer, Guy, *Denn dieser Tage Qual war groß. Bericht eines vergessenen Soldaten* (Wien, Munich and Zurich, 1967).

Schaeppi, Benno H., *Germanische Freiwillige im Osten* (Nuremberg, 1943).

Schlemmer, Thomas (ed.), *Die Italiener an der Ostfront 1942 / 43. Dokumente zu Mussolinis Krieg gegen die Sowjetunion* (Munich, 2005) (*Schriftenreihe der Vierteljahrshefte für Zeitgeschichte*, vol. 91).

Schmider, Klaus, *Partisanenkrieg in Jugoslawien 1941–1944* (Hamburg, 2002).

Schmidt, Rainer F., *Die Außenpolitik des Dritten Reiches 1933–1939* (Stuttgart, 2002).

Schönherr, Klaus, 'Die Slowakei im militärischen Kalkül des Deutschen Reiches', in *Slovensko A Druha Svetova Vojna [Die Slowakei im Zweiten Weltkrieg]*, ed. by the Vojenský Historický Ustav (Military History Institute) (Bratislava, 2000), pp. 151–70.

——, 'Die Niederschlagung des slowakischen Aufstandes im Kontext der deutschen militärischen Operationen, Herbst 1944', *Bohemia*, vol. 42 (2001), pp. 39–61.

Schreiber, Franz, *Kampf unter dem Nordlicht. Deutsch-finnische Waffenbruderschaft am Polarkreis. Die Geschichte der 6. SS-Gebirgs-Division Nord* (Osnabrück, 1969).

Schreiber, Gerhard, *Die italienischen Militärinternierten im deutschen Machtbereich 1943–1945* (Munich, 1990).

——, 'Italiens Teilnahme am Krieg gegen die Sowjetunion. Motive, Fakten und Folgen', in Förster (ed.), *Stalingrad*, pp. 250–92.

Seidler, Franz W., *Die Kollaboration 1939–1945* (Munich, 1995).

Seidt, Hans-Ulrich, *Berlin, Kabul, Moskau. Oskar Ritter von Niedermayer und Deutschlands Geopolitik* (Munich, 2002).

Selder, Emanuel, *Der Krieg der Infanterie* (Landshut, 1985).

Sigailis, Arthur, *Latvian Legion* (San José, CA, 1986).

Stadler, Harald, Kofler, Martin, and Berger, Karl C., *Flucht in die Hoffnungslosigkeit. Die Kosaken in Osttirol* (Innsbruck, 2005).

Stang, Knut, 'Hilfspolizisten und Soldaten: Das 2. /12. litauische Schutzmann-schaftsbataillon in Kaunas und Weißrussland', in Rolf-Dieter Müller und Hans-Erich Volkmann (eds), *Die Wehrmacht. Mythos und Realität* (Munich, 1999), pp. 858–78.

Steenberg, Sven, Wlassow, *Verräter oder Patriot?* (Cologne, 1968).

Stein, George H., and Krosby, H. Peter, 'Das fi nnische Freiwilligen-Bataillon der Waffen-SS', *Vierteljahrshefte für Zeitgeschichte* 14 (1966), pp. 413–53.

Steiner, Felix, *Die Freiwilligen. Idee und Opfergang* (Göttingen, 1958).

Stern, Mario Rigoni, *The Sergeant in the Snow* (Illinois, 1998).

Strik-Strikfeldt, Wilfried, *Gegen Stalin und Hitler. General Wlassow und die russische Freiheitsbewegung* (Mainz, 1970).

Sword, Keith (ed.), *The Soviet Takeover of the Polish Eastern Provinces, 1939–41* (New York, 1991).

The Hidden and Forbidden History of Latvia under Soviet and Nazi Occupations 1940– 1941. Selected Research of the Commission of the Historians of Latvia (Riga, 2005).

Thomsen, Erich, *Deutsche Besatzungspolitik in Dänemark 1940–1945* (Düsseldorf, 1971).

Thorwald, Jürgen, *Die Illusion. Rotarmisten in Hitlers Heeren* (Zurich, 1974).

Thoß, Bruno, and Volkmann, Hans-Erich (eds), *Erster Weltkrieg – Zweiter Weltkrieg. Ein Vergleich* (Paderborn, 2002).

Tieke, Wilhelm, 'Geschichte des "Freikorps Danmark"', In *Im Lufttransport an Brennpunkte der Ostfront* (Osnabrück, 1971), pp. 149–290.

Tolstoy, Nikolai, *Victims of Yalta* (London, 1977).

——, *Die Verratenen von Jalta. Englands Schuld vor der Geschichte* (Munich and Wien, 1980).

Tönsmeyer, Tatjana, *Das Dritte Reich und die Slowakei 1939–1945. Politischer Alltag zwischen Kooperation und Eigensinn* (Paderborn, 2003).

Tys-Krokhmaliuk, Yuriy, *UPA Warfare in the Ukraine: The Ukrainian Insurgent Army* (New York, 1972).

Ueberschär, Gerd, *Hitler und Finnland 1939–1941* (Wiesbaden, 1978).

——, and Wette, Wolfram, '*Unternehmen Barbarossa*'. *Der deutsche Überfall auf die Sowjetunion 1941* (Paderborn, 1984).

Ungváry, Krisztián, *Die Schlacht um Budapest. Stalingrad an der Donau 1944 / 45* (Munich, 1999).

——, 'Die ungarische Besatzungstruppe in der Sowjetunion 1941–1943', *Ungarn-Jahrbuch* (2002–3), pp. 125–63.

——, 'Robbing the Dead. The Hungarian Contribution to the Holocaust', in Beate Kosmala and Feliks Tych (eds), *Facing the Nazi Genocide* (Berlin, 2004), pp. 231–62.

Uustalu, Evald, *For Freedom Only. The Story of the Estonian Volunteers in the Finnish Wars 1940–1944* (Toronto, 1977).

Venohr, Wolfgang, *Aufstand für die Tschechoslowakei. Der slowakische Freiheitskampf von 1944* (Hamburg, 1969).

Vogel, Detlef, and Wette, Wolfram (eds), *Andere Helme – Andere Menschen? Heimaterfahrung und Frontalltag im Zweiten Weltkrieg* (Essen, 1995).

Vogelsang, Henning Freiherr von, *Nach Liechtenstein – in die Freiheit* (Triesen, 1980).

Volkmann, Hans-Erich, 'Ökonomie und Machtpolitik. Lettland und Estland im politischökonomischen Kalkül des Dritten Reiches (1933–1940)', *Geschichte und Gesellschaft*, vol. 2 (1976), pp. 471–500.

Wagner, Wilfried, *Belgien in der deutschen Politik während des Zweiten Weltkrieges* (Boppard, 1974).

Werther, Steffen, *Dänische Freiwillige in der Waffen-SS* (Berlin, 2004).

Wiaderny, Bernhard, *Der Polnische Untergrundstaat und der deutsche Widerstand 1939– 1944* (Berlin, 2002).

Zeidler, Manfred, 'Das "kaukasische Experiment". Gab es eine Weisung Hitlers zur deutschen Besatzungspolitik im Kaukasus?', *Vierteljahrshefte für Zeitgeschichte*, vol. 3 (2005), pp. 475–500.

Index

Because of the frequency of occurrence, the terms 'Germany', 'Soviet Union', 'USSR', 'Russia' and 'Adolf Hitler' have not been included in the index. Bold page ranges signify a full chapter on the relevant subject.

Viipuri
(Vyborg)

Leningrad

LENINGRAD FR

HELSINKI

VOLKHOV FRON

Army Detachment
'Narwa'

Narva

NORTHWESTERN

Tallinn

Demyansk

STOCKHOLM

Pärnu

ARMY GROUP
NORTH   18th Army

Pskov

Riga

16th Army

KALININ FRONT

BALTIC SEA

Daugava

Nevel

W

Vitebsk

Klaipéda
(Memel)

3rd Panzer Army

Dnieper

Kaunas

Vilnius

ARMY GROUP
CENTRE

4th Army

Mogilev

Königsburg
(Kaliningrad)

Neman (Memel)

Minsk

9th Army

Bereztna

Bry

Danzig
(Gdańsk)

Pripyat

Gomel

Szczecin

Białystok

2nd Army

BERLIN   Poznań

WARSAW

Western Bug

Brest-Litovsk

4th Army

Kiev

Lublin

Wrocław

Oder

ARMY GROUP
NORTH UKRAINE

Zhytomyr

Vistula

Lviv

Vinnytsia

PRAGUE

Dniester

Uman

1st Army

Southern Bug

Danube

Bratislava

Prut

Front line
17 April 1944

VIENNA

Hungarian 1st Army

Nik

BUDAPEST

8th Army

Iași (Jassy)

6th Army

Romanian 4th Army

Drava

ARMY GROUP SOUTH UKRAINE

Romanian 3rd Army

ZAGREB

Ploiești

Map source: MGFA (Militärgeschichtliche Forschungsamt)
04833-13; MGFA 4852-01; MGFA 04853-01.